First Published in 2022 by Echo Books

Echo Books is an imprint of Superscript Publishing Pty Ltd, ABN 76 644 812 395

Registered Office: PO Box 997, Woodend, Victoria, 3442.

www.echobooks.com.au

Copyright ©Everald Compton

National Library of Australia Cataloguing-in-Publication entry.

Creator: Compton, Everald, author.

Title: Catching the Linville Train: A Journey Through History, Everald Compton

ISBN: 978-1-922603-13-5 (paperback)

A catalogue record for this book is available from the National Library of Australia

Book and cover design by Peter Gamble, Canberra.
Set in Garamond Premier Pro Display, 12/17 and Bon Vivant Serif.

www.echobooks.com.au

Original paintings on the front and rear covers are the work of Noela Lowien.

Catching the Linville Train

A Journey Through History

Everald Compton

For Helen, who shared my journey
I could never have found a better partner

The Journey

In the faraway year of 1936, I was just five years old when I walked through the front door of the small state school at Linville for the first time. Located in the Brisbane River valley of Australia, it was the village where I would begin a journey to discover what life is all about.

Every day, on my way home from school, I would watch the train from Ipswich pull into the Linville Railway Station to drop off passengers, mail, newspapers and freight before continuing its journey to other small communities scattered around the forests of the Blackbutt Range.

The train was Linville's lifeline to the world. In Linville's 50 homes there could be found only two cars, plus one telephone at the sole local store that was also the post office. The only other commercial enterprises were the timber mill, where my father worked, and the hotel, which was the social centre of a close-knit community.

There were also two churches. The Methodist church was memorable as it was there that I was encouraged to sign a pledge at age six, promising (unfaithfully) that I would never ever touch the wicked booze.

One day, I got to have a ride on the train when it was decided that Linville students should travel once a month to a rural school at a larger town nearby called Toogoolawah where the girls would learn cooking and sewing, and the boys were to acquire the skills of woodwork (at which I was a hopeless failure).

My first journey on this wonderful train was a huge event in my life. I was off to discover the world beyond Linville for the first time, thrilled beyond words.

My grandfather had told me that whenever I saw a train I should make plans to travel on it one day to find out how people lived in other places and discover things that could improve life in Linville. I promised him that I would certainly do that at every opportunity.

One early discovery I made was that every community should have a hospital and a doctor and nurse. Linville did not have any of these, nor did any of the communities that surrounded us. They still do not.

Then there came a day when I was able to go with my family on a train from Linville to Brisbane. The city was just so big that I gasped in awe. I thought it must be the centre of the planet but was shocked when I was told it was a fleabite compared with Sydney and London and New York.

So, I pledged to myself that one day I would catch the Linville train for the long journey that would take me to see those cities and many others.

Significantly, I made a special commitment to visit the holy city of Jerusalem that I'd eagerly learned about at church every Sunday.

This leads me to make an important point. This book you are about to read is not my life story.

It's an objective commentary on events, people and places and attitudes that influenced my life and may well have impacted yours.

My hope is that it will recall in your mind the significant matters you encountered on your personal journey through life because they will be unique.

One day I hope that we can enjoy a pleasant shared experience. It will be delightful to discover that you found a train just like the one I caught from Linville back in the days when I encountered my first major world event, the Great Depression.

It would be the first of many landmarks of history that crossed my path. It had a powerful impact on me that would prove to be unforgettable.

EVERALD COMPTON AO
Brisbane, Australia
Easter 2023
A few months after my 91st birthday

The Book

This is an invitation to you to walk with me through my experience of nine decades of history after I first caught the Linville train and began a journey to a fascinating world.

Since you have shared some of those years with me, you will be able to personally relate to many of my encounters but have a different perspective of them.

May I begin by confessing that history was the only subject at which I excelled at school, meaning that I spent most of my days at the lower end of the class. I loved it and this love has remained with me down the years and steadily grown as a major interest of my life.

So, as I self-isolated during a long struggle to defy COVID-19, I realised that the virus would be recorded by historians as one of the highly significant events of the human saga. Indeed, it is our third most devastating plague in terms of deaths, after the Black Death and the Spanish flu, and certainly the most widespread of them all.

Facing this fact of history caused me to recall some of the other momentous milestones that have occurred during my lifetime. I really did enjoy jotting down my memory of those great events and this led me to think deeply about the profound messages that emanate from each one of them: all still have some influence on our current way of life and our future.

I made difficult decisions as to which events I felt were the most significant of them and easily got to 40. I then pared down the list further to select the most important 25 and began to serialise them on my Facebook page every week during 2020 and 2021. Emerging thoughts eventually expanded the list out to 30 and there I called a halt.

Then, I decided to add to my literary venture by describing my personal encounters with 20 notable people with whom I have worked. Each one of them created some positive change, not just in my life, but in the world at large.

This then encouraged me to expand my thinking even further into the realm of fascinating places I visited in a lifetime of travel. Each one of them revealed a remarkable history that remains relevant to us. This addition has embraced 20 such destinations, but I could have added more with little difficulty.

I reckoned that some personal memories would expand the horizons of the tale of my journey on the Linville train. So it is that you will find five more chapters tucked away near the end that outline some nostalgia about books, movies, musicals, the media and sport. I hope you will regard these as a pleasant bonus.

This led me to write five chapters about what I regard as my life's prime achievements. They each had a public impact in wide-ranging ways that gave me a degree of personal pride.

To gather it all together, I included a final chapter on my return to Linville. It has enabled me to take a fresh look at the world.

All of this has added up to a book of 81 chapters and nearly 100,000 words. None of them are large, just a few pages each.

They combine to contain my original thinking, supplemented by insightful comments made by my Facebook friends each week where they caused me to open my mind afresh and expand the parameters of my old brain. In reality, they are a combination of facts and figures, anecdotes and connections, summation and interpretation.

Enjoy the read.

My hope is that it will lead you to join with me in a wide-ranging debate I plan to foster about where humanity is heading throughout the 21st century as we expand our vision to embrace the countless lessons of our history that don't cease to emerge. You will note that I express some thoughts on this in the final chapter when I arrive back in Linville with Helen, my wife of 64 years, who has been a wonderful partner on my journey. Indeed, I would have been lost without her.

Hopefully, this book will enable my readers to act together with positive endeavour as a team as we strive to make the world a far better, more interesting and challenging place where inequality shrinks, justice expands, compassion abounds and happiness prevails.

It could be that no matter what our age may happen to be, we can have a role in making change happen in the best possible way.

Linville Station 1928

Contents

The Journey	v
The Book	ix
Events	xv
People	xix
Places	xxiii
Me	xxvii
Nostalgia	xxvii
Linville	xxviii

A: EVENTS

1: The Great Depression (1930)	3
2: Abdication of A King (1936)	7
3: I Bring you Peace in our Time (1938)	11
4: Kokoda Saved Australia (1942)	17
5: The Longest Day (1944)	21
6: The Day the World Changed (1945)	27
7: The Holocaust Gives Birth to Israel (1947)	33
8: A Time when Australia Made Things (1948)	39
9: British to the Boot Heels (1949)	43
10: Camelot (1963)	49
11: I Have a Dream (1963)	55
12: The Day Uncle Albert Won The Right to Vote (1967)	61
13: One Small Step (1969)	67
14: Uncle Ho Defeats Uncle Sam (1970)	73
15: The Remembrance Day Coup (1975)	79

16: She Broke the Glass Ceiling (1979) — 85
17: Mr Gorbachev, Tear Down this Wall (1989) — 89
18: The End of a White World (1994) — 95
19: The Rejection of the Turnbull Republic (1997) — 99
20: The Tampa Affair (2001) — 103
21: 9/11 (2001) — 107
22: America Elects a Black President (2008) — 111
23: The Tragedy of Religious Intolerance (2015) — 115
24: America Elects the Wrong President (2016) — 119
25: The Scandal and Tragedy of Child Abuse (2017) — 125
26: The Day Australia Removed the Restraint on Love (2017) — 129
27: An Unstable Decade of Political Coups (2010 to 2020) — 133
28: How Dare You (2018) — 139
29: Pandemics Become a Way of Life (2020) — 143
30: The Era Of Biden and Xi and Putin (2022) — 147
Through the Looking Glass — 151

B: PEOPLE

1: Jeffrey Archer — 155
2: Joh & Flo Bjelke-Petersen — 159
3: Charles — 165
4: The Brothers Costello — 169
5: Zelman Cowen — 173
6: Paul Cronin — 177
7: Elizabeth II — 181
8: Tim Fischer — 187
9: Gerald Ford — 191
10: Julia Gillard — 195
11: Bob Hawke — 199
12: Edmund Hillary — 203
13: Peter Hollingworth — 207
14: Bob Hope — 211
15: John Howard — 215
16: Paul Keating — 219
17: Enid Lyons — 225
18: Jenny Macklin — 231
19: Florence Nightingale — 235
20: Philip — 239
Meeting More of the Greats — 243

C: PLACES

1: Kyoto	247
2: The Great Wall of China	251
3: Taj Mahal	255
4: Victoria Falls	259
5: The Nile	263
6: Jerusalem	267
7: Malta	271
8: The Vatican	275
9: St Petersburg	279
10: Iceland	283
11 The Isle of Islay	289
12: Tarrant Monkton	293
13: Cathedrals	297
14: Quebec	301
15: Philadelphia	305
16: America by Motorhome	311
17: Recoleta	315
18: Waitangi	319
19: The Great Barrier Reef	323
20: Uluru	327
Bucket List	331

D: NOSTALGIA

1: Great Books	335
2: Fine Movies	341
3: Fabulous Theatre	345
4: Magical Media	349
5: Memorable Sport	353
More Dreams	359

E: ME

1: St Andrew's Hospital	363
2: Fundraising	369
3: National Seniors Australia	373
4: Inland Railway	377
5: Advocate	381
Do I Have a Future?	387

F: WALKING THE LINVILLE TRACK

Events

The 30 events I have carefully chosen are listed in chronological order. I have tried to quote an accurate history of each of the events as I recall them, then relate each one to the politics, morals, ethics, religion and culture of their era and estimate their prolonged impact on history.

My hope is that this will lead to a vibrant debate on social media regarding our experience of those events since many of us often see things through a differing lens.

Here they are gathered together in decades.

1930s

I begin with the Great Depression, which has had a huge impact on humanity all the way through to today. This is followed by the abdication of England's King Edward VIII and the hapless Neville Chamberlain's naive and hopeless attempt to sign a peace treaty with Adolph Hitler.

1940s

The invasion of France in 1944 was a massive undertaking. Its failure would have had immense consequences since it was the crucial beginning of the end for Adolph Hitler. Similarly, had we lost the Battle of Kokoda, a Japanese invasion of Australia would have been inevitable. Then came the horrific bombing of Hiroshima, a monumental tragedy that completely changed our world. The ghastly revelation of the Holocaust followed, but then something good happened. Australia produced its own motor car.

1950s

This was the core of the era of Robert Menzies, Australia's longest serving prime minister, who effectively tied Australia's future to Britain. We are yet to break free from it.

1960s

John F Kennedy became president of the United States of America and said that 'the torch had been passed to a new generation of Americans'. Then Australia reversed a terrible wrong by giving the First Peoples the right to vote six decades after all other Australians enjoyed that privilege. Martin Luther King did similarly achieve justice and human rights for African Americans, while his nation became involved in an unjustifiable war in Vietnam. But the decade ended when, incredibly, Neil Armstrong walked on the moon.

1970s

Gough Whitlam was sacked in an illegal breach of the Australian Constitution and Margaret Thatcher broke through the glass ceiling to become Britain's first female prime minister.

1980s

The Berlin Wall came crashing down and communism was destroyed, causing the demise of one of the great ideological movements in history.

1990s

Nelson Mandela brought an end to apartheid in South Africa and, in the process, also destroyed the white man's world, while Australia weakly baulked at becoming a republic.

2000s

Australians disgraced themselves by inhumanely turning back refugees and Bin Laden brought down the Twin Towers of New York on a day that shook the world, but the decade finished nobly when Barack Obama became America's first black president.

2010s

America took a massive step backwards when it elected a demented president. Churches began a significant decline in membership and influence. At the same time, child abuse was exposed as a huge evil that had been occurring in many churches and institutions. Australia finally agreed that those in same-sex relationships are human beings and, immaturely, experienced a decade of pointless political coups.

2020s

COVID-19 hit humanity unexpectedly and hard, but the election of Joe Biden began an era when the world would have to decide whether America or China was the world's superpower and whether they could unite to control an increasingly irresponsible Russia.

2030s

Who knows?

My feeling is that the climate change revolution will reach its peak, as will the ageing population tsunami, all at a time where we enter an era in which robots will become our partners for life.

People

While working on my account of 30 great world events, I began to formulate a plan for an equally important second section of this book.

I finally decided that it would feature 20 eminent public figures, many of whom I met or worked with in my community life, which began at age 24 when I was appointed as CEO of St Andrew's War Memorial Hospital in Brisbane. My task there was to raise the funds to build it, supervise its construction, organise its opening and then manage its administration.

This challenging experience led me into the world of political and financial negotiations in which I was able to master the art of fundraising for a wide variety of projects that were religious and secular, an experience that continued for 65 interesting and productive years from which I have not yet retired and through which I met people who changed history.

In the same way, I became fascinated with the challenge of adequately recording some significant history. I have greatly enjoyed writing about memorable characters.

You will find them in alphabetical order of surnames to avoid the impossible task of grading them for importance. However, to describe them to you more clearly at this moment, I have listed them in groups.

The Royals

There are three. Elizabeth, Charles and Philip. I met and worked with several more, but these three have sufficient history to give us a clear view of royalty.

Presidents

Just one. Gerald Ford.

Prime ministers

First, there is Julia Gillard. Then comes Bob Hawke, John Howard and Paul Keating. Others are mentioned here and there throughout the book. You will have noted that Robert Menzies has already had a place in events since his long term of leadership was a catalyst that changed Australia's post-war direction. Malcolm Turnbull is also featured in the chapter about the referendum to become a republic.

Politicians

Lots of them. Joh and Flo Bjelke-Petersen, Peter Costello, Tim Fischer and Jenny Macklin. They cover left, centre, right and the extreme right.

Governors-general

Two close friends of mine. Zelman Cowen and Peter Hollingworth.

Famous women

Florence Nightingale (in absentia) and Enid Lyons.

Famous men

Edmund Hillary.

Actors

Bob Hope and Paul Cronin.

Authors

Jeffrey Archer.

Clergy

Tim Costello (linked in a chapter with his politician brother, Peter Costello).

Each one of the 20 are people who had an impact on history and, particularly, me.

Places

Travel has been a huge part in my life and it has taken me to about one-third of the nations of the world.

I had extreme difficulty in choosing which destinations made the greatest impression on me since the world is a fascinating place of never-ending revelations. However, I reckon I've picked the top 20 while recognising there are undoubtedly some equally splendid places that I haven't yet visited, and may never do so, as time is running out for me.

I've listed my choices by continents and, in writing the chapters on my visits to each one, I've endeavoured to relate them to the history they created and subsequent impact on civilisation in its many forms.

You will note that I haven't included any glamour resorts since none of them represent any culture of genuine value and are seriously boring in their shallow world of make-believe that will soon fade away.

I've started with Asia and worked westward across the globe so that I finish in my homeland of Australia.

This means that I commence my journey in Japan with a visit to Kyoto, which was once its ancient capital, then move to China's incredible Great Wall, before travelling to India to take in the magnificent Taj Mahal.

A jump then across to Africa to drop in at Victoria Falls in Zimbabwe before going north all the way to Egypt to experience life along the Nile, one of the great rivers of the planet.

There was also a visit to the Middle East where an old Sunday school student like me felt compelled to make an unmissable pilgrimage to Jerusalem.

In heading to Europe, we follow my religious instincts by going first to visit the home of the Knights of Malta and to the Vatican nearby, before venturing north to St Petersburg and far north to enjoy the magnificence of Iceland.

We then journey south to Scotland to taste wee drams on the Isle of Islay, the spiritual home of all whisky drinkers.

Then it was over the border to the south of England at the village of Tarrant Monkton where my ancestors resided. Finally, I couldn't miss a visit to the cathedrals of England for which I had raised a lot of money back in my years as a fundraising consultant.

We cross the Atlantic to Canada for a visit to Quebec, the stronghold of the French in North America, and onto the USA to ponder the birth of democracy at Liberty Bell in Philadelphia before taking a motorhome journey across the American continent with my family during their schooldays when we searched for the soul of America.

Then we were down to Argentina in South America to visit the hidden grave of Eva Peron in Buenos Aires followed by a long journey across the vast Pacific Ocean to where the Treaty of Waitangi was signed in New Zealand, finally heading home to the magnificence of Great Barrier Reef and the spiritual centre of Australia at Uluru.

I would love to have chosen more gems, but all books must endeavour to reach an appropriate ending at a time when readers are, hopefully, thirsting for more.

I should mention that I was 33 years of age when I first left Australia's shores, When I mention this to my children and grandchildren, they are amazed. They all ventured overseas while in their teens.

My greatest disappointment is that I haven't visited either the ice-covered continents of the Arctic or Antarctic, nor have I crossed the vastness of Siberia or travelled the legendary Silk Road in the footsteps of Marco Polo nor ventured up the Amazon River.

Especially, I have not yet been to Tibet where I may experience enlightenment.

Nostalgia

I decided that I should dream of happy days of leisure throughout my 91 years, so I've given a lot of thought to pleasant experiences with books, films, theatre, media and sport.

Writing these five chapters brought out some fascinating memories and reminded me that I haven't spent enough days watching the flowers grow or listening to the songs of the birds.

Me

Readers will be wondering how my life's work impacted on my understanding of the world around me and, therefore, generated the thoughts I've expressed throughout this book.

So, I've outlined my thoughts on what I consider to be the five greatest achievements of my public life.

My first major assignment was in establishing St Andrew's Hospital when I was 24. Then, my long career as an international fundraising consultant is outlined, followed by accounts of two national ventures I founded (National Seniors Australia and the Inland Railway), plus a chapter on my advocacy at various parliaments for community projects that covered 65 years.

I met many influential people of a variety of cultures throughout my career and it was inevitable that the weight of their opinions has influenced my views of life and history. May I say that I'm enormously grateful for their mentoring.

Linville

In this final chapter, I return to Linville.

Within the peace of this unique village, I take an open-minded look at the world of the future based on the many experiences I've enjoyed since my first journey by train from the place that was the ground of my being so many decades ago.

It could be that villages like Linville, where an element of rural history has been lived for more than a century, will acquire a style of life that may well place them in a key role of the creation of a new Australia that has a finer sense of community.

I fervently hope so.

A: EVENTS

1:
The Great Depression (1930)

Greed has always been a dominating factor in human history and will continue to be so forever.

So it is that the Great Depression is best described as 'a perfect storm fuelled by the destructive power of greed'.

It accelerated the expansion of the me society and the progressive depletion of the we society, selfish trends that grow relentlessly in our world of 2023.

I was just a young lad, living in the relative peace of the bush, when the Great Depression was at its peak in the 1930s.

This meant that, at the time, I didn't really understand what was going on. But it was clear to me that something was wrong. People I knew did not have jobs and my father was constantly worried about losing his. The question in my young mind was *why*? It was puzzling to me that someone who wanted to work could not get a job.

Later, in high school, I was challenged to write essays about the Great Depression and, because I've been an avid reader all my life, especially enjoying history, I became fascinated about its origins, impact and legacy. It was easy to discover that it had its birth in the years immediately following the Great War that ended in 1918. People everywhere were weary of the many agonies of war and enthusiastically sought the good life as quickly as they could get to it and by any means that were possible.

This desire rapidly took the world into an era now fondly recalled as the Roaring Twenties when money was cheap and easy to get and too many amateurs fancied themselves as great speculators. It was inevitable that it would end in an enormous social and economic upheaval. The catalyst for this was the financial crash of Wall Street in 1929 when people with huge unrepayable debts jumped out of windows from the skyscrapers of New York.

The sole means of passing the word around the world in those days was by telegraph, but the panic was quickly communicated to us by Australian newspapers and radio stations, and so our money markets also crashed as fear and hysteria set in.

Just five days before the Wall Street Crash, in an unfortunate fluke of unpredictable timing, James Scullin had defeated prime minister Stanley Bruce in a federal election in Australia to become the first Labor leader to defeat a conservative government in 15 years. History reliably records that Scullin made a huge effort to save the Australian economy from the devastation of the Depression that was not of his making, but voters, as usual, needed someone to blame so they unjustly made him the scapegoat for the cause of their plight.

Scullin lost the next election in a landslide to Joseph Lyons who had once been his treasurer but had switched sides to become a conservative. Lyons did a solid job in calming the nation down and creating a slow but steady recovery even though Australia's unemployment rate had risen to a massive 33% at the peak of the Great Depression, more than three times more than that caused by COVID-19.

Over in the USA, Franklin Delano Roosevelt was elected president in 1932 on a promise that he would save his nation by implementing a revolutionary and costly government investment program that he called the

New Deal, which remains controversial to this day, but did the job effectively.

Young though I was, I'll never forget Roosevelt's great speech, broadcast here by the ABC, when he said, 'The only thing we have to fear is fear itself.'

It's a lesson I've never forgotten. Fear is a pointless and useless emotion and experience.

Our former prime minister, Scott Morrison, tried in 2019 to implement a modern version of the New Deal in Australia to save us from the economic devastation of the COVID-19 pandemic. History will eventually judge whether he may have been successful.

Three important issues are clear in my mind as a legacy of the devastation of the Great Depression:

My father was able to keep his job as a labourer, which paid him a meagre wage of three pounds a week, because he was a lifelong member of the Australian Workers' Union and they fiercely protected him and his mates from unemployment. Back in those days, trade unions practised compassion much more than politics and I'm grateful that they did. It's not too late for them to give up their constant quest for power and return to their old ways of doing good.

I lived the first 14 years of my life with just two sets of clothing and no jocks. The result of this has been that to this day trendy clothing is of no interest to me, and I usually don't replace my clothes until they wear out.

I remember the Great Depression years, and those of World War II, as days of a caring society. The dole was almost non-existent, so most people shared what they had with family and friends. You picked up your mates out of the gutter and helped them to regain a place in life. It was a wonderful example of what we can now recall with nostalgia as the *we* society.

Today, Australia is a selfish *me* society where we cherish personal freedom and primarily look after ourselves. This means that our society continually generates greed as a way of life and which operates on a basis of the survival of the fittest.

Sadly, we now have far too many Christians who embrace a so called 'prosperity gospel' that declares that God will help you to become wealthy. However, if you're poor, it's because you're not really practising the Christian work ethic. Of course, this is absolute nonsense. It's simply a respectable excuse to be greedy.

The task of creating a good society in the post-COVID-19 era will be achieved only if we work earnestly to become a *we* society once more.

Strange as it may seem, I look back with some nostalgia at the Great Depression as an experience that moulded my life. I give thanks that I had the opportunity to live through and understand what it meant to me personally and the society in which I lived, then and now.

Ninety years after it occurred, the impact of the Great Depression still has an influence on our lives.

It's unfortunate that politicians, bankers, economists and entrepreneurs have learned little from it.

The unnecessary cycle of boom and bust that caused it still happens regularly now, although thankfully with less damage.

Almost unbelievably, no-one has ever seriously tried to determine how to avoid it and do something constructive about eliminating it in the long term.

Whoever does will become the economic saviour of humanity.

It will be a herculean task because too many powerful people make lots of money out of those frequent booms and inevitable busts and have a vested interest in ensuring that they happen with regularity for themselves.

2: Abdication of A King (1936)

The high-profile demise of King Edward VIII of England marked the commencement of my journey along a pathway that led me to advocate that no nation should have a royal family.

It also caused me to ask why Australia has any need to have King Charles appoint our governor-general.

In addition, I feel the British Royals are such a pampered family. Never have they had to worry about paying the rent.

They have no place in the Australian way of life.

'That woman is seducing and disgracing our king.'

It was the year 1936.

My mother, Thelma, who was a very devout Christian, was telling me with considerable emotion about something dreadful that had happened to the Royal family. My schoolboy brain was in overdrive trying to work out what was wrong with someone wanting to live with a person they loved. And I didn't have a clue about what 'seducing' meant.

I also wondered why this 'scandal' could be considered a crisis when the entire world was struggling to work its way out of the Great Depression and its immense social consequences.

'That woman' was Wallis Simpson.

She was an American citizen who had divorced two husbands and was now the companion of King Edward VIII who had publicly announced his love for her and his intention to marry her, thus making her the queen of England.

The prime ministers of Britain and all its dominions pompously, publicly and indignantly expressed their disapproval of the intended marriage. Indeed, the prime ministers were outraged, even though their own private lives were far from sinless.

Edward decided to defy them and proceed with the marriage, but the killer blow came from the bishops of the Church of England as all kings and queens automatically become the head of that church when they ascend to the throne.

The archbishop of Canterbury announced that the Church of England would have none of it. It would not tolerate a situation where their leader was married to a divorced woman and, furthermore, they would deny her the right to receive any of the sacraments of the church such as Holy Communion, etc. This really was supreme vanity. Most Christians are aware that a couple of close friends of Jesus of Nazareth were known to be prostitutes.

Years later in 1958 when I became an elder of my church and took time to read the detail of the facts of the abdication, I thought that it was more than a bit rich for that the church — originally established by Henry VIII so he could marry six wives — had been so heavy-handed with Edward and Wallis who were saints by comparison. It was clear bigotry.

Most of us totally reject the presumption that people who experience a divorce are sinners. Quite clearly, they are human beings who for any number of valid reasons choose to end their marriage.

So it was that Edward chose Wallis over the British throne. He abdicated and was given the title of Duke of Windsor and a job as governor of the Bahamas. A worldwide debate began over this unjustifiable decision by the Church of England and it very clearly increased the pace of a steady decline in the moral authority of all churches.

The basic question under discussion was quite simple: 'Is Christianity about punishment for sins or is it a source of spiritual power that enables us to handle all the challenges that life throws at us?'

I haven't the slightest doubt that it is the latter. Indeed, a church is a place where goodwill must always flourish.

That the Church of England learned nothing from the Edward experience is revealed by its further actions a couple of decades later when it denied Princess Margaret (sister of the Queen Elizabeth) the right to marry divorced air force officer, Peter Townsend. This intensified the debate on how Christians determine morality. It also caused Margaret to become a chronic alcoholic, hardly a result that the 'compassionate' Christianity would want to boast about.

This attitude of punishment for sins has sadly continued in other forms, with churches taking harsh moral stances of condemnation in opposition to abortion, same-sex marriage and voluntary assisted dying that are simply statements of religious pomposity and vanity. Their judgemental negativity has further hastened a significant drop in membership in mainline churches. Their position is at loggerheads with Jesus who told two utter deadbeats who were nailed on crosses to either side of him that they would be with him in Paradise.

What was also hypocritical was that the church declared Wallis Simpson to be the sole sinner in this appalling saga, but didn't once criticise the moral life of Edward who had at least 10 mistresses prior to meeting Wallis. They just questioned his lack of judgement in his relationship with women. We needed the #MeToo movement to be around at that time so it could trash the primitive belief that, in any casual sexual encounter, it's only the female who is a sinner.

Well, to finish the Edward story, the 'Christian' critics said that his marriage to Wallis wouldn't last because she would give him up when she failed to become consort to a king. She proved them wrong, staying with Edward in a happy marriage until his death 25 years later. They had no children. Some critics claimed that she declined to have a family. Others were certain she was barren and publicly declared her to be so. After Edward's death, his doctor announced that it was he who had been infertile. Such is the way that truth is denied to suit political and religious purposes.

In the end, the undeniable truth is that dogmas, creeds and rigid rules mean absolutely nothing and should be banished from the face of the Earth — they're of no value to humanity.

What seems to me to be of major importance is that we should aspire to enhance a world in which people can fall in love with whoever they choose and, if their relationship fails, we surround them with genuine compassion and understanding that fosters a new beginning in their lives.

This must be our dream for a future that is powered by love and a generosity of spirit.

The irrelevance of the Church of England and other mainline churches gathered pace after Edward's abdication in 1936.

This was caused not just because people worldwide were switched off by the callous way the church treated Edward. It was boosted by the fact that most people could see no valid reason why they would want to be 'saved' from their sins. It is an irrelevant theology that has no place in their lives.

Now, churches are of such small stature in our world that many couples choose not to marry at all and, of those who do, most do not hold their wedding in a church. Of those who do marry, at least one-third end in divorce. Despite their 'sin', Edward and Wallis made a permanent team.

In fact, those whose marriages survive don't relate to churches in death. Their funerals are more likely to be held in a secular funeral home, not a church.

Nevertheless, despite the progressive demise of churches, Jesus of Nazareth is, and will forever remain, the role model of my life and for the lives of many millions around the world. We find him in many places, the least likely being a church.

3:
I Bring you Peace in our Time (1938)

World War II had its genesis in an attempt by Adolph Hitler to ensure that a pure white race, dominated by males, would rule the world forever.

However, his failure to achieve his evil goal did have a side benefit.

It brought to a halt many centuries of crude domination of the world by European nations, ensuring that white men will never again plunder our planet.

The words in the title of this chapter were spoken by British prime minister, Neville Chamberlain, as he climbed out of the small plane that brought him home to London from Munich after signing a 'peace' treaty with Adolph Hitler in September 1938. Huge crowds gathered at the airport and then at Buckingham Palace to cheer him with wild enthusiasm as he waved a white paper containing the treaty.

I remember sitting with my parents listening to ABC Radio as they relayed Chamberlain's words to a worried world.

My father said, hopefully, 'Thank goodness there will not be a war.'

However, we quickly learned that Chamberlain had made a gross miscalculation. He ignored significant errors of judgement made by others throughout the previous decade of Hitler's rise to power. Indeed, he appeared to choose to become a temporary hero by delaying what was inevitable.

In fact, the problem had begun back in 1919 when a vindictive and ridiculous peace treaty had been signed at Versailles in France by the victorious nations of World War I. It placed Germany in an impossible position.

This short-sighted decision had been heavily influenced by United States President Woodrow Wilson and British Prime Minister David Lloyd George with backing from France. They demanded and achieved a clause in the treaty that required Germany to pay huge unreasonable financial reparations for the deaths and destruction caused by the war that had ended in 1918. All sides were equally guilty of starting that war and the Germans had no hope of ever repaying those unfairly imposed debts. The clause's terms were doomed to create failure and generate animosity. When the Great Depression hit the world in 1929, the crippled economy of Germany crashed, causing a humanitarian and economic disaster.

To cut a long story short, this debacle enabled Adolph Hitler to be elected as chancellor of Germany and become the saviour of the demoralised German people after gaining absolute power based on the promise that he would refuse to pay those reparations. He then commenced a decade in which he exterminated five million Jews and one million Gypsies as a first step in the 'purification' of humanity.

So great was his power and influence that the churches of Germany, to their eternal disgrace, backed him by constantly preaching anti-Jewish sermons and praying for his continued leadership in doing God's work.

Dietrich Bonhoeffer was one of few German Christians who bravely opposed Hitler. When Bonhoeffer was imprisoned for his defiance, churches made no effort to intervene on his behalf, and he was shot by a firing squad in 1945.

Then Hitler forced Austria to merge with Germany in 1938 by organising an internal coup, causing the British government to become seriously alarmed. Chamberlain flew to Germany to meet with Hitler and was given a commitment by the dictator that he did not intend to expand his borders further.

No sooner was Chamberlain back in London when Hitler demanded the 'freedom' of people of German origin in both Czechoslovakia and Poland. Again, Chamberlain visited Hitler and was assured that, in due course, Germans in both nations would vote democratically for their own freedom.

Shortly afterwards, Hitler massed troops on the Czech border and publicly declared that he planned to occupy the province of Sudetenland, which had a majority German population. Chamberlain was outraged and demanded that Hitler meet him to sign a peace treaty that would end his planned conquests. The meeting was held in Munich with Italian dictator, Benito Mussolini, present to witness the deal. Hitler insisted on taking Sudetenland after which he would live in peace with all nations.

The Czech government was not invited to be present, nor was their consent sought. Hitler, Chamberlain and Mussolini agreed and signed, and all three went home in arrogant triumph. Within days, Hitler not only took control of Sudetenland by force, but he also invaded the remainder of Czechoslovakia and conquered it, confident that Britain and France would do nothing. He was correct.

Chamberlain then became concerned for the independence of Poland and signed a treaty with them saying that, if Hitler invaded them, Britain would declare war on Germany. This agreement was conveyed to Hitler, but he ignored it and invaded Poland in September 1939, occupying it within weeks. Chamberlain honoured his promise and declared war, but few battles of any significance were fought in the immediate aftermath. Chamberlain was rapidly losing political power in Britain and had no real authority to act aggressively since Britain was ill prepared to become involved in another war.

Chamberlain's position was untenable and he was replaced as prime minister in 1940 by Winston Churchill.

In subsequent letters written to his family, Chamberlain regretted that he had trusted Hitler. He noted in hindsight that it is impossible ever to create a lasting agreement with anyone who is a brutal dictator. It is a lesson the world should never have forgotten. But we have forgotten, as was shown by what has happened more recently in nations like Zimbabwe.

Significantly, Chamberlain had one more role to play in the war before he died of cancer a few months later. It was a crucial one.

Churchill invited Chamberlain to join the War Cabinet as former prime minister along with his new ministers. Churchill also invited Labour Party opposition leader Clement Attlee to join and they worked together splendidly with genuine bipartisanship throughout the war — something Australian prime minister, Scott Morrison, should have done with opposition leader, Anthony Albanese, in the war against COVID-19.

A crisis soon emerged in British politics.

Churchill's defeated opponent in the election for prime minister after Chamberlain's resignation, Lord Halifax, a staunch pacifist, moved at a War Cabinet meeting in 1940 that Britain should abandon the war and make a lasting peace with Hitler, telling the tyrant he could conquer all of Europe if he chose to do so, provided he left Britain and her empire alone.

Churchill hotly opposed Halifax, as did Attlee, but many pacificists in the room backed Halifax to the extent that the vote was tied. Churchill noted that Chamberlain had not voted and invited him to do so. Chamberlain dragged his cancer-ridden body upright and stood tall while he said with conviction, 'My vote is with you, Winston.'

He had redeemed himself and, more importantly, changed the course of history. His decision was the first step in a long and bloody journey that led to the comprehensive defeat of Hitler five years later.

As a young bystander who witnessed these events from afar, I quietly express my everlasting gratitude to, and admiration of, all who fought so relentlessly to remove Hitler and his evil disciples from the face of the Earth.

Neville Chamberlain's monumental blunder in attempting to appease Adolph Hitler is an object lesson for each and every one of us in how to handle any bully who emerges in any aspect of our lives — physical, mental, social, financial, sexual, racial or religious.

Absolutely nothing is ever achieved by appeasing bullies, or pandering to them, or giving in, or running away.

I am unshakeably convinced that the only way to achieve a satisfactory long-term solution to any issue of controversy is to stand up to the aggressor from day one with utter firmness and determination while using every ounce of peaceful wisdom that can possibly be used.

Usually, the bully backs off since they can only dominate those who show fear.

However, the great lesson for me from World War II is that in every war both sides lose.

Australian soldiers and 'Fuzzy-Wuzzy Angles', Kokoda.

4:
Kokoda Saved Australia (1942)

Kokoda was the greatest military victory in the history of Australia.

Sheer guts and incredible bravery by untrained Aussie amateurs overcame the overwhelming odds against Japanese military might.

I was filled with pride for our guys.

They taught me that no challenge in life can ever be regarded as impossible.

On 2 November 1942, I was just 11 years old, and I was, as always, listening to the trusted ABC Radio when they broadcast the great news that Australian troops had recaptured Kokoda in the mountains of Papua New Guinea and the Japanese army was retreating in defeat back towards their landing port at Lae.

Effort had been made by the Japanese to cross the Owen Stanley Range from Lae in a well-planned attempt to occupy Port Moresby where they could set up a base from which they could invade Australia. The long battle lasted from July to November of that year and the Aussies had been outnumbered five to one by well-trained and fanatical Japanese troops who were ready and willing to die for their emperor.

From that day onwards, I've regarded Kokoda Day as a far more important symbol in our nation's history than Anzac Day. Even though few Australians remember Kokoda, let alone observe it, the time has come for us to set the record straight.

Kokoda saved Australia from invasion.

Gallipoli did not.

The significant comparison is this:

At Gallipoli in 1915, Australians were there so we could loyally support Britain in the Great War that was fought over who owned real estate in Europe. It had nothing whatsoever to do with fighting for freedom. Australia was not under any threat. Turkey had done nothing to us to deserve our attack on them and to this day the Turks cannot work out why we were there. But they admire the valiant way that the Anzacs fought and died. As I do and you do.

Kokoda in 1942 was profoundly different in every possible way.

For the first time in modern history, Australia was about to be invaded.

Our future as a free nation was at stake and the British were not there to help us since they were fighting Hitler in defence of their very existence. Our main army was in the Middle East fighting and winning memorable battles for Britain at Tobruk and El Alamein. We needed to bring them home but this could not be done in time so our prime minister, John Curtin, had no option but to send our least trained battalions from our home defence reserves to fight the Japanese in New Guinea.

They were called the Militia.

This title meant that they were not battle-hardened and had no experience of jungle warfare. All they had was guts and tenacity and ingenuity that the Japanese couldn't match. Initially, they'd been forced to retreat after hard fighting day by day from Lae, back across the mountains at Kokoda almost to the outskirts of Port Moresby. There, they threw everything into one last battle, which they won. This enabled them to drive the Japanese back all the way to the top of the mountains at Kokoda where a colossal battle was fought and won with courage. This will be remembered for centuries.

They had saved Australia. The Japanese army was in full retreat. At the same time, other valiant Aussies were winning another battle further south at Milne Bay where they drove the Japanese back into the sea.

These days, groups of athletic tourists regularly climb the mountains from Port Moresby to Kokoda with all possible logistical support and find it to be an experience that takes them to the brink of mental and physical exhaustion. And when, with huge relief, the tourists finally reach Kokoda, they just cannot comprehend how Aussie soldiers did it while also carrying guns and supplies and with the Japanese constantly shooting at them.

As our veterans themselves acknowledged, our victory was aided greatly by the American navy who cut off Japanese supply lines by winning the Battle of the Coral Sea.

Added to this was the extraordinary bravery of the locals who joined the Aussies in a brave attempt to stop the Japanese from destroying their villages. Our guys called them the 'Fuzzy Wuzzy Angels'. They did not cease to carry supplies up the mountains to keep our troops fighting and then carry our wounded safely back to Port Moresby.

It must be recorded also that our men on the battlefields were let down badly by the top brass of Allied forces, especially our supreme commanders, MacArthur and Blamey, who had no idea whatsoever of the terrible terrain on which battles were being fought and issued orders that were impossible to carry out in such dreadful conditions. However, the Aussies did what all good Aussies do. They ignored these incompetent bosses whom they justifiably despised and got on with winning the battles.

The cold statistics of war reveal that in those five months of battle at Kokoda, we lost 625 valiant Australians who fought and died with bravery. Another 1050 were wounded and 4000 suffered from malaria, often fatally. No-one seems to have counted how many Fuzzy Wuzzy Angels died or were wounded, but we know that their casualties were heavy.

Former Australian prime minister, Paul Keating, summed it up magnificently when he visited the graves of Kokoda heroes at Port Moresby on Anzac Day in 1992.

His words were among his finest:

> 'They died in defence of Australia and the civilisation and values which had grown up there. For this reason, the battles in Papua New Guinea were the most important we ever fought. They fought in the most terrible circumstances. Surely no war was ever fought under worse conditions than these. Surely no war ever demanded more of a man in fortitude. And the support given to our soldiers by the people of Papua New Guinea constitutes one of the great humane gestures of war. In the end, our soldiers who died here believed in Australia and the future that their country held.'

Proudly and gratefully, I pause to remember them on 2 November every year even though few join me in doing so.

And, whenever I experience the inevitable tough times that hit all of us in life, they inspire me to fight back and win.

When Michael Somare became prime minister of Papua New Guinea in 1985, I worked with him to raise funds for his subsequent election campaigns.

He was a great leader whom they called *The Chief* and he was able to create a new nation out of the hundreds of tribes who each had a different dialect and little in common. An incredible achievement.

He told me that, before the war, his people were very suspicious of Australians because they were acutely aware that Australia did not treat the First Peoples of their nation as the equal of whites.

But, when they fought side by side to repel the Japanese invaders, the 'Fuzzy Wuzzies' and the Aussies hit it off incredibly well.

They were brothers in arms in war and remain so in peace.

5:
The Longest Day (1944)

In the history of the survival of humanity from oppression, the invasion of France by British and American forces and their allies was as an important and memorable occasion as I have experienced in my life.

Its failure would have been catastrophic for the cause of freedom.

Its success meant that those who were seeking to dominate us faced the inevitability of defeat.

Dwight Eisenhower, who eight years later would become president of the United States, was the American general appointed as supreme commander of the Allied invasion of Europe. It took place on 6 June 1944 and is usually recorded by historians as D-Day.

He predicted that it would be the longest day of his life and most of humanity thought likewise. Indeed, it was.

I was in my final year at primary school at the Toowoomba North State School when at 3:00 pm that day our headmaster spoke on a loudspeaker to tell us that the invasion of Hitler's Nazi empire had begun. He told us that it was one of the most significant of days in the history of the world. It would decide whether tyranny or democracy governed the world in our lifetime. The invasion just had to succeed. He asked us to observe a minute of silence for those who were dying on the beaches of France at that very moment. I was greatly moved by this tremendous event and went home to listen to reports from the BBC and to be assured that our troops were getting a firm foothold on the French province of Normanby and heading towards Berlin.

The vision for this magnificent day became a possibility when Churchill, having survived by one vote in the infamous coup attempt led by peacemakers in the War Cabinet, went to the House of Commons to make his finest of many tremendous speeches that would follow.

'We will fight on the beaches, we will fight in the fields and in the hills, we will fight on the seas and in the air. We will never surrender. And if the British nation and its dominions shall live for a thousand years, people will say, "This was their finest hour".'

The British parliament erupted in unanimous cheering and millions of British people listening to him on radio vowed to stand with him to the death. On his way out of the House of Commons at Westminster, Churchill said to his colleagues, 'The fighting must be on their fields, not ours.'

He immediately ordered that preliminary planning commence for an invasion of Europe that would destroy Hitler. It would take four hard years of relentless toil for it to become a reality.

Churchill's immediate and urgent task in 1940 was to get 300,000 British and French soldiers off the beaches around Dunkirk and brought safely home. Except for the sea, they were surrounded on three sides by the German army.

Then, Hitler made a fatal mistake.

He decided to go all out to capture Paris quickly and leave the 'inevitable' destruction of the defenders of Dunkirk for a week or so. In that short gap of timing, Churchill organised every available navy boat into action and invited thousands of British people to sail their private boats across the channel to Dunkirk. They did so magnificently and evacuated 99% of the troops. Many of those troops went back to France on D-Day. It was a decisive factor in winning the war.

Then Churchill organised the constant bombing of Germany to weaken their war capacity, the most famous raid being the work of Guy Gibson in leading the Dambusters squadron in flooding the industrial heart of Germany in the Ruhr.

So it came to D-Day.

The great side benefit was that D-Day created a second war front that forced Hitler to take thousands of troops from the Russian front so he could attempt to defend France. This enabled Russia to halt his advance towards Moscow and commence a fightback that would also lead all the way to Berlin.

One hundred and fifty thousand troops from USA, Canada, Britain, France and Poland were progressively assembled in southern England ready to cross the channel, while 100,000 navy and air force personnel were ready to transport them over there and back them with heavy fire. An Australian squadron was part of the team. It was the largest seaborne invasion in history. Indeed, the greatest logistical exercise in the history of warfare.

They were already on the boats on the evening of 4 June when severe bad weather set in. Eisenhower delayed them for a day, but the weather got worse, causing considerable sea sickness and dwindling food supplies. Unless they went now, the battle-ready troops would be demoralised by having to disembark. If they did go, many could drown in rough seas while wading ashore with heavy gear. A decision had to be made. It was unavoidable.

Eisenhower's top brass — de Gaulle, Montgomery, Patton and others were divided in their views. Churchill was in favour of taking whatever risks were necessary, but some in his War Cabinet were not.

The decision was left to Eisenhower alone.

He went for a walk by himself in blinding rain, across the fields surrounding his headquarters in southern England. Being a solid sensible Christian, he quietly prayed for the safety of his troops no matter what he decided to do. After a considerable time, he walked back into the War Room dripping wet.

He said just two words, 'Let's go.'

The invaders set forth in progressive waves of assault just after midnight on the morning of 6 June and, by midnight on the next evening, they had secured solid beachheads at seven places on the Normandy coast to such an extent that the Germans had no hope of being able to drive them back to sea. Hitler had once more guessed wrongly. He had most of his troops based further north at Calais where he was certain the Allies would land since it was the shortest crossing of the English Channel.

Four thousand four hundred Allied troops died on the beaches that day. Another 6000 were wounded. The Germans lost slightly less because it is easier to defend than attack. Many more on both sides would die on the pathway to Berlin. But D-Day was an enormous blow for Adolph Hitler, the greatest mass murderer in history.

What have we learned from this?

Great victories only occur when you have outstanding leaders. Eisenhower was sound, solid, practical and calm. Churchill was an inspirational motivator and a huge risk-taker in everything he did every day. They formed the perfect team.

Hitler lost because he ruled by fear and would never take advice, believing he was infallible. His team served him loyally but only because the alternative to obedience was to be shot. Eventually, they simply fell apart. The lesson is this — never work for a bully or live with one.

But there is one message for every one of us.

All wars are stupid.

There are the victors and there are the vanquished, but never are there any winners.

PS. The book *The Longest Day*, written by Cornelius Ryan and based on the experiences of a variety of people on that great day, is a wonderfully exciting read. A movie of the same name is an absolute ripper. It has a huge array of superstars: John Wayne, Sean Connery, Henry Fonda, Robert Mitchum, Richard Todd, Richard Burton, Kenneth Moore, and more.

Also, a great song was composed to celebrate it, with the lyrics 'Come ye back ye British soldier, it will be the longest day.'

There has been much speculation about which event in the Second World War forced Hitler to face the reality that he had lost.

Many say it was absolutely D-Day.

Others reckon it was when the German army suffered an enormous defeat at the Battle of Stalingrad in Russia that halted any possibility Hitler had of conquering the Russians. Indeed, it put him into retreat.

Another thought was that it occurred when he allowed the British army to escape from Dunkirk.

Perhaps it was when his ally, Benito Mussolini, was crushed into humiliating defeat by the Allied armies in Italy and then assassinated by his own people.

I believe that Hitler never accepted the possibility that he could be defeated

He took his own life to avoid having to acknowledge he had lost.

I find it quite amazing that, many decades later, an utterly different person was elected to the role he once had as chancellor of Germany.

Angela Merkel.

And she held the post for much longer than Hitler — 16 years.

She was a person of peace and compassion and ability who possessed the negotiating skills that were lamentably absent in the life of Adolph Hitler.

Above all, Merkel established an undeniable acceptance that there is no role anywhere in the world that a woman cannot fill, and do so with excellence and achievement.

Her legacy is enormous.

6:
The Day the World Changed (1945)

The day of the nuclear bombing of Hiroshima was the most appalling day in world history.

In our desperation to bring World War II to a rapid conclusion, we opened the door to a means of destroying humanity that had not existed before and it was all absolutely unnecessary.

One day, a powerful maniac will make use of this limitless power to eradicate all forms of life on our planet,

It is inevitable.

On 6 August 1945, an American bomber named *Enola Gay*, commanded by Colonel Paul Tibbets, dropped a nuclear bomb that had never before been used in warfare. It instantly killed 100,000 people who lived in the Japanese city of Hiroshima.

As Tibbets' plane rapidly gained height to avoid the deadly mushroom cloud that rose rapidly towards him, he looked out the cockpit window and quietly said to his crew, 'What have we done?'

As the news flashed around the world, millions of people asked exactly the same question and came to realise that our world had entered an era in which humanity could be extinguished in a matter of days.

To begin to find an answer as to why such an horrendous event occurred, we need to take a close look at the history of PROJECT MANHATTAN.

This was the name given to the venture that paved the way for Tibbets to be flying on his fateful mission that day carrying a bomb that had cost two billion dollars to produce.

In 1938, Adolf Hitler held a meeting with Germany's finest scientists at which he instructed them to design a bomb so powerful that no-one would have the capacity to stop him from controlling the entire planet. Shortly afterwards, Japan set its scientists to the same urgent task.

The USA spy network got wind of these plans and the Americans set out to be the first to achieve such a weapon, giving it a local name of MANHATTAN so that its purpose could not be easily detected. Working in secrecy, they made much faster progress than their enemies. Their scientists had greater funding and skills, one of their advisers being no less than Albert Einstein. To cut a long story short, they were able to create a mini version of what they called an atomic bomb and successfully exploded it in a remote desert in their own state of New Mexico in the early months of 1945.

They then built a far more deadly version of the bomb that enabled the US military to press President Harry Truman to allow them to drop it on Japan before the war ended. They presumed that they could not test its war-winning capacity once peace had been achieved. The compelling rationale for their request was that it would prevent the deaths of millions on both sides if they could avoid a land invasion of Japan necessary to end the war.

At the same time, American intelligence learned that an internally organised coup against Japan's fanatical war leader, General Tojo, was imminent and had the tacit blessing of Emperor Hirohito. The coup makers had deliberately sent a message to the Americans that said they believed they could gain power within two weeks and would then negotiate peace as a matter of urgency.

For reasons that few of us will ever be able to accept as being genuinely justified, America decided that they should test the bomb before the wartime opportunity was lost. Truman records in his personal memoirs the reasons why he accepted the advice of his military chiefs and signed the order to bomb Hiroshima. He then recorded that he slept soundly because he also saw it as a huge opportunity to let Russia know the depth of power that America would have in the world when the war ended, and difficult peace negotiations would be on the table.

After the initial blast on Hiroshima had instantly killed so many, another 50,000 died over the next few days from radiation burns and, in the decades thereafter, many more died from cancer, particularly leukaemia, as the winds carried the deadly radioactive clouds to other parts of Japan. There was also a significant increase in birth defects and mental retardation for the next generation after the Hiroshima bomb.

The bombing of Hiroshima nullified plans for the internal coup in Japan. Japanese military leaders defiantly decided that the nation must unite to fight on after the terrible assault on its civilians. It didn't occur to them that they had brutally and sadistically slaughtered many more civilians in Asia and the Pacific over the previous five years than would ever occur if the nuclear bombing of Japan continued.

Truman responded to their defiance by dropping a second bomb on Nagasaki three days later on 9 August, with similar devastating results, immediately and for years later.

Japan again resolved to fight on so Truman advised them that he had two more bombs he could immediately drop on other cities if forced to do so.

What changed the minds of the Japanese with greater urgency than the threat of more bombs was that Russia, having just helped to defeat Hitler, declared war on them at that moment and began to assemble an army at Vladivostok in Siberia ready to stage an invasion of Japan, hopefully before the Americans could get there. The Japanese made the wise decision that it was better to have Americans take over their nation than Russians and so they surrendered to US General Douglas MacArthur on a ship in Tokyo Bay on 2 September 1945, just four weeks after Hiroshima had been hit.

The peacetime world then began to embrace nuclear power for industrial purposes by building power stations on every continent except Australia, but the spread of its usage subsequently slowed down in the long term after old, poorly designed and defective power stations exploded at Three Mile Island in the USA, Chernobyl in Russia and Fukushima in Japan. Had this not happened, nuclear power, which does not release greenhouse gases, would have by now replaced coal as the world's greatest provider of clean energy.

In the meantime, military, worldwide, has moved forward rapidly in developing more powerful nuclear armaments to such an extent that the bomb that was dropped on Hiroshima was soon revealed to have been a popgun compared with the nuclear weapons that are now available and which have at least 100 times more destructive power than the original that hit Hiroshima.

These bombs can now destroy a city of 20 million people in one hit.

And the huge worry for you and me is that the trigger to use those bombs has too often been in the hands of grossly unstable people like Trump, Putin and Kim. Even a far more stable leader like China's President Xi does not often give the impression of being our favourite uncle either.

About 15 years ago, I visited Japan with some of my family and during interesting holiday we took a trip on the bullet train from Tokyo to Hiroshima. We went to the Hiroshima Peace Memorial Park, which marks the exact place where the bomb hit. It is now a World Heritage Site.

We paid a visit to the museum there which is filled with the most horrific photographs you could possibly find anywhere on the planet. Crowds of bewildered people are shown aimlessly walking the streets with no clothes, no hair, all their skin hanging from their bodies like many large plastic bags, and their eyes burned out.

After a while, my grandson, Nic, who then was still in his school days, said to me, 'Grandpa, can we go outside? I have had about as much of this as I can take.'

'Yes, Nic. I feel the same way.'

We sat on a park bench beside the Genbaku Dome, which is built around the dark remains of one part of a wall that was unbelievably left intact after the enormous blast. Embedded on it is a shadow in the form of a person. Someone had been standing there when the bomb hit. No part of the body was ever found. Only the shadow remains of a human life.

We gazed in astonishment at this sight and Nic asked me a significant question. 'Why is it, Grandpa, that we live in a world where one lot of human beings want to do something as awful as this to another lot of human beings?'

I said, 'I do not know Nic, I just don't know. But I do know that you and I must do our best to make sure it never happens again.'

Now, I often wonder how we can achieve such a goal.

I just cannot envisage the possibility.

Nevertheless, I will never forget the responsibility that you — my readers — and I have to strive ceaselessly to achieve a world of peace in which nuclear power has only peaceful uses for its awesome potential.

Australia has not embraced nuclear power except for one small reactor at Lucas Heights near Sydney, which fosters excellent initiatives such as nuclear medicine. It has the capacity to be expanded and used to develop other innovative uses.

Our current policy is a significant mistake. Nuclear power as an energy source is climate friendly with no contaminating emissions unless it self-destructs as it did at Chernobyl. But this was clearly due to negligence and irresponsibility in both its construction, operation and maintenance.

It's time that we find the ways and means to safely invest in nuclear power and also find safe means of storing nuclear waste.

7:
The Holocaust Gives Birth to Israel (1947)

The burning desire of Jewish people to re-create their ancient nation is understandable, and not surprising, when it became an unstoppable force at the end of World War II.

I was only 16 years old when the modern nation of Israel was born, and politically immature, but my gut feeling was that it should not have been allowed to happen since it was likely to create a permanent state of war in the Middle East.

It has not pleased me to note that I have been proved right.

My fervent hope is that one day I will be proved wrong.

In 1947, the United Nations, in a very close vote, approved the division of the British Mandate of Palestine into two independent states. The one along the Mediterranean coast was called Israel and the remainder retained the old name of Palestine. Quite irresponsibly, the exact borders were not agreed upon.

Arab nations reacted in anger and immediately invaded the territory claimed by Israel. The war lasted less than a year after which a fragile peace treaty was signed in 1948, enabling Israel to formally declare its independence.

Yet, wars have persistently continued over Israel's right to be there and show no sign of abating soon.

The history of all this is a long one. Scientists have traced instances of some form of primitive life in the Holy Land back to a period of one and a half million years ago and, as the Bible reveals, many wars have been fought on its soil and there are, lamentably, more to come.

In Old Testament days, many thousands of Jews were sent as slaves to Babylon.

More modern history reveals that the Jewish people were driven out of the Holy Land in the year 632 when Arabs, who had adopted the Muslim faith, conquered the region and gave them no hope of remaining there. This resulted in their being no option for Jewish people but to gradually seek new lives all around the world even though they suffered persecution wherever they went.

The pertinent point to fix in our minds at this moment in history is that Palestine has been the homeland of Muslim people for more than 1300 years and they are therefore indelibly entitled to believe that the land is theirs even if only judged on sheer length of occupancy.

In 1492, Jews began to return to their original homeland when shiploads of them fled persecution in Spain to settle permanently in the land where their faith was born despite its domination by Muslims. Steadily, they came back from all over Europe and North America and began to dream that one day they would become an independent nation that would, once more, be the custodians of the Holy Land.

Finally, after countless battles over a couple of centuries, they achieved their dream in 1947 and did so principally because of the worldwide sympathy they received after the horror of the Holocaust that occurred during World War II. Hitler's decision that Germany must become a pure white nation had resulted in millions of Jews and Gypsies being rounded up, locked in prison camps, herded into gas chambers and burned to ashes.

Hitler was not the only murderer of Jews.

Stalin killed at least two million of them in Russia and another million were murdered in Vichy France by the puppet government that Hitler established there under the incredibly pathetic leadership of Marshall Petain.

Indeed, historical records have revealed that, in every nation to which Jews had ever migrated, they suffered persistent and unending hostility.

Inevitably, a worldwide movement began that sought to enable them to reclaim their homeland and live in peace. It was regarded as minimum repayment for their prolonged suffering.

So it was that in 1947, as the result of their relentlessly passionate commitment to their cause, the Jews gained control of a significant part of their homeland, but not peace. That still looks a long way off since the wars they have fought to defend their nation over the last 70 years have resulted in them being in control of Palestine territory on the West Bank of the river Jordan (where the Jews have illegally established settlements) and the Golan Heights in Syria, as well as virtual military domination of the Gaza Strip. But this control is hotly disputed by the Arab world, and they will never accept it.

My understanding of the complexity of it all was greatly enhanced by twice reading the magnificent novel by Leon Uris that he gave the biblical title of *Exodus*. Written in 1958, it sold more than a million copies at the time and it still sells well. Its characters are fictitious, but the events it outlines actually happened, a fact affirmed by eminent historians. It vividly portrays how the three major religions in the Holy Land at that time were each divided into factions — spiritual, cultural, racial, political, financial, social — with hatred, bitterness and violence dominating their existence. These divisions still exist right now.

While these situations remain, there will be no peace. The question is how and when will peace ever be achieved? No-one really knows, but there are some small glimmers of hope.

Let me tell you of a personal experience I had that offers a tiny ray of hope.

About a decade ago, Helen and I visited Israel. We didn't travel in a tour group since the leaders of those routine forms of travel give cheap canned commentary, so I retained the excellent services of a professor of religion at Tel Aviv University. He was an eminent expert in three faiths — Christian, Jewish, Muslim. He drove us around in a comfortable and modern black Mercedes with bulletproof windows and took us to special places that were important to all three faiths. (By the way, his name was Moses.)

When we arrived at Bethlehem to visit the site of the inn where there had been no room for Joseph and Mary, the queue of people waiting to enter the Church of the Nativity was enormous. Moses suggested to us that if we paid US$25 each to a church caretaker he knew, he would get us to the top of the queue immediately. We decided this was a good investment and, after paying up in cash on the spot, were taken underground through a maze of dark corridors and up some stairs to the place where legend says the manger lay.

As we were leaving, after pondering for a few moments on the enormity of this birth on the history of humanity, I spoke with the visitor immediately behind us to apologise for our queue jumping. He was an Arab in full Muslim gear. I politely expressed surprise that a Muslim would wait for two hours in a long line to see the birthplace of Jesus Christ.

I will never forget his response, spoken in clear English, 'Jesus is a revered prophet of my faith whose teachings mean much to me. I am here to pay my respects to the man whom Christian people regard as their saviour and whom I hold in the highest regard.'

We had an instant bond.

It is possible for Christians and Muslims to relate peacefully with one another and work positively to achieve meaningful goals. Jews can participate also, as Jesus was crucified when he was proclaimed to be their messiah and the Romans declared him to be the King of the Jews.

In my own small way, I work on building that relationship as I participate in interfaith groups in Australia, but there are far more powerful forces in the field than religion, such as money, power, greed, corruption and political ideology, plus pure bigotry.

Even so, we have no option but to live in hope of an enlightened advance in religious and political tolerance and help to seek peace for all who live in the Holy Land, even though it is now one of the most violent places on our planet.

Most people yearn for a world at peace even though we have never been able to achieve it. The tragedy is that we keep making short term, fix-it-quickly decisions. Another prime example of this was the disastrous decision to divide the Indian sub-continent into three nations — India, Pakistan and Bangladesh and break up Yugoslavia.

Looking forward at the future of Israel, will peace be possible if it survives?

No.

Will there be peace if Israel is destroyed?

No.

How then will we achieve peace in the Holy Land?

There will be some hope if Israel recognises Palestine as a nation and they sign a peace treaty. And if many agree also that Jerusalem should be an independent nation state that becomes the centre of world religions.

On the world scene, we will take a huge step towards achieving peace when it occurs in our own souls and within the local communities in which we live.

8: A Time when Australia Made Things (1948)

There was a time when Australia made things. A day I now look back on with considerable nostalgia and pride.

Australia achieved something quite special.

We manufactured our very first homemade car.

Now, we don't make any cars at all. In fact, we make very little of anything.

This is extraordinarily sad because we have destroyed the proud heritage of those who built our nation by using their ingenuity to create whatever we needed to serve a purpose.

Our First People pioneers made everything they needed to survive on our continent for 65,000 years. Subsequently, settlers from other lands who first came here two centuries ago did likewise.

The fact is we need to experience significant attitude change so we can choose to use our creative talents far better than we now do.

At Port Melbourne on 29 November 1948, Prime Minister Ben Chifley proudly unveiled Australia's first homemade car — the Holden. Until that day, our cars mostly originated from Britain, USA, Germany, France and Italy. Chifley declared the new car to be 'a beauty' and announced that there were 18,000 advance orders for it at a competitive price of 733 pounds each (1466 dollars).

The name Holden had first appeared in the world of business in Adelaide in 1856 as an enterprise that made saddlery. This small company eventually progressed into creating upholstery for vehicles.

Then, in 1918, General Motors from the USA contracted with Holden to venture into making car bodies and they did well with that until they became one of the many victims of the Great Depression that began in 1931. General Motors bought them out that year but kept their name. Immediately after World War II ended in 1945, General Motors decided that Australia was now ready to produce its own car made totally in Australia and be called a Holden. They achieved it magnificently in three short years.

Others gradually joined the field as competitors — Ford, Toyota, Nissan, Mitsubishi, Vauxhall — but Australia didn't have a large enough population to sustain a car market of that broad competitive capacity. This meant that those car manufacturers depended on annual government subsidies to stay afloat and this eventually became politically unsustainable since other industries demanded equal treatment.

The government axe fell first in 2014 and finally hit in 2017 and it was all over for Holden and its successors. The hardest hit state was South Australia. Holden had its largest plant at Elizabeth, just north of Adelaide. The tragedy was that, at that moment, all the splendid skills the car industry had accumulated over 70 years were lost. Many talented people were tossed out into the ranks of the unemployed and had to retrain to do other work.

It was handled incredibly badly. The Abbott government was hugely negligent in failing to develop a plan to channel those skills into new industries that had the potential to use them. Instead, all over Australia, we steadily ceased to make things and so our cost of imports has risen dramatically. It need never have happened. We had, during the war years, already clearly proved that we could be creative manufacturers that operated profitably.

When World War II broke out, Australia was isolated from its allies in the UK and USA and so we had to get organised to defend ourselves against a high possibility of an invasion by a militaristic powerful Japan.

Prime Minister John Curtin, and Chifley, who was then his treasurer, enlisted the services of Essington Lewis who temporarily left his role as CEO of the nation's largest steel manufacturer, BHP, to coordinate and manage the local production of the armaments we needed and to do so within Australia using only local minerals and other resources.

It is now an indelible part of our national legend that Essington Lewis proved to be a born leader who created manufacturing enterprises virtually overnight. He organised the production of ships, planes, bombs, tanks, guns, armoured cars and ammunition in sufficient quality and quantity to equip us to win the war.

His initiatives created new opportunities for thousands of Australian craftsmen with skills that were acquired via all of his incredible achievements. These were quickly taken up post-war by General Motors-Holden and other industries such as makers of agricultural equipment and boats.

Incredibly and irresponsibly, we have tragically lost it all.

The general excuse given for this tragedy was that our wages were too high for us to be competitive. We had fallen behind in the acquisition of technology skills, our local markets were too small, and the tyranny of distance kills us competitively in reaching world markets.

May I say in blunt Australian language that these explanations are, quite plainly, a total nonsense that no rational person could possibly accept.

We have simply been asleep at the wheel, lacking initiative and having little vision. We have complacently enjoyed the good life while we let the world pass us by. It is nothing short of a disgraceful piece of unjustifiable neglect by successive governments of both left and right.

So, can we start again right now?

We have proved that Australians are naturally creative and venturous risk-takers. We can re-start making things as soon as we make up our minds to do it.

We can become world pioneers in making electric and hydrogen vehicles. It just needs some innovative and fearless leadership and courageous investors.

Clearly, we have the opportunity to make this our prime national initiative in creating a new economy in the wake of the economic devastation of COVID-19.

Australia is a continent that possesses an abundance of resources needed to manufacture anything we choose to make.

However, we've convinced ourselves that other nations can do it better than we can and have more specialist skills to do it more efficiently.

This attitude is negative and stupid and lazy. We have demeaned ourselves to the extent that a huge reformation is needed to turn around our ingrained negativity and regain the resourceful attitudes of our pioneers.

Be this as it may, the date of 29 November 1948 must be indelibly etched in our national legend. It is a day to be remembered.

9:
British to the Boot Heels (1949)

From time to time, every nation produces a leader who stays in power for so long that they dominate history to the extent that we have difficulty in comprehending what life would have been like without them.

Such was the case in Australia with Robert Menzies.

He was in power as the nation's prime minister for almost two decades and was the last of Queen Elizabeth's men.

His term in office and his departure were significant events in Australian history as it marked the beginning of a slow, but persistent movement towards the inevitable removal of the Crown from its ability to select our governor-general.

But this is a goal that remains unachieved.

I first met Robert Gordon Menzies at the Old Parliament House in Canberra six and a half decades ago. I was impressed by several things.

He was tall, large and formidable, a powerful orator with an exceptional brain and a huge amount of political nous. This explains why he was prime minister of Australia on two separate occasions, totalling 19 years, a record that is not likely to be surpassed.

He presided over a prosperous era of our history, although there are many critics who say he retarded our social and economic development by lulling us into a comfortable sleep rather than stirring our pioneering spirit.

I have several memories of his eminent career to share with you as the result of contact with him down the years:

He had close links with Queen Elizabeth and with everything British. Indeed, when World War II began, he actively sought and failed to gain an appointment in London to serve in Churchill's War Cabinet. Thereafter, he was often accused of spending too much time travelling to Britain. Indeed, he gave the impression of being more British than Australian.

When the young Elizabeth first visited Australia in 1954, Menzies' emotional farewell speech contained these words that were quite over the top, 'I did but see her passing by, but I will love her till I die.'

He was a liberal, not a conservative. I recall listening to his speech on ABC Radio in 1943 when he launched his new Liberal Party. He said, 'This is a party of liberals, not conservatives. The Country Party is on the right, Labor is on the left. I invite you to join me in the centre.' His successors have unwisely strayed a long way from this carefully chosen path in which he sensibly sought and succeeded to occupy the middle ground of politics.

When Menzies became PM for the second time in 1949, there were only nine government departments. The chief secretary of every one of those departments was a professional public servant with a minimum of 20 years' experience as a bureaucrat. There were no political appointments to the top jobs. Those guys knew how to run an efficient government. We sorely need them again rather than the political appointees who have now contaminated our bureaucracy with their ideology.

Menzies tried to be bipartisan in his dealings with his political opponents. His relationship with Ben Chifley was a classic of Australian politics. When Chifley was prime minister and Menzies was opposition leader, they met for a drink at the start of every session of parliament to agree on what legislation would be passed after minimal debate and what they would fight over. When their positions were reversed in 1949, they continued the tradition.

Especially noteworthy is the fact that they never abused one another at Question Time, unlike the crude behaviour of today's political leaders.

On the night that Chifley died of a heart attack in 1951, Menzies was presiding over the Jubilee Ball in Canberra to celebrate 50 years since six states had joined together to establish the nation of Australia in 1901. Chifley had apologised for not attending as he wasn't feeling well and remained in his room at the Hotel Kurrajong where he died quite suddenly.

When the news of Chifley's death was conveyed to Menzies, he instantly rose from his seat to address the illustrious crowd of high-powered attendees. He announced that Chifley had passed away and the ball would cease. With tears in his eyes, he said, 'He was my friend.'

Can any of us imagine this happening in an era like that of Abbott/Gillard.

A year or so before Menzies retired as prime minister, at a time of his own choosing, a feat achieved by few other prime ministers, I was invited to be a guest at a reception Menzies held at Parliament. The great man was running late.

While sitting alone sipping away at a splendid glass of red of a quality that the pollies always ensured was available, I was befriended by a new member of Parliament who was also enjoying a red.

His name was Gough Whitlam.

In his trademark style of very colourful language, Whitlam proceeded to tell me with great conviction what a pompous old Pommy-lover Menzies was, totally unable to relate to the average 'ocker Aussie' and sadly devoid of all vision.

After a while, Menzies entered the room and took it over like a colossus. Whitlam instantly jumped to his feet, way ahead of anyone else, and dragged me up with him.

I said, 'What are you standing up for, Gough? You have just graphicly informed me that Menzies is a total misfit.'

'Everald, no matter who occupies the office of prime minister, it is vital that we respect the office, not the person. Besides which, Menzies just happens to look like a prime minister, even though he is not fit to be one.'

Not long before Menzies died, he decided to raise funds in Australia to save a Presbyterian mission hospital in Pusan, Korea that had fallen on hard times. In his early life he had a maiden aunt who served there as a missionary for many decades, so he wanted to honour her very committed Christian life. As I was a Presbyterian elder and had worked on Menzies' fundraising team when he founded the Churchill Trust in Australia, his private secretary called me to ask if I would accept the position of honorary organiser of the campaign, which Dame Pattie Menzies would chair as the old prime minister was not well enough to do it. It was an honour I gladly accepted.

We launched the campaign at an evening rally at the Melbourne Town Hall, which was packed to the rafters with a huge crowd of old Presbyterians. Dame Pattie performed like the champion she was, an elegant person who spoke from the heart. At the end of the meeting, she joined the appeal committee for supper. After about an hour she asked me if I would take her to her car since she wanted to get back to her Toorak home as soon as possible since Bob was quite unwell.

When we reached the front door of the town hall, we were warmly greeted by hundreds of people who had waited outside for an hour to see her go home.

Ever the professional, she whispered in my ear, 'Let's make a grand departure.'

With that, she took my arm as we paraded down the steps to rapturous applause. I had to clear a pathway to the car and protect her from far too many people who were reaching out to touch her. Then I had to go to the front of the car to clear a pathway so it could move.

As it drove slowly away to ever increasing cheers, a nice and wise old lady who was standing near me said, 'Mr Compton, they are not really cheering Dame Pattie. They are yearning for the grand old era that she represents. It is a tragedy that it will never return.'

A few years earlier than this, when Menzies retired as PM, Queen Elizabeth appointed him as Lord Warden of the Cinque Ports (i.e. the five ports along the channel coast of England). This honour, backed by centuries of tradition, meant that he had the responsibility of defending England against French invaders. The title also awarded him a seat in the House of Lords at Westminster.

Menzies was home at last, and returned to Australia only to face his death in the land where he was born.

His state funeral was the largest ever seen in Australia, before or since, and his life can be defined as a clear era of our history, a benchmark on which all other histories are based.

Menzies was born and bred in a small rural community in north-western Victoria called Jeparit.

It is a long way from London in distance and culture.

Yet he was entranced by old England and believed that Queen Elizabeth represented the law in a manner that no commoner ever could.

For this reason, he didn't want to cut ties with her.

So far, no subsequent Australian prime minister has seriously tried to change the view that the integrity of the law still rests with her.

Will this belief die with her?

I think it will.

It's time for Australia to stop clutching the apron strings of Mother England and stand on our own two feet as an independent nation.

10:
Camelot (1963)

This is the story of a day when I first came to terms with the fact that any leader of any nation anywhere can be assassinated at any time by a zealot or a nutter and very little can be done to prevent it.

I'd read several books about the murder of Abraham Lincoln, but had wrongly regarded it as having happened in an era of primitive politics that no longer applied to the 21st century.

From the moment of the Kennedy shooting, every national leader was placed at high personal risk.

Does any rational person really want to become a national leader?

The answer always is YES.

I was at a meeting in Hollywood on 22 November 1963, with Danny Kaye's manager, negotiating (ultimately unsuccessfully) for the great stage and screen legend to visit Brisbane to launch the Children's Hospital Foundation.

His PA, in considerable distress, ran into the room to tell us that President John F Kennedy, better known as JFK, and only 46 years of age, had been shot and killed in Dallas, Texas. By mutual agreement our meeting was terminated, and we agreed to continue our discussions by telephone.

As I walked back to my Los Angeles hotel, I encountered people openly weeping in the streets and shops closing early in respect for the president. I wondered if Australians would break down in tears if one of our prime ministers was assassinated. From my room, I watched Lyndon Johnson sworn in as president, followed by the unforgettable memory of Jackie Kennedy arriving back in Washington with large blotches of the president's blood splattered across her pink dress.

By sheer coincidence, my planned itinerary through the United States took me to Dallas the very next day. After I'd finished my meeting there, I walked to Dealey Plaza where Kennedy had died. It was covered with the largest volume of flowers I have ever come across in my travels and all traffic was being diverted away from the scene where huge crowds were paying their respects.

I looked up at the Texas School Book Depository from where his assassin Lee Harvey Oswald had fired the fatal shot. I reckoned he would have had a clear view of his famous target. There is no way he could have missed, and it made me wonder how any of the president's bodyguards could ever offer total protection when their chief is in a motorcade in an open vehicle.

A couple of days later, I watched the president's funeral on television from a friend's home in Fort Lauderdale, Florida. When JFK was laid to rest at Arlington Cemetery in Washington, the glamorous era of Camelot was over.

It was Kennedy himself who chose 'Camelot' to describe the purpose of his presidency. This was the title that King Arthur of England, by legend, had given to his castle and his kingdom 1500 years earlier. It was intended to be a place of peace and prosperity but didn't achieve that splendid goal. Kennedy planned to plant this vision once more in the hearts and minds of Americans, but he'd made only small progress towards achieving it when he was struck down.

Like Barack Obama, JFK was a charismatic leader and orator, but lacked the political skills to convince Congress to pass most of the legislation he placed before them. He also wasted too much time on a stream of affairs with famous women, the most notable being Marilyn Monroe and Marlene Dietrich. Such were his exploits, he made Bill Clinton and Donald Trump look pure.

Forgetting his inept politics and immature personal relationships he will, in cold reality, be remembered for two significant matters other than his assassination.

The most dramatic and successful was his confrontation with Russian President Nikita Khrushchev in October 1962, over nuclear missiles that Russia has installed in Cuba with the approval of their president, Fidel Castro. Those missiles could hit any American city in minutes. Kennedy demanded they be dismantled. Khrushchev refused and immediately sent a fleet of nuclear armed vessels across the Atlantic to protect his missile installations.

In an urgent and high-risk response, Kennedy dispatched the American navy and air force out to meet the fleet with orders to sink them. The world held its breath. We were on the brink of war. I lay in bed that night trying to work out how many days it would take for the nuclear cloud to float out to Australia. Fortunately, the Russian ships turned around and went home, thus making my concerns pointless.

Kennedy showed courage and nerves of steel in this enormous crisis. He became an instant hero in the non-communist world, his poll ratings rising to 80%. But unfairly, few gave any praise to Khrushchev for having the common sense to back off. It cost him heavily personally as, not long after, he was removed from power in a Kremlin coup.

JFK's other significant initiative was civil rights legislation that he had presented to Congress with considerable personal commitment a year before his death. The legislation was planned to give to African Americans many basic rights they had been denied in the century since Lincoln gave them their freedom. It was stalled in a political deadlock for many months before Kennedy died, with little hope of it ever going to a winning vote. But when Lyndon Johnson took over as president after the assassination, he asked Congress to pass it as a memorial to Kennedy and he skilfully twisted every political arm that he could to score one of the greatest legislative victories of all time since most white Americans were strongly opposed to it. In the end, Johnson dedicated the victory to Kennedy who had designed and launched it.

However, the finest memory I personally have of Kennedy is the speech he made at his inauguration in 1960 when he said: 'Ask not what America can do for you. Ask what you can do for America.'

In the crucial battle the Australian nation is fighting against COVID-19, and which has caused huge social and economic chaos, we should remove the word 'America' from that inspirational sentence pronounced by Kennedy and replace it with 'Australia'.

We have a unique opportunity to create our own Camelot, or an improved version of it, right here, right now.

Be that as it may, let me conclude with a few interesting asides:

Years after he was removed from power, Khrushchev was asked this question by an author of a book on his life, 'What difference would it have made if you had been assassinated instead of Kennedy?'

The great Russian thought deeply, then said, 'I can tell you with absolute certainty that Mrs Khrushchev would not have married Aristotle Onassis.'

The *New York Times* reported that Jackie Kennedy Onassis was highly amused and made it a point of hilarity at dinner parties she attended.

We should note that three other American presidents were assassinated in similar fashion to Kennedy (i.e. death by firearm, the great plague of all life in the USA):

- Abraham Lincoln, 1864
- James Garfield, 1880
- William McKinley, 1901

Two presidents survived assassination attempts:
- Ronald Reagan, 1981
- Gerald Ford (twice), 1975

The only death of an Australian prime minister that was not the result of natural causes was that of Harold Holt when he drowned at Portsea near Melbourne in 1967.

The most interesting political question that has been asked all my life is one that will continue to be debated forever and remain unresolved.

'Should we have leaders of charisma who give us hope and vision but usually disappoint us, or is it better to have dull leaders who achieve some good?'

Kennedy had a magic about him but was only a moderate achiever.

Angela Merkel had little charisma but achieved great things for Germany, Europe and the world.

Ideally, we should have charismatic achievers, but there have been few of them around in our past, present or future.

The closest to it in my lifetime was Nelson Mandela.

To find an equivalent in Australia, we must go all the way back to 1904 when Alfred Deakin became our second prime minister. I hold the view that he was our greatest.

11:
I Have a Dream (1963)

I have spent my life endeavouring to be a practising Christian who tries to serve humanity, and I have found that there are only a few Christian leaders of the modern era whom I respect or revere.

Martin Luther King is at the top of the list, followed by William Wilberforce and Dietrich Bonhoeffer.

King was a person who took his Christianity beyond the church and out into the world in the way Jesus of Nazareth would have done in the same situation. Few others have done this. Mostly, they only tried to ensure the survival of their church and that proved to be a pointless exercise.

He had more impact in the United States of America than elsewhere, but many Australians like me felt the inspiration of his life.

Right now, Christianity desperately needs more leaders of his calibre, faith, commitment, courage and ability to reach out far beyond the confines of churches.

In Christian folklore, one of the highest honours that one can receive is to be invited to preach at St Paul's Cathedral in London. Many of the great and mighty of our era have lobbied hard to achieve that privilege, whereas Martin Luther King achieved it without ever trying.

I asked a question about this when dining with my longstanding friend, the then dean of St Paul's, Eric Evans, over lunch at a restaurant nearby the cathedral in 1990.

'Tell me, Eric, who preached the finest sermon in St Paul's during the twentieth century?'

Without hesitation, he answered, 'Martin Luther King. I was a parish vicar out in Gloucestershire at that time, but I came up to London to hear him. The cathedral was packed out and he held the congregation spellbound. It was powerfully inspirational stuff. He motivated me to get out into the world and march with him in spirit to achieve justice for all humanity at that very moment.'

Just as our meal was ending, a friend of the dean's came to our table and asked if he could join us for coffee.

'Everald, meet Andrew Lloyd Webber. He is one of my flock at St Paul's. A regular at the cathedral when he is in town. You know him as a great musician, but let me tell you that he is the son of a humble Anglican vicar.'

This explained to me in part why Webber composed two of his musicals with religious themes. *Jesus Christ Superstar* and *Joseph and his Technicolour Dreamcoat*.

As our chat proceeded, I asked the great composer the same question as I had asked the dean. Same answer. Martin Luther King.

I've never listened to a recording of that great sermon in the cathedral, which was preached when King stopped over in London on his way home to America after receiving the Nobel Peace Prize in Sweden in 1964. But I did watch a film of his most famous speech from the steps of the Lincoln Memorial at the culmination of the Great March on Washington in 1963 before the largest crowd ever assembled in Washington, before or since.

His immortal words still ring out in my soul, 'I have a dream that one day my children will be judged not by the colour of their skin but by the content of their character.'

The life journey of Martin Luther King that led him to that great day had been a tumultuous one. There had been many marches that he led in southern cities where a majority of whites were racist. In addition, he led transport boycotts against laws that forced African Americans to sit in segregated areas of buses and trains and could not use the same toilets as whites. He served jail sentences often, but he steadily achieved results.

History will record that his greatest achievement was to work with presidents Kennedy and Johnson to have significant civil rights legislation passed by Congress.

His many campaigns were not just about racial discrimination and justice. His significant impact was in seeking to lift his people out of poverty. And he had a burning personal conviction that his work was a Christian calling. He was born for this task.

So it came to pass that, on 4 April 1968, he was standing on the veranda of a motel in Memphis talking to a church organist about a hymn they would sing at a rally planned for that evening.

He said, 'Please play it real sweet.'

A shot rang out. He was dead before his body hit the floor. His assassin, James Earl Ray, can simply be described as a bigoted racist nutter with mental health issues.

When I heard the tragic news, I relived the impact of his epic words at the conclusion of the Washington Rally, 'Free at last. Free at last. Thank God almighty, we are free at last.'

At King's funeral, it was noted that he had received honorary doctorates from 52 universities worldwide. I doubt that this record will ever be surpassed.

Posthumously, President Jimmy Carter, a fellow Christian, awarded King the Congressional Medal of Honour, the highest award he could receive in America. A national public holiday has also been named after him.

Years later, at the turn of the century, Gallup conducted a poll to determine who were the 100 most respected people who lived in the 20th century. Martin Luther King came second, close behind Mother Teresa, a person whom he greatly admired.

May more leaders like King respond to a personal calling of faith to serve our world at this moment when humanity is more divided as a society than at any time in our lives. Hatred and greed and violence and inequality are growing curses that we must remove with urgency and replace with finer aspirations.

As a well-meaning postscript, may I say also that Martin Luther King would not have been impressed by the ridiculous controversy that arose in Australia that forced the manufacturers of Coon cheese to change its name.

He would have regarded it as an absolute piece of pointless publicity-seeking trivia. Coon is a word that for centuries has been used described a famous cheese-making process. Turning it into a crude racial issue will create consequences that can only be damaging to the cause of equality, especially as most people know that 'coon' is only occasionally used in Australia as a stupid slang word by a few ignorant racists to describe someone from the First Peoples.

King was called offensive names daily throughout his life.

He ignored them all as he concentrated his mind, and the minds of millions, on the great cause of justice. It will never be achieved by playing silly games with words.

King hit the big issues by taking huge risks. It was his life's purpose never to flinch when this caused him pain.

Throughout whatever years I have left, I will never forget Martin Luther King.

He has been one of the great role models of my life, along with William Wilberforce, Winston Churchill, John Flynn, Mother Theresa, Nelson Mandela, Angela Merkel, Dietrich Bonhoeffer and Jesus of Nazareth.

King was not a saint.

Among other things, he publicly admitted to being unfaithful to his wife, Coretta, thereby acknowledging that he was, like all of us, a human being with frailties.

But, above all this, he was a giant.

12:
The Day Uncle Albert Won The Right to Vote (1967)

At the time, I didn't fully understand the significance of the historic 1967 Australian referendum, but I knew that it righted a great wrong.

White Australia had, at long last, come to recognise that First Peoples were human beings who had sufficient mentality to be able to vote in elections.

I constantly ask myself why it took so long to hold this referendum when we note that it resulted in a vote that was 94% YES.

It was 1967 and it was a long-awaited recognition. Sixty-six years earlier the First Peoples had been given no recognition when the Constitution of the new nation of Australia was approved.

At the referendum held that year to amend the Constitution, the First Peoples finally won the right to vote, become citizens and therefore eligible to be counted in a census. Prior to that they were non-persons. The vote in favour was the largest majority ever attained in a referendum in the history of the nation. White Australia had decisively voted to turn its back on racism that had plagued our land for far too long.

For Uncle Albert Holt, a respected Elder of his proud people from the Cherbourg Aboriginal Mission in Queensland, and a personal and valued friend of mine, it was a memorable moment of his life. He told me that tears came to his eyes when, a few days later, whites who had previously called him Holt or Abo, addressed him as Mr Holt. It was an experience he had never expected. It had been a long journey for his people.

The First Peoples heritage has been accurately calculated by eminent white anthropologists to have begun on the Australian continent 65,000 years ago, after a long journey from Africa via Asia that had taken many centuries.

When James Cook sailed up the east coast of Australia in 1770, he encountered a few small groups of First Peoples, but saw no buildings. When he reached Cape York, he hoisted the British flag on Possession Island and claimed the continent to be a sovereign territory of King George, saying it was 'unoccupied'. He had acted in the manner his king had ordered him to do once he found the Great Southern Land.

When Governor Arthur Phillip arrived at Botany Bay with the First Fleet two decades later, he had instructions to find means of living in peace with any native people whom he may encounter. Quite predictably, this proved to be an impossibility since the natives had no alternative but to defend the land that was theirs by right of continued occupation for many generations. Had I been one of the First Peoples at that time, I would have fought with passion to defend my heritage without hesitation.

The land battle lasted 100 years and resulted in the deaths of 30,000 First Peoples and 3000 whites. It was an unfair fight. The whites had guns; the First Peoples had spears. Worse still, another 100,000 First Peoples died from diseases brought by whites for which their immune system had no defence. It was far worse than COVID-19. Added to this was the atrocity in which white men stole First Peoples women, resulting in the unwanted arrival of many people of mixed race who were rejected by both whites and blacks. This wanton irresponsibility was a human tragedy.

So, when Australia became a nation in 1901, the Constitution simply recorded that First Peoples were the responsibility of state governments who were their guardians and, therefore, they were not Australian citizens. This caused New Zealand to back away from its intention to be part of the Federation since they had recognised Māoris as citizens in 1840 and couldn't understand why Australia hadn't done likewise.

Despite this disgraceful act of racism, the Australian Government enlisted the First Peoples to serve in its army in two world wars where they fought with valour. At the end of each war, they were denied the war pensions that all whites received. It was declared that they were not citizens and therefore ineligible, a callous and shameful act.

So, what do we do about it now as a nation populated by migrants from 100 countries with numerous cultures and religions? We can rightly say that all of this was not our fault. The responsibility clearly lies with colonial Britain. Nevertheless, we are living with its consequences, and it is a huge social challenge that is eating away at the very fibre of our being as a nation. We cannot brush it away any longer even though most whites may continue to try to do so.

It is easy for non-First Peoples Australians to think that the problem lies solely with the First Peoples themselves. Far too many of us are prone to say that First Peoples must restore their culture and heritage themselves, saying billions of dollars of welfare has been thrown at them with no identifiable results. This is a very convenient excuse. But the reality is that many whites do the same and often worse.

Yet we rarely look at the quite extraordinary talents that so many First Peoples have. Clearly, we need a treaty, something like that 1840 Treaty of Waitangi that the British signed with New Zealand Māoris, to end it all and establish a culture of mutual respect and responsibility and a pathway to a cohesive society in which most people get a fair go on a level playing field.

Of one thing we can be very certain — throwing more money at this challenge will achieve absolutely nothing.

The adoption of the Uluru Statement from the Heart would be a great start.

Additionally, we can then move to recognise in the Australian Constitution that First Peoples heritage was founded when their people became the first settlers. It is a simple statement of fact. We can then move to negotiate a Treaty or perhaps a Bill of Rights and Responsibilities that unites us all.

I suggest we should also vote on this wording as a preamble to the Constitution:

'Australia was founded 65,000 years ago. It is now a nation in which its original inhabitants live in peace with migrants from more than 100 nations. We share its prosperity while respecting its laws and participating in its pursuit of justice for all and equality of opportunity.'

I support this as a proud descendant of a convict who was treated just as badly as the First Peoples population.

It has been an honour for me to join Uncle Albert Holt and Henry Palaszczuk as the three characters in a book about understanding Australia titled *Goondeen*. It was published in 2017 (and you can buy it online at goondeen.com.au).

In the book, Albert speaks on behalf of the original inhabitants of Australia.

Henry represents migrants. (He escaped from Hitler's Europe.)

I represent convicts and the people of the bush where I was born and bred.

As you read and enjoy *Goondeen*, you will note that I have enormous respect for both Albert and Henry. However, in this chapter of my book, I honour Albert who served with distinction as a police liaison officer. He represents a basic common dignity and decency that is the cornerstone of our nation.

Henry and I try to follow in his respected footsteps.

Note that in First Peoples folklore, a Goondeen is 'a father figure, a very wise, smart and respected person; a clever fella'.

To be recognised as a Goondeen is an honour that I hugely value, knowing that I don't really qualify for it.

I'm unable to comprehend how I could ever accept a situation where I lived in a nation that had a constitution that did not recognise me as a person with basic human rights, especially when my ancestors had lived on the continent for 65,000 years and been responsible custodians of it.

I reckon that I would have done my best to lead a physical revolt against this enormous indignity.

Being jailed for it would have been no worse a fate than the indignity of living in a community where I had the same status as a dog or a cat.

So it is that I will work until I drop to have the intent of the Uluru Statement enshrined in our Constitution as a basic first step on the pathway to justice.

13:
One Small Step (1969)

As parts of history quietly fades away in the minds of our generation, one event will never be forgotten by future historians.

It is the day when a human being from our planet stepped onto the surface of the moon and, thankfully, was able to get home again.

Neil Armstrong's arrival there opened the door to the possibility of finding life somewhere else in the universe.

One day, it will be discovered.

Nothing is more certain.

When I was just a little boy, I remember pointing my finger at the large bright light that appeared in the sky at night-time and asking my mother what it was. She told me that everyone called it the moon, that it was made of cheese, and there was a man in the moon who just loved eating cheese. Wow, I thought, what a life. I just loved cheese. Still do, as my overindulged frame clearly shows.

One of the many books written about Neil Armstrong reveals that, when he was a boy, he had an expectation about the moon that greatly exceeded mine. Armstrong was sitting on the veranda of his family home in

Ohio with his grandfather looking out at a magnificent full moon when he said, 'One day I am going to fly to the moon.'

His grandpa told him that it was impossible.

'No, Grandpa. Judy Garland says that you can do it.'

Then he sang a few lines from one of Garland's most popular songs, 'Somewhere Over the Rainbow':

'Somewhere over the rainbow blue birds fly. Birds fly over the rainbow why, oh why, can't I?'

He got there on 20 July 1969, watched by billions, the greatest viewing audience in history at that time.

His pathway there was predictable for a life that was utterly committed to his chosen destiny. He took his first flying lessons at age 16 and studied aeronautical engineering at Purdue University, joining the US Air Force to serve in the Korean War where he flew 78 bombing missions. A few years later, he joined NASA and quietly became part of their moon program, steadily working his way to the top ranks of astronauts. He was certain that the goal set by President Kennedy to put a man on the moon by 1970 was achievable and he personally wanted to prove it.

He first went into space on a *Gemini* flight before being chosen for the moon landing on *Apollo 11* with Buzz Aldrin and Michael Collins. The world held its breath in sheer wonder as almost everyone watched the take off. Most people, and especially their families, felt they would never see the astronauts again.

As they circled the moon a few days later, Armstrong and Aldrin climbed into the lunar module and started their descent, leaving Collins behind to keep circling the moon alone until they came back. As they neared the moon's surface, the computers failed. The flight command team back in Houston told them to abort the mission and return to link up with Collins. Armstrong ignored them, switched off the computers and flew it in manually to land safely.

I was looking at a television set in my office, entranced, wondering in awe at the technology that enabled them to send a picture from the moon all the way to Brisbane. I watched Armstrong step down onto the moon's surface to make the first human footprint.

Then he said words that would ring throughout history forever, 'One small step for a man, one giant leap for mankind.'

The astronauts stayed on the surface for a couple of hours collecting rock samples and such. Finally, they left an American flag on a small pole that they drove into the ground. The American people had earned the honour. It had been a huge investment of time, skill, money and courage that was extraordinarily and excellently done.

At last, they climbed back into the module to come home. No-one knew if the computers would function normally again, but Armstrong and Aldrin had agreed that if they failed to take off, they would spend their final days trying to work out what went wrong so the next crew to fly to the moon could do it safely. To the relief of the whole world, the computers worked. They joined up with Collins and all three made it back safely to one of the greatest public welcomes of all time.

Eventually, they even flew to Australia to give us a small piece of moon rock and received a rockstar welcome.

Sadly, after a couple more trips to the moon by American astronauts, America stopped manned flights for the time being and looked past the moon to send unmanned rockets to Mars and other planets. This is great for science, but it doesn't have the excitement and impact that Armstrong created.

Armstrong then decided to walk away from all publicity and lead a quiet life as a university professor. Even when he journeyed to the North Pole with Edmund Hillary's son in 1985, it was done in private. He had seen the North Pole out of the windows of *Gemini* and *Apollo* but wanted to find out what it was actually like.

He died in 2012, aged 82 and, at his request, he was buried at sea, near where he'd splashed down at the end of his history making journey.

He'd achieved his life's work, and with huge honour and, to my eternal disappointment, he discovered that there was no cheese on the moon.

He had often asked himself a blunt question about life that we all should ask of ourselves, 'Why am I here?'

He knew exactly why he was born, and he answered the question magnificently when he stepped onto the moon.

On many occasions after he returned from the lunar landscape, he was asked, 'Why didn't you find heaven out there? If you could not find it, where is it?'

He was reported as saying, 'You tell me where you think it is and I will fly out there to find it.'

The mystery of it all creates the power that enables Christians to keep searching for an answer and, while we are doing this, we can have great admiration of the life and work and commitment of the first man on the moon.

But let us get back to Earth for a moment and ponder the profound challenges of being a legend.

Armstrong was enraged when he discovered that his barber always kept his hair clippings, stored them in small bags and sold them to customers for $3000 a bag. There was a waiting list of willing buyers. At that moment, the barber lost his most famous customer, but by then his bank account was substantial and he was happy with his fate.

The fact that Armstrong could find no trace of heaven out there in the vast universe enabled me to affirm a personal decision.

He enabled me not to feel comfortable by not identifying myself a Christian.

This once treasured title has been demeaned by those who call themselves the 'Christian right' and who are people who shamelessly use Christianity as a political weapon.

Years ago, when Neil Armstrong reached the moon without finding either heaven or hell out in realms of space, I rejoiced that the myth had been shot to pieces, as I did not believe in either.

I give thanks that this enables us to get rid of the rubbish elements of theology and concentrate on Jesus the Man.

Now, I identify myself as a 'Working Partner of Jesus of Nazareth' and I walk with him to create a more compassionate world.

14:
Uncle Ho Defeats Uncle Sam (1970)

Wars achieve nothing except death and destruction.

No nation or leader ever wins a war — everyone loses.

In particular, the Vietnam War achieved nothing for the invaders of the land. They lost much and there was no valid reason that can even remotely justify it.

It revealed yet again that all participants in wars are scarred forever, physically, emotionally and financially.

Australia has partnered with the USA in four major wars over the past 75 years: Korea, Vietnam, Afghanistan and Iraq.

Important lessons can be learned from all four, particularly Vietnam where many more people died than in the other three combined. However, there was a result in Vietnam that united that nation, whereas the conflicts in Korea and Iraq are ongoing and, while Afghanistan has technically ended with the Taliban taking control, the battle will continue since their internal enemies will strive forever to remove them.

Most significantly, history will record that, at the time of the war, Vietnam was a small nation whose population was then only 30 million, yet it defeated a much larger nation of 350 million Americans (plus its allies) in a very decisive manner in circumstances that were quite extraordinary.

The tragic tale is quite fascinating.

Vietnam has been a nation for at least 4000 years, often dominated by China throughout that period, but continually proclaiming its independence. This ceased when France made it a colony in 1848 and inhumanely plundered it for a century. Japan successfully invaded Vietnam in 1940, but allowed Vichy France (Hitler's allies) to be a puppet government that helped supply their army while it conquered Malaya, Singapore and Indonesia.

When World War II ended, civil war broke out in Vietnam after they defeated and removed France. Communists took over North Vietnam with French Catholics and political conservatives occupied South Vietnam. It continued for 20 years. In 1963, America decided to support the proclaimed independence of the South. Their involvement lasted pointlessly for a bloody and disastrous decade.

For purely political reasons, Australia answered America's call for help and sent troops into the battle in 1965. Our prime minister, Harold Holt, adopted the slogan, 'All the way with LBJ', acknowledging his friendship with US President Lyndon Baines Johnson. North Vietnam eventually won and two profound messages came from this huge tragedy.

A key factor was that North Vietnam had a remarkable leader, who gave the impression of being benign and insignificant, but had a soul of steel. His name was Ho Chi Minh, now known to the world as Uncle Ho. This name was chosen deliberately as a play on the nick name of his enemy, Uncle Sam.

He spent his early life working as a slave labourer of French ships, then took up work in Paris as a waiter in a restaurant. He joined the French Communist Party and was sent to Russia for training as a revolutionary. From there, he returned home to Vietnam where he became leader of the Communist Party of Vietnam and devoted his life to defeating France, America and all their internal and external allies of which Australia, disgracefully, was one.

The simple reason for his victory was that the anti-communist allies were fighting for a shallow ideology based on capitalism and power. Uncle Ho and his people (known as the Vietcong) were fighting with passion for the freedom of their homeland. This made an enormous difference.

History has since proven that Uncle Ho was far more a nationalist than he was a communist. His name means 'Bridge of Light'. The former capital Saigon was renamed in his honour as Ho Chi Minh City. It is a well-deserved accolade since he did not start the war. That honour belongs solely to France. In an exercise of colonial greed when the Japanese were defeated, the French refused to return their illegal colony to those whose heritage covered thousands of years.

Why did Australia get involved?

Our stated rationale was that we wanted to stop the advance of communism in South-East Asia, while at the same time affirming our commitment to a long-term alliance with America.

We eventually sent something like 60,000 troops to Vietnam over the long course of the war, basically peaking at 7500 at any one time.

Most were young Aussies doing their compulsory national service. They were chosen for this honour by a ballot that decided who would serve according to the month and year of your birth. Five hundred and twenty-one of our conscripts were killed in the jungles of Vietnam. Another 3000 were wounded. Most of the remainder came home traumatised and many remain so to this day, receiving little help with their suffering. A disgraceful blot on our image as a civilised nation.

But we did do one good thing.

We accepted thousands of Vietnamese refugees as the war was coming to a close. They were on the losing side of the internal battle, but most became citizens of Australia, with one rising to become a distinguished governor of South Australia. Disgracefully, our current policy on refugees is now the oppositive. Totally inhumane.

When all is said and done, we failed once more to accept that all war is undeniably stupid.

While we should continue our alliance with Uncle Sam, we must do so with independence and not become involved in unnecessary confrontations that America has with China or any other nation. President Xi has the firepower, technology and skills to lob a rocket on Sydney from anywhere in China and destroy it completely. All our new expenditure on weapons of defence amounts to zero in terms of our ability to respond.

I have one shameful remembrance:

Australia helped America use chemical warfare against the Vietnamese. We sprayed their jungle with a lethal concoction called Agent Orange, which was intended to drive the Vietcong out into the open as well as contaminate their food supply. This had a cruel impact on the health of the Vietnamese civilians and the quality of their crops and livestock still evident half a century later. We are unable to put forward any justifiable excuse for this and must never ever do it again. It is not the Australian way.

Nevertheless, I proudly honour of the valiant Aussies who were given no option but to go to war in Vietnam. They faithfully served our nation even though they knew they should not be there and did not want to be there. They yearned to return to those they loved. They should never have left them in the first place. Now, many lie in lonely, unmarked graves covered by jungle.

It is important to remember that Uncle Sam also used conscripted troops in Vietnam and that many Americans publicly opposed the war and conscription

The most high-profile one was Muhammad Ali who fought conscription through the courts for years and won. He famously declared, 'I ain't got no quarrel with them Vietcong.'

Billions shared the same view.

But we must also not forget that the Vietcong were not saints. They fought with unrestrained brutality.

A prime example of this was on display when revered American senator and presidential candidate, John McCain, who died only recently, was a pilot in Vietnam who was shot down and captured. He was treated with gross inhumanity during five years as a prisoner of war. Incredibly, he bore them no malice.

Will there ever be a time when the world manages to go for a century without there being a war anywhere? I have dreamed of it, but am very certain it will never happen.

Wars are simply an extension of personal habits.

While we allow domestic violence to continue in our society, it means that we are condoning family wars.

When we have violent protests in our streets, we are saying that negotiations never work, but violence does.

Even the Bible recognised the problem. In the Bible's very first chapter, it records that Cain killed his brother Abel.

While the story is a myth, its message set the scene for others to do likewise anywhere at any time.

15:
The Remembrance Day Coup (1975)

A disgraceful abuse of democracy was carried out via the blatant manipulation of the Constitution of Australia by Governor-General John Kerr and achieved immortality for Gough Whitlam.

He will be remembered for centuries to come as the first, and hopefully the last, prime minister to be sacked by a governor-general.

It must never be allowed to happen again.

It was 11 November 1975.

At 11:00 am, I joined with millions of Australians in a minute of silence to remember all who served Australia in World War I, the Armistice for which had been signed on the 11th hour of the 11th day of the 11th month of 1918, 57 years previously.

Shortly afterwards, the news broke on the ABC that the governor-general of Australia, Sir John Kerr, had sacked the prime minister, Gough Whitlam, and appointed opposition leader, Malcolm Fraser, as caretaker PM until an election could be held in December. A mixture of both anger and joy broke out across a nation that was hopelessly divided in its initial reaction.

The three prime participants, Whitlam (prime minister), Kerr (governor-general) and Malcolm Fraser (leader of the opposition), were a flawed trio who by a fluke of history were in positions of power in the same place at the same time when there was an opportunity for a political crisis to be contrived.

Kerr was a person of personal insecurity who had severe problems with alcohol and had yearned since his schooldays to go down in history as someone who had done something memorably significant for the nation. He foolishly achieved his goal. His action will be debated for centuries to come. It was a profound breach of the Constitution of Australia.

Whitlam was a well-educated, intelligent and visionary prime minister. Nevertheless, he was also a poor manager of projects and people, who didn't suffer fools gladly. He was often discourteous to Kerr and badly underestimated his ability to make any decision of consequence. However, he had that very day won a vote of confidence in the House of Representatives and was therefore not remotely eligible to be sacked unless laws were to be broken.

Fraser was a blueblood who had the belief that he was born to rule and felt that this entitled him to have secret conversations with Kerr that enabled him to encourage the governor-general in his plan to sack Whitlam. It was a huge breach of protocol. He knew that Kerr could receive advice only from the prime minister. He also had no sense of timing. He didn't need to stage a coup to ensure he reached the Prime Minister's Lodge. He only had to wait six months for Whitlam's three years term to reach its end.

On the day of the sacking, Kerr advised Fraser that he was about to become prime minister before he told Whitlam that he was to be dismissed. The pointlessness of it all was that Whitlam was bound by the Constitution to call an election the following year, one which Fraser would have won in a landslide. Fraser needed only to exercise some patience to become PM without tearing the nation apart.

There were two other villains.

They were the Chief Justice of Australia Sir Garfield Barwick, and Justice Anthony Mason, who would later become chief justice. They met Kerr separately to give him constitutional advice and privately, without the knowledge of their prime minister, and recommended to him that he dismiss Whitlam. Had Whitlam gone immediately to the court on the day of his dismissal to take out an injunction to stop Kerr from sacking him, as he was entitled to do, they would have been in a compromised position of not being able to dispense justice especially as some of the other justices subsequently disagreed with the advice they had given Whitlam.

Queen Elizabeth was also involved indirectly.

Kerr had informed her of his concerns. As revealed in 2020 when the High Court of Australia authorised the release of Kerr's correspondence, the queen's private secretary had exchanged many letters with Kerr who had sought her advice on the legality of dismissing Whitlam. The secretary clearly encouraged Kerr to do so.

Several questions arise:

1. Does a governor-general have the power to dismiss a prime minister? Yes, so long as they operate within the confines of the Constitution.
2. Should Kerr have used that power? No.

The reserve powers in the Constitution were put there by Queen Victoria when she approved the Federation of Australian states in 1901. She was in her dotage and had opposed Federation because she wanted the six Australian states to become counties of England and elect representatives to the House of Commons at Westminster. Barton and Deakin threatened to follow the example of the USA and leave the Empire if her wishes were implemented. She only gave in when they agreed to add a clause enabling her to dismiss any prime minister who did not personally obey her wishes. Whitlam had many flaws but, at no point in his tenure as prime minister, did he ever disobey the queen.

The stated reason for Kerr dismissing Whitlam was that the Senate had for a month refused to grant supply to the Whitlam government. This meant that the government would shortly run out of funds for its daily operations.

The Senate had no constitutional right to do this. It has the right to reject individual money bills, but not deny basic funding for a government to function. It was Kerr's duty as governor-general to instruct the Senate to obey the Constitution. He did not.

So, almost half a century later, where does this leave us?

The coup established a tradition that now enables the Senate to hinder and defeat any government in any way that it chooses even though the government has the confidence of the House of Representatives and has been given a mandate at the previous election to carry out its stated policies. This outrage means that crossbench senators, who often get only a thousand or so primary votes in their state, and are elected by a fluke in the allocation of preferences, decide what laws will govern 25 million Australians. It is an abuse of democracy.

Now I will calm down for a few moments and chat about how life subsequently panned out for the protagonists.

A year later, Fraser asked Kerr to resign after he became hopelessly drunk on Melbourne Cup Day before a huge crowd at Flemington. Kerr went on to live in London. He died there, utterly ignored by Buckingham Palace and Westminster and Australia.

Gough Whitlam lived to a ripe old age, almost making it to his century, giving him time to reflect on how ineptly he handled his dismissal. Had he instructed his senators on that historic day to deny funds to Fraser's government, he would have foiled Kerr's decision and rendered it void.

Nevertheless, almost miraculously, he and Fraser eventually reconciled their differences and worked as a team on various causes, often appearing together as speakers at major public events. I attended one of them and it was a delight to witness their extraordinary reconciliation.

Malcolm Fraser was never able to live with his guilt. He became an ineffectual prime minister as a result. After losing to Hawke in 1983, Fraser fell out with the Liberal Party and resigned his membership when he publicly declared that they had moved to the extreme right and he could no longer accept this. While it is true that they have moved far to the right, Fraser had moved left at the same time.

At the end of the day, there were no winners of this coup. The prime loser was Australia. Politics produces few saints.

But there is often a touch of humour in any crisis.

At the election that followed the coup, Whitlam was harassed at a campaign rally by a woman.

'You are the devil incarnate, Gough. When you die and get to the gates of heaven, how are you going to convince the Lord that he should not send you to hell?'

'Madam,' replied Gough, 'I want to assure you that I will treat him as an equal and debate the matter vigorously.'

Fraser's most memorable words were, 'Life was not meant to be easy.'

The only words of Kerr's that will be remembered are the absurd ones he used when he gave his unjustifiable reasons for sacking Gough.

The Australian people had the final say when they elected Fraser at the subsequent election, but their votes were emphatically not an endorsement of what Kerr had done. They simply took to opportunity to remove Gough — he had lost their confidence.

The power of the governor-general in relation to Parliament and the ministry is now a matter for urgent review and, then, subsequent constitutional changes.

The Constitution does not mention a prime minister.

The sole right to appoint ministers is given to the governor-general.

By tradition, the prime minister advises the governor-general who should be appointed, but the governor-general is under no obligation whatsoever to accept that advice. They can appoint whoever they want to and the prime minister can do nothing about it.

Given the reality of these powers, the people of Australia should have a say in who becomes governor-general. The power to make such an

appointment now rests solely with the prime minister and the UK monarch even though the prime minister has no status under the Constitution.

This defect in the Constitution reveals a general breakdown of the functioning of a democracy. It is clearly unsatisfactory and must be changed via a referendum.

16:
She Broke the Glass Ceiling (1979)

Margaret Thatcher was an incredible woman who was either loved or hated.

Very few people were able to take a moderate position in commenting on her.

Nevertheless, for good or ill, she was a powerful leader who had a passionate view of how to change the world via conservative ideology and she gave it a 100% commitment.

But, at the end of the day, her dedication to her agenda brought her down in dramatic fashion.

Margaret Thatcher was the daughter of devout Methodists who owned a small shop at Grantham in England. They took her to church every Sunday. She often became bored with the church but experienced bursts of enthusiasm whenever the parson talked about John Wesley, legendary founder of the Methodists 400 years earlier.

Wesley's ministry was based on solid fundamentalism that reached out to the poor and dispossessed, and his brand of Christianity became the core of Thatcher's faith too. She believed that if Christians followed Jesus of

Nazareth in caring for the downtrodden, then there would never be a need for any government to hand out welfare. In her view, governments were forced to get involved only because churches failed to take up their calling. Thatcher became a generous, lifelong donor to Wesley Missions but held a low opinion of church leaders who were not like Wesley. For this reason, she attended church only when duty called.

Just like many people with a Christian background, she felt a calling to reform the world politically and economically by taking up politics as a progressive conservative. As you know, she became prime minister of England about four decades ago, the first woman to achieve that honour while remaining in power for 10 years. She 'broke the glass ceiling' that had denied women their right to achieve political equality with men.

Of course, she was not the first woman in the world to do this, but she was probably the most famous. Indira Gandhi had been elected as PM of India much earlier and Golda Meier had done likewise in Israel. She was not the last either. Angela Merkel followed her when she gave superb long-term leadership to Germany. Similarly, Julia Gillard got the top job in Australia as well Jacinda Ardern in New Zealand and Michelle Bachalet in Chile.

Hilary Clinton failed to break the glass ceiling in the USA. She should have beaten Trump easily, but ran the most pompous, out of touch campaign such as I have rarely seen and did so in a juvenile performance against an unstable bloke she should have wiped out.

So, the crusade goes on. The glass ceiling has not yet been broken in the workplace where women are still consistently paid less than men and must try twice as hard to get a promotion in any profession.

I was in the Australian Parliament in Canberra in 1974 when Gough Whitlam had legislation passed granting women equal pay for equal work. I stood and cheered. It was a historic moment for our nation. But the misogynists in Parliament couldn't cope with the threat of equality and rose up immediately in cynical anger and declared falsely that no woman did in fact work which was equal to that of a man in any field of employment.

So, to this day, while the gap has narrowed, equality is still an unfulfilled aspiration of what should be a civilised society, and this is to the eternal disgrace of Australia (and the world). Nevertheless, we have made some progress. Australia has one female state premier, Annastacia Palaszczuk, at my time of writing and our chief justice is a woman.

However, let us return to Maggie.

Even though some of her legislation was based on extreme right-wing ideology, and she was very rigid in too many of her public statements, there can be absolutely no doubt that she was an extraordinary leader who revolutionised the British economy and led her nation to victory in the Falkland War with Argentina. She overstepped the mark with an excessive privatisation of government assets and services and may have caused the world to rethink the wisdom of governments aspiring to have only a small role in society and the economy.

Throughout her era, she dispensed no political spin. What she said she would do, she did. If you got in the way, that was your bad luck.

The world needs more people of conviction in the Thatcher mould — leaders who follow an ideology and whom we feel we can trust even though we may often disagree with them. They are a significantly scarce commodity in modern life.

It is fascinating that John Wesley's great social mission was a cornerstone conviction of Thatcher's life. She was not driven by a religious faith as he was, but she believed that you were not Christian unless you were a hard and tireless worker and a responsible citizen. We will not see her like again for a long time.

This is a pity because she had graduated in science at university and, conservative though she was, she became the world's first political leader to advocate action on climate change. One of the several reasons why her colleagues voted her out was that she proposed legislation on it. Even now, few conservatives are in the climate team in any nation. A tragedy of closed minds.

There are many more glass ceilings to be broken and one day they will be. I hope that some of them will be inspired by the example of John Wesley, just as Maggie was.

John Wesley's theology is one of the founding pillars of the beliefs of the Uniting Church in Australia of which I am an elder and 44 of his most famous sermons are embedded in the Basis of Union agreed by the Methodist, Presbyterian and Congregational churches in Australia 45 years ago.

Thus, we can all be assured that Wesley was a leader of people who aspire to have a mission in life.

Thatcher's life and work have given us the same assurance.

Given that Margaret Thatcher became the leader of Britain in 1979, it is extraordinary that, 44 years later, the United States of America has not yet elected a female president.

This fundamental question must be asked, 'Is the USA a misogynist nation?'

It is hard to answer that question in the negative.

However, it is heartening to know that in 2020 the Americans elected a female vice president, Kamala Harris, so it remains possible that an American woman may yet break the glass ceiling.

Time will tell.

17:
Mr Gorbachev, Tear Down this Wall (1989)

The collapse of the Berlin Wall signalled the end of the Cold War between the USA and Russia and advanced the pending collapse of communist governments in Eastern Europe.

This marked a significant event in world history even though Putin has the destruction of Ukraine on his agenda.

Thus, the demise of the Soviet Union did not create a more peaceful world.

The can has quite simply been kicked down the road.

As Eisenhower led the Allied army across France following the D-Day invasion in June 1944, the Russian army was rapidly driving the Germans back through Poland. It became a race to see who would reach Berlin first. Eisenhower should have been the one to get there first, but he was delayed by Hitler's desperate decision to stage one last mighty battle to save his evil empire.

The insane dictator launched the Battle of the Bulge in the Ardennes region of Belgium and sent the Allies into retreat as he threw at them every last resource that he had. There were heavy casualties on both sides, but the German offensive eventually ran out of steam, allowing Eisenhower to advance again. The delay enabled Stalin to take Berlin and go far beyond to lay permanent claim to everything he had captured.

So it was that in the post-war negotiations, two nations were formed, East Germany and West Germany. Berlin itself was divided into four zones that were controlled by Russia, USA, UK and France. After three million East Germans fled to West Germany over the following decade, the East German communist government built a wall around the Russian sector of Berlin. They also fenced the entire border that divided Germany and laid one million land mines along it. They even went to the extreme of having 3000 attack dogs patrolling it constantly.

This caused Winston Churchill to remark that 'An iron curtain has descended upon Europe.'

The prime place to try to escape from the East to the West was called Checkpoint Charlie, which was the connection artery between the divided city where over the years 150 people were shot dead trying to run across it to gain freedom from communism.

A change began when Gorbachev became president of Russia. He was the first Russian leader with the courage and ability to acknowledge that communism throughout Europe was in its death throes, economically, politically and socially. He tried to reform the structure of communism and formed a political friendship with Margaret Thatcher who gained agreement from Ronald Reagan that as much as possible should be done behind the scenes to quietly cooperate with Gorbachev in his reformation strategy.

Reagan went to West Berlin to make a speech containing the famous words, 'Mr Gorbachev, tear down this wall!'

Thatcher had told Gorbachev of it in advance. It was all part of a three-way strategy to make genuine changes happen. It worked successfully for a while.

On 9 November 1989, the infamous Checkpoint Charlie, the scene of many deaths, was opened to free movement, and people were allowed to move without hindrance around Berlin. Five hundred thousand residents of Berlin emerged with axes, hammers and shovels to knock down the wall brick by brick. Some tore it down with their bare hands. It was one of the most extraordinary scenes of freedom in the history of the world.

At the same time, the East German government collapsed and the reunification of Germany began. One of those who took part in the merger negotiations on behalf of East Germany was a young Angela Merkel who was a science teacher at the time but recognised by powerful mentors as a potential leader of the future. It was the beginning of her impressive political career.

The reforms that Gorbachev bravely initiated caused the rotten, old inefficient economy of Russia to collapse quickly.

In a coup that I regard as an enormous tragedy, Gorbachev himself fell two years later. He was universally blamed for the inevitable chaos and Boris Yeltsin, a hopeless alcoholic, took his place. This opened the doors for Putin to easily remove Yeltsin and become yet another infamous dictator of Russia. Thankfully, communist governments throughout Europe were gradually replaced and, hopefully, are unlikely to ever return.

If we can be objective for a moment, may I put forward the view that it is possible to imagine that communism in its purest form was a splendid concept for creating conditions for equality of humanity. However, none of the proponents of it, especially Lenin, Stalin, Mao, Castro, Tito, and so on, ever made the slightest effort to practise it in its purest form.

They used it as an ideal they could promote solely as a weapon to gain power. They then deliberately made sure that they failed to implement the equality they espoused. They concentrated on retaining power through constant bloodshed and fear while they enjoyed grand lives that personally made them far more equal than anyone else.

The original aim and impact of communism in its purest form was not unlike that of Christianity, but it didn't ever have a leader of the quality and compassion and honesty of Jesus of Nazareth.

Interestingly, Mahatma Gandhi once remarked, 'The tragedy of Christianity is that no-one has ever tried to practise it in the manner that Jesus intended.'

Nevertheless, it is Christianity, not a revival of communism, that is most likely to enable us to live in hope of a better, fairer, more honest world that can be enjoyed without fear. The major obstacle to this is the so called 'Christian right' who use their 'faith' as a political weapon, just as the communists did with their ideology.

So, may I suggest that if you have not yet visited Berlin, you should do so as soon as the post-virus world makes it easy to do.

It is a magnificent city that almost became the capital of the world when Hitler was at the peak of his power. I visited there a decade ago and experienced the memories of war and peace.

I made it my business to walk across Checkpoint Charlie and retrace the steps of those who died trying to escape across it to the bright lights of the West and away from the repressive gloom and torture of the East. I saw it as a symbol of the hope that will always lie deep in the soul of humanity, never to be repressed.

I also visited the Jewish Museum Berlin that graphically tells the history of the Holocaust, one of the most terrible events in the history of humanity. It is an experience of inhumanity not to be missed.

Above all, it will commit us to the cause of breaking down all the walls — political, religious, racist, economic — anywhere in the world that have no place in civilised society.

Gorbachev was followed as Russian Leader by Boris Yeltsin, an alcoholic incompetent. Yeltsin's arrival provided an advantage for Vladimir Putin in his quest for power.

Putin was a common thug who removed Yeltsin without raising a sweat.

This leads us to ask ourselves some crucial questions:

'What has been achieved by the knocking down the Berlin Wall and the subsequent fall of Gorbachev?'

A reunited Germany certainly did well. It was led to prosperity by Angela Merkel, but Putin led Russia away from communism and embraced an aggressive form of fascism that is far worse.

Thus far Russia has consumed Crimea and is endeavouring to do likewise in Ukraine. The Baltic states will surely follow.

Be this as it may, when Gorbachev died in 2022 at age 91, I took a moment to remember him in a silent tribute. He rid the world of the yoke of communism oppression and gave Deng a convenient excuse to reform the communist government of China, transforming it into a bastion of state capitalism by avoiding the political mistakes that Gorbachev made in his haste to achieve reform.

18:
The End of a White World (1994)

Forgiveness was once a pillar of the Christian faith that will hopefully return one day.

Nelson Mandela did not openly embrace Christianity, but his life and work had many similarities to that of Jesus of Nazareth.

He fought fiercely for justice and peace, then won it with compassion.

I was at Bloemfontein in South Africa working on raising finance for a reforming venture at the University of Orange Free State. It had been an all-white university for more than a century, but it had recently made the controversial decision to admit non-whites as students for the first time. It planned to allow them to qualify for admission by studying on campus at minimal cost. This was a ground-breaking change that apartheid whites had great difficulty in accepting.

My phone rang.

It was Zach de Beer, parliamentary leader of the Progressive Federal Party.

His party had been formed many years earlier by the legendary anti-apartheid warrior, Helen Suzman, who was the valiant leader of the minority section of the white community that alone advocated inevitable change to the white domination of South Africa. The Progressive Federal Party had been fundraising clients of mine for five years. Together, we had raised sufficient money to enable them to increase their number of seats in parliament from 10 to 36 over two elections.

Zach said, 'Parliament has just voted to let Nelson Mandela out of jail.'

It was a breathtaking day in South Africa's history of white supremacy and Zach's party had made it happen.

For far too long it had been clear to almost the entire world that South Africa had reached such a state of international disrepute that it had no option but to set Mandela free after having made him work as a slave in disgraceful primitive conditions in a prison on Robben Island near Cape Town for two decades.

President Willem de Klerk, who led a white supremist government that had been in power for decades, made a courageous but inevitable decision to release Mandela but, when he put the vote to parliament, 30 of his own party crossed the floor to sit with the ultra-conservative opposition and deny him the votes he required.

Zach de Beer then led his liberals from the crossbenches to sit with de Klerk and give him the numbers he needed to win.

Mandela was a free man.

The news caused me to sit down and take several very deep breaths to regain my composure because I had experienced a small personal role in changing the course of history.

I recalled a challenging day of my life when, while Mandela was still in jail, I was organising capital for a foundation that helped Zulus set up small businesses. I went to a village outside of Johannesburg to meet a man who was a close friend of Mandela and who had offered to help with fundraising. He had once been in the same jail as Mandela for several years. Our conversation was both riveting and heart-rending.

Suddenly, the South African police raided the village and informed me, at gunpoint, that I was under arrest.

I produced my Australian passport, plus a letter that Bob Hawke had given me commending my work in South Africa. The senior police officer told me that he'd never heard of Hawke but wisely decided it would be smart to back off instead of creating a possible international incident. However, he insisted on following my car all the way back to my hotel. On arrival, he told me to never again contact anyone associated with Mandela, an instruction that I did not comply with.

I never met Mandela, but I have read several books about him and had long and fascinating conversations with people who knew him well. He was clearly an extraordinary person of great compassion and a hugely inspirational leader.

When he won the subsequent election in a landslide, he publicly forgave all who had imprisoned and tortured him, and he retained the services of the white public servants who had worked for years with the apartheid government. He deliberately said to them that he had no experience of government and needed their knowledge of how a government worked. Incredibly, they agreed to stay and served him loyally.

For many centuries, European nations conquered vast sections of every continent and ruled them ruthlessly and inhumanely as they plundered their resources. South Africa was a prime example of extreme white arrogance and injustice. Many colonial nations such as India, Pakistan, Indonesia and Algeria gained their freedom long before South Africa did, but when Mandela walked free, his fame was such that it was the symbolic end of a world once utterly dominated by whites. Never again will any nation become a colony dominated by foreign racists.

When Mandela made state visits to the old colonial masters of South Africa, the British and the Dutch, he was greeted by enormous crowds. People reached out to touch him, seeking forgiveness for what their ancestors had done to him and his people. He warmly responded. Everyone understood that the age of slavery was at an end.

My most vivid memory of him was the day when the white South African Rugby Union Team won the World Cup final in Cape Town, defeating an overwhelmingly white New Zealand team, ironically called the All Blacks. Mandela walked out on to the field and put on a Springbok jersey to show that they were his team. He was one of them. They greeted him warmly and formed a rugby ruck around him to show that he was their leader.

Sadly, racism still lives and thrives in our world.

It always will. Every generation produces a more radical brand of bigots, mostly Christian, Muslim, Hindu and Jewish plus a lot of thugs who are blatantly fascist. Fortunately, society usually rises above them.

For Christian nations, this is important because there is no evidence whatsoever that Jesus of Nazareth was a white man or a racist or a zealot.

He is a role model for us all and a leader worth following.

I am a committed working partner of his.

There are two significant ways in which we can judge leaders of nations:
- **by the economic prosperity they create, or**
- **the spiritual, moral and ethical leadership they give and the inspiration they provide.**

Critics say that Mandela did not create prosperity, but this was a near impossibility in a nation where most non-whites had not previously received even a minimal education that would equip them to be moderately productive.

What few can deny is that he gave his people freedom, dignity and hope to begin a long journey out of poverty.

19: The Rejection of the Turnbull Republic (1997)

Three questions must be answered before there can be any changes to the Australian Constitution that will create a republic.

Is there any need for Australia ever to become a republic?

Can we remove the powers of the British Crown that are currently in our Constitution and have an Australian head of state while still retaining the legal status of being the Commonwealth of Australia?

Will we be better off without the Crown?

Malcolm Turnbull is one of the most intelligent people I have ever met. He had the ability and opportunity to be a successful and revered prime minister of Australia and should have been for at least a decade. He could have gone down in history as one of our greatest prime ministers. He looked and acted like a prime minister.

Sadly, he was a disappointing failure due to three significant personal flaws:
- an immature belief in his personal destiny
- the inability to be a team player
- a lack of basic political nous.

These traits were vividly on display many years before he ever became prime minister and were prime reasons why he, to the disappointment of thousands of volunteers who backed him, led them to the loss of the Australian republic referendum in 1999.

Unwittingly, he made it a referendum on his personality and leadership, not the virtues of becoming a republic. He was certain that Australia's voters would see him as the creator of a significant piece of Australian history when we rejected the British Crown. Hindered by this delusion, he naively allowed himself to be outmanoeuvred by John Howard on the framing of the words put to voters that he thought were a minor bit of trivia in comparison to the big picture. Added to all of this, in all the planning of the campaign, his decisions were those that prevailed in the organising and conducting the campaign, not those of his team. Had he listened to them, he would have won.

I can speak with some personal knowledge of those dramatic events since I was an active member of his broader team. This occurred when it became clear that Turnbull's referendum campaign was struggling. Andrew Robb, a longstanding friend of mine who would later become an MP and minister, invited me to join him in forming a new team called *Conservatives for an Australian Head of State*. I did so with alacrity and determination.

Our original plan was just to advocate a simple change to the Australian Constitution by deleting all references to the 'British Crown and replacing them with the words *The People of Australia*. By doing this we would not need to become a republic. We could retain the title Commonwealth of Australia. These two issues alone would have turned defeat into victory.

We also planned to retain the office and title of governor-general because the word president created many negative images.

Additionally, it was our opinion that the matter of how the governor-general would be elected could be decided in a separate referendum.

Because Malcolm Turnbull was not interested at all in any of the above, Andrew Robb and I campaigned solely on one vital issue that an Australian should be our head of state, not the British monarch.

However, we were not Malcolm's biggest problem.

He refused to consider making a deal with a powerful group of committed republicans led by former Brisbane Lord Mayor, Clem Jones, who wanted the president of a republic to be elected by Australian voters, not appointed by Parliament. They decisively destroyed Malcolm's vision of a republic by asking their supporters to vote with the monarchists as a protest against his intransigence.

An analysis of voting estimated that only 21% of voters supported the retention of a role for the monarchy in Australian Government. The rest were republicans who were unnecessarily and hopelessly divided. So, we all fell together.

A quarter of a century later, should we now hold another referendum on the republic?

Yes, but not for the moment.

In the aftermath of a pandemic and its devastating social and economic aftermath, 90% of voters regard the issue of becoming a republic as an enormous piece of trivia they can do without while we sort out how to prepare for and manage the next pandemic.

More importantly, a much more pressing need in the minds of most voters is to hold and win a referendum to enshrine our First Peoples heritage into the Constitution.

Can we make these and other significant constitutional changes at an appropriate time?

Absolutely.

Regarding Malcolm Turnbull's vision of a republic, we do not have to use that word ever again, especially as most voters regard it as American. We simply need to have a vote to remove our legal ties with Britain, and we also must design a means whereby voters can have a say on who will be our governor-general and not leave that power to the prime minister alone as is wrongly done now.

At the same time, we must vote to clearly define the powers and composition of the Senate, which was established for the sole purpose of protesting the rights of the smaller states in any power struggle to curb the dominance of New South Wales and Victoria. It should only have the right to delay legislation by recommending changes to the House of Representatives, but after three such delays, it must pass it.

And we do not need each state to elect 12 senators who have two terms without facing voters. It is disgracefully ridiculous that Tasmania has 12 senators, but only five members of the House of Representatives.

So, we must continually seek to reform the great work that the Founding Fathers achieved in 1901 as, 120 years later, we live in an entirely new world and must adapt to it. But, when we vote on changes, they must be founded on and come from the grass roots of society, not from the thoughts of one leader or any group of politicians.

Malcolm Turnbull himself would not make that mistake again, even though he still retains those three flaws. They were the fundamental reasons why he was removed as prime minister in a primitive and unnecessary coup in 2018.

Two-thirds of the nations that are members of the British Commonwealth of Nations are republics that no longer have the British monarch as their head of state, but happily retain an informal link with the British Commonwealth of Nations.

Australia's tragedy is that we always appear to be hesitant to follow their pathway of independence.

We say that it's because we're reluctant to offend the Crown, but this is nonsense. Queen Elizabeth was not offended at all when so many of Britain's former colonies chose to become republics. They revered her as a person, as most Australian Republicans clearly did.

Australians are simply too frightened to cut the apron strings with Mother England.

We are in fear of living alone in a potentially hostile world and, because we are so paranoid, our stature on the world scene is hugely diminished.

20:
The Tampa Affair (2001)

The events surrounding the Norwegian ship Tampa and its human cargo of refugees degraded Australia's status as a benevolent nation and a responsible one.

Nevertheless, it enabled John Howard to turn a highly probable electoral defeat into a significant political victory.

Can Australia be proud of the way we handled the Tampa incident?

Emphatically, NO.

In August 2001, an unseaworthy vessel named the *Palapa* that was operated by people smugglers was carrying 433 refugees from Afghanistan to Australia. It sent distress signals saying it was sinking in the Indian Ocean not far from Christmas Island. The Australian coast guard picked up the messages and broadcast a crisis call to all ships in the area.

Captain Arne Rinnan of Norway, who was sailing to Australia on a freighter called *Tampa*, responded immediately. Our coast guard determined that he was commanding the ship that was closest to the *Palapa* and invited him to go to their rescue.

Rinnan was a decent man with years of maritime experience. He had no difficulty in accepting this responsibility since it was an international custom of all seafarers — and part of their folklore — to which both Norway and Australia are signatories.

The tradition has for centuries been that those in peril on the seas must be saved if at all possible by the nearest ship in the area. Guided there by an Australian coast guard plane, Rinnan quickly reached the *Palapa* and transferred the refugees, plus five crew, onto the deck of the *Tampa*. He had nowhere else to put them. The holds were packed full of freight bound for Australia,

He found that 43 of the refugees were children and four were pregnant women. Many were suffering from dysentery.

Because Christmas Island was the closest place to take the stranded refugees and was an overseas territory of Australia, Rinnan set sail for there. He assumed that this was what the Australian coast guard would want him to do since they were the ones who contacted him and sought his cooperation. But on arrival offshore from Christmas Island, the Howard government refused to take the refugees and directed an Australian SAS regiment to board *Tampa*, inspect the passengers and, if they were deemed to be fit to travel further, to instruct Rinnan to take them to Indonesia.

It was an act of piracy for Australia to direct the SAS to aggressively board a Norwegian boat in international waters. It is important to note that Rinnan later reported that the Australians who boarded his ship had apologised to him, but said they had no alternative but to follow orders from their superiors.

To add to the appalling fiasco, Indonesia also refused to take the unwanted human cargo. The refugees were left in limbo.

To cut a long and complicated story short, the refugees were eventually sent to Nauru, New Zealand subsequently took 131 of them and Australia accepted 92. The remainder had varying fates, but their treatment as human beings was disgraceful.

While all of this was happening, John Howard made his famous speech saying, 'We will decide who comes to Australia and the manner in which they come.'

At the time, Australia was just a few months away from a general election and the polls were showing clearly that the ALP, led by Kim Beasley, would win decisively.

In the emotional parliamentary debates that followed on urgent legislation that Howard rammed through Parliament to 'legalise' his decision, he dominated Beasley, whose sympathy was with the plight of the refugees but was wedged on its politics. The prime minister swiftly rose in the polls. He had correctly read the minds of voters and subsequently won the election.

We could be both cold-blooded and pragmatic about this and say that Howard was far more astute than Beasley in reading the anti-refugee mood of the electorate, and we would not be wrong.

The aftermath resulted in a major political rift between Australia, Norway and Indonesia and criticism from the United Nations. There was worldwide media condemnation of Australia for the way in which Captain Rinnan had been abused and humiliated, when his sole sin was to respond to a request from the Australian coast guard to save hundreds of people who were drowning at sea as they fled from a war in Afghanistan in which Australia was an active participant.

The undeniable blame for this fiasco lies entirely with Australia and we should admit it with shame.

Rinnan subsequently was given several international humanitarian awards as well as being granted the highest honours Norway could give him.

He deserved these accolades because the refugees staged an unsuccessful physical revolt against his crew when it became clear that Australia would not take them. They declared him to be weak for not forcing Australia's hand in the matter. Unfortunately, they conveniently forgot that he had saved them from drowning.

Australia's reputation took a huge battering internationally, but most Australians rarely ever get upset about what the world thinks about us, and the international community has now, 20 years later, largely forgotten this disgraceful incident.

Of far greater concern is that our harsh policies on refugees still remain in place two decades later and are very primitive and without a hint of compassion. But life goes on despite all that. Politics is without compassion.

Nevertheless, there is an undeniable fact to be absorbed by every Australian.

We must acknowledge that our economic history proves that the waves of migrants who have come by boat to Australia for two centuries have always boosted our prosperity. They have never created unemployment or caused an economic recession.

We now need more of them to come here and, if we're smart, we will admit them with a legal requirement and motivational policy that they must live and work for at least a decade in our sparsely populated rural regions, not our crowded capital cities.

Inland Australia is far more liveable than most of the places from which many refugees have fled — it's time to look more seriously at resettling refugees in more regional areas.

Australia's harsh policies on refugees are in contravention of international treaties signed just after World War II ended.

Basically, we are obliged to grant asylum to refugees fleeing wars.

We accepted that responsibility when we allowed thousands of refugees from Vietnam to settle here after we'd been heavily involved in that conflict.

The Vietnamese refugees proved to be good citizens, yet we now treat other refugees like animals with no rights.

Our position on this issue of humanity really is indefensible.

It's long overdue for us to change it permanently.

21:
9/11 (2001)

We live in a violent world.

Indeed, the inescapable fact is that the world has always been violent.

9/11 is a classic example of violence at its worst.

It was caused by religious bigotry and was accompanied by a renewal of fear, greed and lies at many levels of society that are now permanent elements of life.

The reality of it is that it is the responsibility of each and every one of us to eliminate religious bigots from our personal society.

I was staying overnight at a hotel in Sydney on 11 September 2001. When I stirred from my slumbers, I went to the door of my room to pick up the morning newspaper. The headlines hit me like a sledgehammer, as did the almost unbelievable front-page photo of a plane crashing into one of the Twin Towers in New York.

Immediately, I tried to call my son Paul who lived and worked in New York. I could not get through. The American telephone system had collapsed.

My wife, Helen, called from Brisbane to make sure I'd heard the news. She too was having no luck with phone calls.

Then Paul sent us both a message to say he was okay, but was trying to find his wife, Andrea, who was attending a meeting at a building right next door to the Twin Towers. We breathed a huge sigh of relief when he was able to let us know they had found one another and were walking across Brooklyn Bridge to their home because the transport system was in lockdown. In what was an absolute miracle, Andrea had caught one of the last trains out of Ground Zero just before the subway collapsed.

Two decades after what Americans refers to as 9/11, we can look back with some degree of calm and, importantly, try to understand why it was that 3000 people died and 25,000 were injured on that dreadful day. What exactly did the terrorists achieve?

Without in any way wanting to praise Osama bin Laden, who was an evil killer, it must be acknowledged that it was a brilliantly planned and executed operation that no-one except Al Qaeda could have ever contemplated as a possibility. It took years of planning and organisation to enlist and train zealots and fanatics who were willing to die to make it all happen.

The response by America was to invade Iraq after falsely claiming that Saddam Hussein had weapons of mass destruction. Australia joined them in what was to be a pointless operation that killed millions and is still unresolved. Sadly, President George W Bush didn't pause to ask himself what caused Bin Laden to even think about this awful atrocity. He should have been stunned into self-reflection when he learned the news that large numbers of people in many nations had openly clapped and cheered when they heard what had happened.

Regrettably, he took no steps to find out and no-one since has seriously tried to resolve the differences that generated this hatred in the first place. There is fault on both sides for taking up polarising positions.

I can think of at least 10 reasons why it happened and why it should never have happened. Ultimately, it was a lethal mixture of international politics, religious intolerance, personal greed and primitive minds.

But, out of every disaster, come wonderful tales of people risking their lives to search for and save others. Too many of those heroic volunteers died as they tried to help people they had never met before. They set an example of compassionate humanity and incredible bravery we must treasure and never forget.

A photograph I will never forget is one of a man and a woman who held hands as they jumped out of a window in one of the stricken towers 80 floors up. It was the only alternative that they had. They were to be incinerated by the scorching hot fires that surrounded them. Their deaths were initially recorded as suicides, but a court subsequently changed that by correctly declaring it to be an act of voluntary euthanasia. The judges ruled that, because they faced certain death, they made the choice that a jump would be less painful than burning and so they chose to die together. It was a small step in ensuring that justice could prevail for all who died on that shocking day.

Years later, as the result of immense diplomatic risks taken by President Obama, Osama bin Laden was shot and killed in Pakistan by American soldiers in a skilful operation. He was buried at sea without ceremony that very day. Few people in the Western world mourned him. But, to the people of the Middle East, he has become a revered legend, a hero of the Muslim faith, whose memory will live forever.

So, the crucial question is this: will an event like 9/11 ever happen again?

Yes.

With absolute certainty.

Lethal weapons have more power over the behaviour and responses of humanity than goodwill.

Those of us who want to try to change this have a lifelong challenge ahead of us. This fact is blot on the human conscience.

Many believe that violent acts like 9/11 will always originate in the Muslim world and be aimed at nations whose origins are Christian.

This is not likely to be the case.

It is now a greater possibility that an equivalent to 9/11 will originate in nations that are basically 'Christian', such as Russia or in the Balkans. Even more likely is that it will originate from the United States itself.

Of great concern also is that it is already happening via religious persecution in India where Hindu nationalism is profusely aggressive against Muslims and Sikhs and Buddhists.

22:
America Elects a Black President (2008)

The election of Barack Obama as president of the USA was a huge step forward, culturally, spiritually and racially, for the American people.

Their next step of similar impact will be to elect a woman as their leader.

This will open the door to an LGBTIQ person winning the top job.

I won't live to see it, but it will be a wonderful achievement.

They have already proven they can break with tradition as, back in 1932, they elected a person with a disability, Franklin Delano Roosevelt, to lead their nation. He stayed in office for 12 years despite suffering from severe polio.

I really should change the title to African American president, but I chose to say 'black' so as to highlight the huge difference in the lives of white and black Americans.

We can begin by going back to origins of this tragic humanitarian issue.

Commencing from the 1700s, slave traders from European nations, most of whom identified themselves as practising Christians who believed they were God's chosen people, invaded Africa and violently herded Africans into filthy boats for an inhumane journey across the Atlantic to North America. Many died on the way. Those who arrived there were sold as slaves to the owners of wealthy plantations where they worked in primitive conditions for no pay. Most were subjected to appalling brutality, with no semblance of human rights acknowledged.

Eventually, despite heavy opposition, action to stop this was taken in Britain by an MP named William Wilberforce who showed extraordinary leadership to have legislation passed through the House of Commons banning British ships from participating in slave trading. This was a wonderful first step in a long journey and it took 15 years of intense political negotiations for Wilberforce to achieve it despite receiving persistent abuse.

A disturbing factor to note is that he did it despite powerful opposition from the Church of England who were the receiver of regular financial support from slave traders who gave the church significant sums of money in return for not condemning or opposing their inhuman activities.

In 1860, the whites in the southern states of the USA began a civil war to maintain their God-given right to continue to have slaves doing all the hard work for them. Thankfully, they lost, and Abraham Lincoln, the finest president in American history, convinced Congress to pass legislation freeing all slaves. He paid a huge personal price for doing this. He was the first American president to be assassinated.

Even so, slaves were only nominally free. Every possible obstacle was put in their way to prevent them from being accepted as human beings with a right to equality and the freedom to vote.

Then, one day, a century and a half later, a miracle occurred.

A black man was elected president of the United States and he was sworn in for the first of his two terms of office in January 2008. It was almost unbelievable. Non-whites openly wept in public. Barack Obama, most probably the finest orator of my lifetime, was expected to do his best to fix all that was wrong with the hugely divided American society.

But, for a wide range of reasons, it didn't happen and many felt a sense of betrayal. This has been proven to be an unfair attitude.

Just before Obama won office, America had been stricken by the Global Financial Crisis that hit the world in the latter part of 2007 and the solving of that consumed his first two years as president. Then, he lost control of Congress in the mid-term elections and didn't have the votes to get significant legislation passed.

Also, as a relatively young president, he did not have the political skills of master legislators like Lyndon Johnson and Joe Biden who knew how to twist arms to gain assent. Much as I admire Obama, his record indicates that he was as a moderate achiever as a reformer. But he did get elected twice, thus showing that a majority of Americans sought change from being a racist, gun-toting society.

Now, a series of African American deaths, notably that of George Floyd, caused by unjustifiable police brutality, has created the Black Lives Matter movement. It will burn relentlessly for years. It will not go away. Tumultuous days lie ahead with no-one really knowing how it will play out. There have been gutless efforts to fob it all off by glibly saying 'All Lives Matter'. While this is true, it is nevertheless a coward's way out of avoiding any responsibility for racism.

So, we now have a clear option facing us.

We can really get specific and serious about particular acts of discrimination that occur too regularly. We could win the support of most of humanity in asserting that Women's Lives Matter or we can choose to overlook it. Additionally, we can highlight LGBTIQ Lives Matter, Disabled Lives Matter, Refugee Lives Matter along with thousands upon thousands of others who are always trampled upon by the powerbrokers who look after the privileged and ignore injustice.

It's clearly obvious that the best path forward for society is to hear and follow the calling to turn a selfish world into one where most people are given the chance to attain a good life in the sun by fully expressing the talents that they have

---

If you would like to get a refreshingly authentic view of Barack Obama, then I strongly recommend that you buy the book *Renegades*, the story of Obama's friendship with Bruce Springsteen.

They jointly wrote it and it is a cracker of a read.

It's an inspirational encounter of two guys who came from nowhere to reach for the stars and get there.

It may motivate you to read Obama's autobiography, *A Promised Land*. It is powerful literature, as is Springsteen's book *Born to Run*.

23: The Tragedy of Religious Intolerance (2015)

Throughout my lifetime, God has, conveniently, been blamed for everything we are unable understand or want to run away from.

His name is now far too often used to justify the deeds of guilty people.

Some are well-meaning but misguided souls, but most are pure evil.

Their activity reached a peak in the middle of the last decade when it caused many to decide that the God in whom they believed was an irrelevance in their lives and it is no longer necessary to have a God of any type for any reason.

This was a sad time in the history of religion. Some of us still sincerely believe that God is an important spiritual power that leads us to achieve good things for humanity.

Just a few short years ago, a schoolteacher in France was brutally beheaded, an action that shocked the world to its core.

Solely for the purpose of providing illustrative teaching, Samuel Paty had drawn a caricature of the Prophet Muhammad which in no way mocked the prophet and he respectfully discussed it with his class at school as part of their studies on religion. The Muslim community took exception to his educational initiative, saying that he had publicly ridiculed Muhammad and must be punished. Their grossly violent reaction ended tragically.

The killer, who was shot by police, had claimed that he'd carried out this evil deed 'in Allah's name'.

A similar event to this happened again in France in the same era when Muslim extremists shot and killed many of the staff of a Paris newspaper called *Charlie Hebdo*, citing similar reasons as the murder of the schoolteacher. It caused the people of France, and most of the non-Muslim world to be outraged and rightfully so. But their rage has not curbed religious violence. Indeed, soon afterwards a religious extremist drove a truck into a crowd at Nice in southern France, killing dozens.

These horrific acts have caused Christians like me, and hopefully those of other faiths, to be careful and thoughtful of the way in which we say we do things 'in God's name'.

In centuries past, our practice of tolerance has always been bad. Christians regularly burned 'sinners' at the stake and did so by the thousands, claiming that it was the will of God.

During the era of the Hitler regime in Germany, Christian churches publicly condoned his violent persecution of Jews and Gypsies, whom they believed were not God's people.

More recently, the horrendous sexual abuse of children had been brought into the public eye in churches worldwide and there has been little sign of repentance.

So, where does all this leave people like you and me?

It means that religious intolerance now dominates our society. Human endeavour is no longer solely dominated by the money and power battles that occur between disciples of capitalism and socialism and communism.

In its place we have a constantly growing worldwide feud for the control of minds between Muslims, Jews, Christians, Hindus, Buddhists and many other religions. Tragically, it is too often violent and always insincerely done 'in the name of God'.

For a long time now, I've held the view that I cannot ever say that I'm doing anything in the name of God even though I pray sincerely that my plans are based on Christian principles. To do so is sheer arrogance and cowardice on my part. I have no right to blame my personal hang-ups on God. I can feel powered by my faith, but I can never claim that my endeavours are the work of God. I am responsible for all my actions. And I cannot ever claim that any act of aggression or violence was done in God's name. Sadly, this is proved by the history of World War II, which records that both sides believed that God was on their side.

Finally, it always comes down to personal actions and responsibility. Our participation in mob hysteria can far too often end in tragedy.

Through my participation in an interfaith group in North Brisbane, I try to live in good relationships with friends and acquaintances in my local community who are Christians, Muslims, Jews, Sikhs, Hindus, Mormons, Bahai, Buddhist, atheists and others. We strive to discover good ways to live and work together to create a better world and we will continue to do so.

It simply proves that nothing can or should separate us from living with goodwill to all.

There will always be extremists who will do evil, but their numbers are relatively few in a world of eight billion people. They just have an impact far beyond their size.

Media in all its forms must act far more responsibly than they do now. This presumes that they are in fact capable of doing that and can refrain from giving evil people the publicity they crave.

The Great Spirit in whom I believe never sits in judgement of people.

Neither should we.

The spirituality in our lives, no matter what its religious origin may be, is a gift of the power to do good. We do have the power to create compassionate societies in which we live and move and have our being. The tragedy of religious intolerance has rapidly overshadowed compassion.

May grace and peace be the cornerstones of our lives and our society.

While God is blamed by many for almost everything that happens in the world, he (or she) has nothing to do with any of it. Hopefully, one day the God blamers will acknowledge that the sole purpose of the Supreme Being is to be the source of our spiritual power.

Because the word 'God' is now so demeaned I try not to use it except for general public understanding of what I am talking about.

I follow a Great Spirit without whom my life would be greatly diminished.

I do nothing in the name of the Great Spirit, and never will.

24: America Elects the Wrong President (2016)

It is painful for most people to make any comment about Donald Trump at any time.

We know he is best ignored and hopefully forever forgotten, but it is certain that this will prove to be a forlorn hope.

Even if he fades away, a legacy will be perpetuated on his behalf by his devotees for many years to come and so we have no option but to face up to this as a reality.

Before writing a word of this chapter, let me first make a confession.

It will be difficult for me to say anything that is in any way complimentary about Trump. I hold him in the lowest possible regard. I have the firm view that history will record that he has been the worst president the United States of America has ever had or could ever possibly have in the centuries ahead.

Indeed, I'm also perplexed as to how America reached a point in its history where 70 million people voted twice for a person of such gross instability, blatant dishonesty and crude decadence.

Having told you this, I feel a bit better and will now make an honest attempt to be objective in searching for an answer to the perplexing question of how the most powerful nation on Earth experienced this huge bleep of insanity in its practice of democracy.

Firstly, let me say that Trump did not win the 2016 election. Hilary Clinton lost it.

She held the naive belief that she was taking part in the equivalent of a royal procession to the White House. She was certain that it was her destiny to be the first female president of the USA and was convinced that all she had to do on election day was to turn up and she would be voted in. Not only did she live in this personal state of unreality, but she was also certain that American voters would never be so dumb as to elect an idiot like Trump as their president. (Actually, too many of us felt the same way.) So, she ran a pompously arrogant and unprofessional campaign that was doomed to fail, and did so spectacularly.

On top of all this, huge numbers of Americans were sick to death of their nation being run, year after endless year, by an arrogant, corrupt and insensitive political establishment that was run by the powerbrokers for a privileged few. Hilary looked and acted like a seasoned member of the Establishment. In actual fact, she and her husband Bill had been powerful figures in that Establishment for a long time.

So, when Trump turned up and declared over and over again that he would 'drain the swamp in Washington', far too many Americans decided that this was a long overdue, first-class idea, especially those living in what Americans called 'the rust belt': the little towns everywhere whose industries had closed down because time had passed them by, and the intense competition of international trade finally killed their ability to compete.

What was absolutely astonishing was that Hilary did not recognise their plight. Incredibly, she said on the day after the election that she had been unaware that they were so angry. This from a person who had spoken at more than 300 campaign rallies across America in the previous two years and had sensed none of their anger. The facts of the matter are that she had not visited a single one of those dying towns and did not appear to give them a second thought.

Trump did.

Added to all of this were many voters who felt that Barack Obama had failed to live up to their expectations of him. Irrespective of whether this allegation is true or false, they felt hugely let down and, as Hilary had been a high-profile member of his team as secretary of state, she took the brunt of their punishment.

It is most bewildering that few of those who voted for Trump ever got round to enquiring as to whether or not he had the political experience and management skills to drain the swamp and replace it with something that was better. The reality is that he did not have that ability.

His record shows that he had been bankrupt three times because he had the sparse ability to handle money or people. The latter is highlighted by the fact that he has had three wives, a dozen broken relationships and still has many women filing rape charges against him. He simply cannot relate to people, and this has been proven by the fact that the entire White House staff changed three times in four years.

It would take many pages for me to list the entire scope of his sins, so I will not try.

Just let me say that when he legislated his promised tax cuts, the result was that he helped only his wealthy mates and vastly increased national debt. Those in the rust belt who had voted for him in droves got no benefit from those cuts whatsoever. And his handling of COVID-19 was an exercise in disgraceful incompetence and irresponsibility.

Having said all of this, I must admit that I feared there was a real chance that Trump would win a second term as president at the November 2020 election. A lot of voters were still angry and disillusioned with their world and they once more blamed it on the Establishment, not Trump.

Joe Biden had been a leader of the Establishment for 40 years as a senator and vice president before becoming the Democrat nominee to run against Trump. He too was a member of the Obama team and, unfortunately, he did look somewhat elderly and frail.

It seemed at one point that the only person standing between Trump and a second term as president was Kamala Harris who has now become Biden's vice president. She has leadership skills and ability and acts unlike Hilary Clinton.

She also has some humility and so a growing number of voters appeared to believe that if Biden's health cracked, she would be a splendid replacement. We wait to see how the cards will fall. Anything is possible in America.

After all, Clinton got three million more votes than Trump in 2016 and lost because she did not win enough states to get a majority in the Electoral College. The only thing that is certain in life is that nothing is certain.

But, fortunately, Biden did win and he even though he will never set the world on fire, he seems to be a creator of sensible change.

However, most Americans will never forget that Trump tried to win by fraud, plus threats and bribes to those who counted votes. When that failed, he actively promoted a physical attack on Congress, the first president ever to do so. And he did that even though Biden had beaten him by seven million votes.

So, history will remember him as a cheap thug from the deepest part of the gutter who has a magnificent talent to tell dozens of lies daily, believe them to be truth, and be able to convince millions of naive voters that he is a god.

A sobering thought for us all as we tread along the way to an uncertain future is a necessity to never forget that, in two successive elections, so many millions of Americans voted for Trump.

Can we really avoid the question as to why so many voters could be so dumb twice? And why were so many of them certain that he was robbed of victory in 2020?

Are the foundations of democracy under threat? Should irresponsible people like that have the right to vote without passing an intelligence test?

Thomas Jefferson, in my view, was as fine a president that the United States ever had, exceeded in stature only by Abraham Lincoln.

Jefferson made this comment, at the time when he drafted the Declaration of Independence that divorced the British colonies from their colonial masters in Britain:

'If Americans are set free from the tyranny of the king of England, and are in control of their own nation, they will vote sensibly in the election of their leaders.'

As we are all aware, this did not happen and never will.

People always vote for a government they think will enable them to respectably practise greed and they will likely do so again in the United States in 2024.

Australians often do the same.

25: The Scandal and Tragedy of Child Abuse (2017)

It goes without saying that no child should ever be abused, physically or mentally, for any reason whatsoever.

That they have been abused for centuries by 'Christians' and their churches is an abomination.

An unpalatable fact is that every one of us who is a member of a church is guilty of turning a blind eye to awful atrocities in order to preserve the reputation of our church.

The question is this: What are we now doing to stop such atrocities from happening ever again?

I have been attending church on all but a few Sundays for nine decades.

During that time, I have been a member of only five church congregations — Linville Methodist, Toowoomba Presbyterian, Nyngan Methodist, Brisbane City Presbyterian and Aspley Uniting.

At none of them did I ever come across any evidence of child abuse, nor did I ever meet any who could have been clearly identified as a paedophile.

Maybe I was naive or unobservant, but it came as a shock to me when Prime Minister Julia Gillard, despite opposition from her constant political opponent Tony Abbott, a Roman Catholic zealot, found it necessary and urgent during the 2010 term of Parliament to establish a royal commission to investigate child abuse in Australia.

I had read novels and seen movies that were based on paedophile activity that was happening predominantly in Catholic churches, but I irresponsibly considered that these were isolated incidences of depravity that were given public prominence beyond their danger to society.

Then, in 2014, I learned that two Protestant pastors whom I knew well had been charged for child abuse crimes, so it was obvious that it was time to take the matter far more seriously than I had done previously and get involved in planning to give victims a genuine chance of a new life while ensuring that their predators were adequately punished.

Like most people, I asked myself 'How did we allow this to happen?' and 'Why did we turn a blind eye to it?' and 'Did we do this deliberately?'

In reality, it proved quite easy for me to do some research to discover that child abuse had been very actively going on for many centuries and had been covered up, not just by churches, but also in respected institutions such as the Scouts as well as government orphanages, sports clubs and schools.

Appallingly, in the case of churches, the offending priests were usually moved on to another parish as if nothing had happened. Scout leaders were never reported to police. To my complete surprise, there were clear instances of paedophile crimes within the Salvation Army that shocked me to the core. Undeniably, those omissions are unforgivable especially since many thousands of children were abused.

The high-profile criminal trials of Cardinal George Pell that began in 2017 highlighted the issue but did not result in any solutions being found to solve the problem in the long term. Eventually, in 2021, Pell was found to be not guilty. The Australian High Court ruled that the case against him was not proven beyond reasonable doubt. This result was not satisfactory to either Pell or his alleged victim and, predictably, it created a widely divided community of opinion that has fostered bitterness and mistrust.

Beyond the realm of religion, young women have been sexually abused by too many depraved people such as Jeffrey Epstein, Harvey Weinstein and, allegedly, Prince Andrew. And all the evidence is that this curse of society is rapidly growing.

So, the perplexing challenge is this: just how do we give significant and meaningful help to victims of any form of abuse to ensure they restore their lives when they have suffered so horribly.

Money alone will not fix it and the funds so far paid to them in compensation has been too pitiful and disgraceful to make any difference in easing their plight. All that we have done is to kick the can down the road for the next generation to worry about.

Mainline churches have suffered with declining attendances as a result as well as a loss of commitment from those who remained. Fortunately, Christianity has not been irreparably 'downgraded' as a faith. Those who committed the crimes were, absolutely, not truly Christians even though they claimed that they were. Nevertheless, the community at large holds long-term suspicions of churches and Christians, and there is a lot of work to be done to turn that situation around.

Despite all this is the fact is that Jesus of Nazareth is the role model of my life.

However, solutions must be found and implemented that will remove violence and injustice in all its forms everywhere, especially from the world of religion.

Not only do child abuse victims deserve and need compassion, so do domestic violence victims, abused elderly, people with disabilities and those humiliated by racism, especially refugees and the First Peoples. This means that we all have a huge amount of work to do to create a more caring and compassionate society for all humanity.

At this moment, the indisputable fact is that humanity is steadily descending towards the primitive and so we cannot remain inactive and allow this decline to continue.

We have it in our power to remove those days of darkness from our society and convey hope and decency and honesty to the communities in which we live and make them safe for everyone, especially those who are young and vulnerable.

A major reason why churches become a haven for paedophiles is that, at worship on every Sunday, we are told that our sins are forgiven.

I shudder in disgust every time I hear it. It means that people such paedophiles have adopted the view that they can continue their evil because they know they will be forgiven next Sunday.

Churches must decide right now not to continue to perpetuate this appalling lie.

The only person who can forgive us is the person we have hurt. We cannot appoint God as a third party to intervene on our behalf. That is an act of cowardice.

26: The Day Australia Removed the Restraint on Love (2017)

Having grown up in a fundamentalist 'Christian' environment, I always believed that people became homosexual by choice and against the 'will of God'.

I learned that this assumption was pompously wrong and am hugely grateful that I was able to help rectify this indictment on the lives of so many decent people.

On 7 December 2017, the Australian Parliament acted with great wisdom when it passed legislation that made it possible for people of the same gender to marry. There were only three dissenting voices (plus some walkouts, irresponsibly led by Prime Minister Scott Morrison).

The public debate that preceded the passing of this significant legislation was often quite bitter and divisive and this meant that the postal vote that gave Australians the right to express a view on it was hotly contested.

Despite this, I rejoice that, finally, when all the votes were counted across the nation, the margin for approval was decisive 2 to 1.

I voted YES because I oppose discrimination in all its forms. Indeed, I publicly campaigned strongly for a YES vote.

The truth is that I have no right to tell another human being who they will fall in love with and what will be the status of their relationship.

Since I am a lifetime elder of the Uniting Church in Australia, I was persistently criticised by leaders of churches when I made a public stand on my support for this issue and declared my intention to vote YES on the matter. But I expected that and did not try to retaliate. Life is too short to waste on bitterness. The church leaders attacked me in the same way when I had a leading role in passing legislation in Queensland to make voluntary assisted dying legal, but I have come to accept that far too many Christians are nasty people.

I'm not a theologian and have no aspirations to be one. But it is possible to mount a strong case that asserts that the text in the Old Testament on homosexuality that says it's a sin for a man to leave his wife to lie with a man also says nothing about a man who has no wife.

It also fails to mention the sexual preferences of women, so the biblical passage ignores 50% of the population.

But this primitive fundamentalist debate about words written thousands of years ago is just nitpicking nonsense. The key issue is that Jesus told us to love one another and not to 'throw stones' at anyone unless we are without sin ourselves.

And it is pointless to say that those in same-sex relationships should have been granted some form of civil union that is not actually marriage. This pompously says that heterosexuals are more decent and honourable people than those who are not. It seems to me that this is simply a blatant example of bigotry. I have homosexual friends who are fine Christians, generous givers and good citizens. They are not lesser humans than the rest of us.

When I was at school, there was a fellow student who was quite clearly effeminate. He was born that way, but I, and others, to our eternal shame, gave him a hard time calling him by the nickname of 'Pansy' and making it clear to him that he was not one of us. Years later, I just happened to meet him and his male partner by pure chance at a shopping centre one day. Quite clearly, they enjoyed a strong relationship.

I apologised for my behaviour back in our school days. He bore no malice whatsoever and told me that he had learned from the experience. He had rightly decided that he should never sit in judgement of other human beings who have different attitudes and habits than he does.

Pointlessly, a debate continues about whether or not churches and their priests are now compelled by law to marry same gender couples. In Australia, they are not obliged to do this. The law clearly says that any marriage celebrant, whether religious or secular, can refuse to marry any couple of any sexual orientation without giving a reason. Celebrants are protected by law from any persecution.

My local church has correctly decided that if a gay couple come regularly to our church for worship, and are formally received as members of the congregation because they declare their Christian commitment without being forced to do so, then we will welcome their marriage.

We would have an entirely different attitude to those who casually walk in from the street and wanted to marry because they think we have a nice building for wedding photographs.

So, there can be no doubt that Australia made the right decision on same-sex marriage in 2017.

We removed a restraint on love and that has got to be a wonderful and honourable and decent thing to do.

Too many Christians wrongly believe that our faith is based on being saved from our sins.

If this version of theology is correct, then it infers that homosexuals in a sexual relationship are sinful people and therefore they cannot possibly be Christians.

It goes without saying that this is childish nonsense. Indeed, I have no desire to be saved from my sins.

Christianity is about living positive lives of service to all humanity, not just the pious few who are certain they are holier than others and want to make a public issue of it.

27:
An Unstable Decade of Political Coups (2010 to 2020)

The Australian Constitution is unclear as to whether or not the appointment of a prime minister is to be determined by Parliament or the governor-general or the voters of Australia.

Indeed, the Constitution only mentions ministers, not a prime minister. It also has no mention of political parties.

For the past decade, political parties alone have been consistently deciding who will be prime minister and this practice is fundamentally wrong.

There were four occasions in the decade of 2010–2020 when serving prime ministers of Australia have been removed from office by a vote of MPs of their own political parties.

It is very possible to develop a convincing case to prove that none of these leadership coups should have happened, but the stark fact is that they did.

The first victim was Kevin Rudd, challenged by Julia Gillard.

He was nearing the end of his first term as prime minister and was leading comfortably in all public opinion polls. In normal circumstances, he should have been safe from challenge but the cause of his demise was personal, not political, as he is considered a difficult person to deal with and was callous about the way he treated his ministers and his staff day by day. Additionally, he was often pompous and discourteous in the way he greeted and held discussions with visitors. A rebellion against him as a person was inevitable.

It was all over in three turbulent days. Out of a caucus of around 100, Rudd finished with only eight firm supporters and had been completely unaware of it. John Howard, as astute a politician as I have ever met, would never have been caught out like that. He would have smelled the plot in the air long before it could have developed a power base and quietly quelled it.

Second was Julia Gillard, Australia's first female prime minister, and in my view one of our better ones. She was challenged and replaced by Rudd.

After almost losing the election that she called far too early after her defeat of Rudd, she survived by leading an extraordinary minority government that passed more than 500 pieces of legislation despite having to rely on the votes of five independents every day. She proved that genuine democracy can work successfully.

However, she was constantly harassed by Rudd who wanted his old job back. This created a situation where her own team decided she would lead them to defeat in the forthcoming election and enough of them agreed that Rudd was the only one who could save them, so they brutally crucified her. Rudd did not save them and there was never the slightest chance that he would. I believe that if Julia had survived the coup she would have won.

The removal of Gillard by Rudd after he re-challenged her was a huge error for which the Australian Labor Party has paid a long-term political price.

Number three was Tony Abbott, who was challenged by Malcolm Turnbull. And he deserved to be kicked out right from the opening day of his term.

He was out of his depth as prime minister, very incompetent and absolutely dominated by his chief of staff, Peta Credlin. And always lagging considerably behind the opposition leader in the polls.

Few wept at his departure. He had achieved very little. Indeed, he took Australia backwards.

Last was Malcolm Turnbull, who was initially challenged by Peter Dutton, but this led to a second ballot where Scott Morrison won party leadership.

As bad as Abbott was, Turnbull had difficulty mustering sufficient votes to beat him. Turnbull had to sell his soul to people on the political right of him to get the required votes and he had to buy the votes of too many rusted-on conservatives by making them promises that contrasted with his basic political beliefs.

So it was that the scene was set for his eventual defeat.

The Christian right did not let him govern so he decided that, to stay on as prime minister, he needed to sit on the fence on far too many key issues. His tenure simply could not last and everyone on both sides of Parliament knew it, except him.

Many Australian voters were upset by those four coups, and still are, and rightfully so.

They believed that at every election they chose a prime minister who should not have been so callously struck down since the belief was they were the only ones who could remove them, not the politicians.

The only way to stop this in future will be to hold a referendum to change the Constitution to say that, when a prime minister is deposed by his or her own party, the governor-general must swear in the new leader only as acting prime minister and then immediately call a general election so that voters can express their approval of the change or otherwise.

It is important to note that Rudd, Abbott and Turnbull reacted bitterly to their removal and went out of their way to destroy their assassins and, indeed, their own parties.

The only one to behave with dignity was Gillard.

She gracefully agreed to retire from Parliament at the following election, which was only three months away, so as not to be a negative factor for her party in endeavouring to be re-elected She has retained a dignified silence ever since and made a successful life for herself outside of politics.

The other three are still wailing in anger at their demise and will do so relentlessly until the day they die.

It must be carefully noted that none of the four coups were carried out because the nation was in crisis at the time. It was declining but not disastrously enough to warrant a coup. All four coups were done in the cold pursuit of personal power and had no other reason to justify them except for a breakdown in human relationships fuelled by excessive egos.

It was good for democratic stability that Scott Morrison was able to finish his elected term as prime minister without facing a coup, even though there were rumblings of one. He was finally removed by Anthony Albanese in a legitimate election.

The undeniable fact is that only the voters of Australia can pass their judgement on who will lead our nation, not the powerbrokers who exist in Parliament and whose existence is to the detriment of the basic principles of democracy.

Australia must not tolerate another coup.

Nevertheless, I feel certain that someone will give it a go sometime as the quest for power lurks in too many souls.

Most voters are unaware that the Constitution of Australia does not mention political parties but they naively vote for parties that have no legal right whatsoever to be involved in Parliament.

So, if they are to remain in existence, a referendum must be held to add clauses to the Constitution that make their existence legitimate and their operations honest.

A fundamental clause should be one that ensures that all elections held by political parties for officers of branches, state councils and federal councils, as well as election candidates and leaders must be supervised by the Australian Electoral Commission.

This will mean that for the first time in their existence, political parties will have to practise democracy instead of serving as power groups controlled by political thugs.

28:
How Dare You (2018)

Throughout history, some extraordinary people have, from time to time, stepped forward to make an impact on events that change the course of history without ever holding political office.

Joan of Arc was one. St Patrick was another. Jesus of Nazareth was the most notable of all, but in our era, an extraordinary one has been Greta Thunberg.

Indeed, her story is quite spectacular and successful and not yet finished.

Greta Thunberg stormed onto the world scene like a thunderclap in 2018, then departed silently in 2020, but returned in 2022.

In those high-profile years, she created more debate about climate change than anyone else in the world.

She even surpassed David Attenborough, the world's most famous and respected environmentalist, in coverage on both mainstream and social media and that is saying something. I hold the view that David Attenborough is one of the finest proponents of great causes in my lifetime.

Greta is not someone whom we can regard as a 'normal human being' (if there is such a person anywhere in the world).

She was born in 2003, which means that, at my time of writing, she is just 20. Her family are intense people who have spent their lives being tumultuously involved in revolutionary causes. They swept Greta along with them and she was a committed participant in their crusades.

At age 11, Greta became passionately involved in advocating climate change and, largely due to her immaturity at that point in her life, she quickly became distressed that she was getting nowhere. It impacted her to such an extent that she lost the ability to speak a single word and stopped eating at the same time. In addition, she was diagnosed with autism. She was close to death, but made an incredible recovery against all the odds. Indeed, her doctors were baffled by the cause of her recovery.

In 2018, she organised a student strike for climate change at her school in Sweden, advertising it on Instagram. It was an astonishing success but her campaign would probably have died there and then were it not for a famous journalist who happened to stumble across her activity and sent her story around the world. Schools everywhere began strikes in support of her initiative and it spread to almost every nation even though Greta had no team and no money. I have never before seen this happen so quickly.

Unsurprisingly, she clearly despises money as an evil commodity that finances the destruction of humanity.

Without ever requesting it, she was invited to be a keynote speaker at the United Nations Climate Change Conference in Copenhagen. This was followed by an address to the United Nations General Assembly in New York and then a meeting with the powerful Climate Committee of the American Congress in Washington. She went to the USA from Stockholm on a yacht, supplied and crewed by friends. It took 17 days to travel there and another 17 back. She refuses to fly in any aircraft because they 'destroy the atmosphere'.

In all three speeches, she challenged her influential listeners by repeatedly using the words, 'How dare you destroy our planet?'

Then, quite suddenly, and without a dramatic announcement, she went back to school and kept silent. The world wondered whether we would hear from her ever again. But, just as suddenly in 2022, she returned and revived her crusade, not so intensively as before, but with as much passion.

It is impossible to produce facts and figures that can accurately measure her impact on the war against climate change but, at least partly because of her advocacy, education around the science of climate change has become more prevalent. Deniers are now an illiterate and decadent irrelevance even though they will never stop spreading their negative views. The only debate focuses on what we do about it right now and how we do it in a way that gets measurable results. Obviously, pragmatic answers must be found, and soon.

A powerful world leader, or leaders, will soon be needed to step forward to back Greta and help find a pathway to success right now that also sets out a clear plan to ensure it creates prosperity.

In reality, positive ways must be found to fix our climate in a responsible and sensible approach that does not destroy basic livelihood.

We have the skills to do this and anyone who claims that fixing climate change will bankrupt the world is simply a childish fearmonger as well as being a dangerous purveyor of misinformation.

Greta, enjoy the rest of your schooldays. Keep up the good fight no matter what abuse you face.

The rest of us can continue to ask ourselves the powerful and embarrassing question that Greta has placed before us.

HOW DARE YOU DESTROY OUR PLANET?

And then do something about it.

Greta, I think that the leader of renown who backs you will be female. The stark fact is that most of the deniers of climate change are male.

Throughout history, there have been many Greta Thunbergs in addition to the people I named in the prelude to this chapter.

They have arrived in a burst of flames, mesmerised people, then departed the scene in spectacular ways.

John the Baptist was one. He was beheaded.

So was Lawrence of Arabia who died in a road accident.

As was William Wilberforce when he stopped the British slave trade. His health deteriorated badly quite soon after achieving this.

Greta Thunberg will, at some point, flame out too, but I hope it happens after we have achieved her dream of making the climate change challenge an unstoppable success.

Nevertheless, the world will always need more people like Greta.

May they keep arriving.

29:
Pandemics Become a Way of Life (2020)

Medical scientists consistently tell us that there can be no doubt that COVID-19 and its variants and relatives are with us forever.

We will never eradicate it, but we can discipline ourselves and adapt to live with all viruses.

The current pandemic has been caused by the way in which, since the beginning of time, humanity has endlessly contaminated our air, water, land, flora, fauna and sea, thereby giving viruses many plentiful breeding places.

Centuries ago, extraordinary pollution caused the Black Plague and the Spanish flu and other mass killers. History endlessly repeats itself.

It's time we got smart and stopped contaminating ourselves.

I hold the view that, of all the crises that happened during my lifetime and have impacted on all humanity, COVID-19 ranks third.

The Great Depression of the 1930s was by far the worst in terms of human suffering, followed by World War II, which caused far more deaths than the pandemic.

This does not mean that COVID-19 is not a serious matter. It is and it warranted a far more urgent response than Trump gave it in the USA or Modi did in India.

Despite some political blunders and careless disorganisation, Australia has done well to contain and survive it. I can find no valid reason to doubt that. Fortunately, being a big island located far away from the rest of the world has helped to shield us.

Nevertheless, there are lessons to be learned from our experience of it so we can handle pandemics better in the future.

In political terms, there have been some unfortunate defects in our performance. Australia was torn apart by six warring states regularly insulting one another about their management of COVID-19 and acting as independent nations. It was not necessary for that to occur. Indeed, it was hugely divisive. However, in the end it produced a reasonable result that was to our mutual benefit. The political backlash will come later.

A concern has been our obsession with avoiding death from any virus, and this fear resulted in us overlooking the fact that we unintentionally ruined the livelihood of millions of Australians by destroying their jobs and their small businesses and, even worse, we created an enormous crisis in mental health problems that tragically caused the rate of suicides to double. I can say that because I am an honorary fellow of a university in which I serve in their mental health research institute.

What we can do now is to establish a permanent national crisis authority and we should do it with urgency, so we are ready for regular pandemics that are inevitably on their way. We live in an overpopulated world, one that is also massively polluted.

To achieve the creation of this authority, the Australian Parliament must call a referendum so we can vote on approving an addition to the Australian Constitution via a clause, which could read something like this:

'A national crisis authority shall be established, chaired by the governor-general, and consisting of the prime minister, state premiers and territory chief ministers. Their decisions will be decided by a majority vote and will be observed as enforceable national laws until the crisis is deemed to be over. The governor-general will have sole power to decide that a crisis exists, and its conclusion will be determined by a majority vote of the authority. At no time during a crisis will states have power to close their borders for any reason.'

Let me make six observations in conclusion:

- Our vaccination program would have been far more efficient and effective if it had been managed by a national crisis authority rather than the ineffectual National Cabinet, which was a talkfest without teeth.
- Despite all the rantings of anti-vaxxers and freedom lovers, I happily had four vaccination jabs. There was pointless panic about the remote possibility of blood clots. I didn't get my jabs because of any personal fear of COVID-19. I reckon I could beat it by myself. It was simply the responsible thing to do for the overall good of society and so I'm ready to have more jabs any time they are recommended and available.
- The aftermath of COVID-19 was tough, and could have been avoided if we had taken national action that locked down hotspots, not closed state borders. Because viruses will be with us forever, further closure of borders will achieve nothing but chaos. We can and will find ways to live with pandemics responsibly and never again operate by panic and fear.
- It is a disgrace that the Australian Government doesn't have quarantine facilities strategically placed throughout the nation. We had them in use in the days of my youth, especially during the polio epidemic, but we closed them down as cost-cutting measures. Hotel quarantine was an irresponsible and unsafe response and must never be used again.
- We must forever practise physical distancing and improve hygiene practices.
- In particular, we must renovate all public toilets in every part of the nation and install some technology in them so no-one has to touch a door or a tap or a flush button. Public toilets are potential disease-spreading hotspots that are a primitive disgrace in a civilised society.

I'm happy to debate these issues with anyone at any time. I have no doubt that my recommendations can be further improved.

During such a debate, I will consistently emphasise that I am a proud Australian who happens to live happily in Queensland. However, I strongly object to being called a Queenslander. I'm an Aussie to the boot heels who just happens to be a contented resident in the Sunshine State. Unlike too many who live in Queensland, I like people who live in other states. I haven't found them to be the economic and social enemies that intensely parochial Queenslanders fear them to be.

Any reflection on the COVID-19 pandemic reminds us how easy it is to create panic among the majority of the population.

Never before in my lifetime have I seen many people become stricken with fear every time there was a surge in virus numbers. Sadly, some people became abusive of others whom they thought were not responding to the virus as seriously as they were.

Even worse has been the appalling attitude of anti-vaxxers who stoked fear of death by vaccination in a manner that was irresponsible and vicious. They ranted about their right to freedom but don't seem to have ever considered what their responsibility was to the community. I have never before come across such selfish people and I hope I can live my remaining days without running into them again. This may well prove to be a false hope.

Disturbing also was the clear evidence that some of those politicians and bureaucrats who were in positions of authority in controlling lockdowns and border closures became so drunk with personal power that they would resist any attempts to challenge their power.

Nevertheless, Australia appears to now be a more mature nation in our social behaviour than we were before COVID-19 first hit us.

30: The Era Of Biden and Xi and Putin (2022)

The world is constantly changing physically, socially, economically and politically — and has been since the beginning of time.

Right now, we stand on the brink of greater changes than history has previously recorded, and we have 'leaders' of our greatest nations who at this moment show clear evidence of not being our prime choices to handle challenges, but I hope that my presumption will be proved wrong, at least with two of them.

My final chapter on the historical events of my life that began in 1931 has reached a moment where, having debated the past, we can express concern about our future.

I have called it THE ERA OF BIDEN AND XI AND PUTIN for want of a more descriptive title. They are the three key powerbrokers in the world at the time of writing.

Joe Biden became president of the USA in 2020 at a point in history when his nation still retains its place as a powerful nation on Earth, militarily and economically. It will have a huge influence on our future even though China will inevitably overtake it as number one in a decade or two. This is because China has four times the population of the USA and far more land and mineral resources. However, Russia, in actual fact, occupies more land than both of them combined, but has little chance of challenging China's dominance.

Xi has total power in China, whereas Biden must deal with a deeply divided Congress in achieving the passing of his policies. Since Xi does not have to face a legitimate democratic election, we can take it for granted that he will become the dominant influence in our lives for a long time to come. Putin conducts elections with predetermined results that can only be described as a farce, but he has the personal power to dispense fear in a way that Biden never can.

Biden has inherited a nation that has been torn apart by the past, and the continuing influence of Donald Trump, who remains utterly divisive and destructive. This loads Biden with the immense task of repairing and restoring a world order that Trump did his best to destroy.

Biden is still having to concentrate a major portion of his efforts on leading the USA out of the economic and social consequences of a continuing pandemic that was out of control when he inherited it due to enormously irresponsible 'leadership' by Trump, someone who was significantly out of his depth. This will continue to be a hell of a job for Biden to manage in the long term, especially as he also has to conquer the curse of inflation.

On the other hand, Xi seemed to have the pandemic under control simply because of his greater power to dominate and regiment the entire population. Despite this, the pandemic continues to break out on a regular basis.

Putin hides his COVID-19 statistics. Even so, we can safely presume this and the resultant economic fallout have been bad.

Additionally, Biden leads a nation hugely divided between the haves and the have-nots as well as great racial division. This is an even greater challenge than COVID-19.

Trump accidentally but correctly identified the problem in 2016 when he declared that inequality was caused by the corruption of the political establishment. He promised to 'drain the swamp in Washington'. However, he proved that he didn't have the intellectual capacity to make even the most minute difference. If he did, it was to make corruption worse.

There are many haves and have-nots in China but the overall gap is not as vast as in USA. Be this as it may, the have-nots are powerless to do anything about it in China, whereas there is always at least a glimmer of hope for them in the USA.

Russia is controlled absolutely by Putin and his oligarchs.

The rest of the world now looks on and wonders what to do about it.

Most are looking to China for leadership, not the USA or Russia, because President Xi has the political power and will to deliver his promises, whereas Putin's hold on power is quite questionable. This has now become frail due to his unjustifiable invasion of Ukraine and the worldwide economic sanctions that have been placed upon his nation. Biden still battles with rabid opposition from the hugely negative Republicans who oppose everything he does.

My view is that Australia should adopt a long-term plan that will lead us to be able to maintain peaceful trading relationships with all three of China, the USA and Russia, while building and continually expanding closer trade and cultural ties with the natural partners of our region, namely India, Indonesia, Japan, Singapore, New Zealand, the Pacific nations and Chile.

In doing this, we must also accept that we will not be returning to anything that resembles what we personally regard as 'normal'.

There never has been a situation in any phase of life that can be described as 'normal' and there never will be.

We can only look to a future that is a mystery and be prepared to change everything in our lives in regular attempts to find better ways to live well.

The alternative is to slowly perish.

The war with Ukraine has revealed even more starkly that Russia is the least stable of the three superpowers and the most irresponsible.

When Putin finally goes, hopefully in whatever way is best for humanity, Russia will cease to be a threat to the world and could experience a much-needed reformation.

Xi will be around for a long while yet,

Biden may have only one term as president and of particular concern is the possibility that his successor may be from the extreme right of the Republican Party.

So, Xi will become the world's most stable leader.

Only one thing is certain. The future is uncertain.

So, it would be better if leaders of finer quality could be found than Biden, Xi and Putin, but the nations they lead have no obvious alternatives.

We live in hope that a messiah may yet emerge.

Through the Looking Glass

Is it possible to forecast what will be the notable events in the remainder of our current decade and the decades beyond?

What will grab the headlines and remain in our memory in the same way as the events of my 90 years have left an indelible impression on me?

My global thinking is centred on the way in which the world handles *climate change*. It is the premier crisis event for every nation and will change the way we live, especially in determining the level of our health and prosperity.

Within Australia, a powerful issue will be recognition of the *First Peoples* in our Constitution, a matter of justice that we have delayed for the 120 years since Federation and can be put aside no more.

Another essential constitutional addition that awaits achievement is the compelling need to create a *national crisis authority* that has genuine power to handle future pandemics much more by learning from the experience of COVID-19 and improving every possible aspect of it.

Then there will be the pursuit of *gender equality*. Australia is handling this so poorly that it will cause a lamentable rift in the way we live as a society.

At the United Nations, there will be created a new and long overdue charter on human rights to protect *refugees* and *minorities*. It will take many years to achieve, but it is inevitable.

Over and above all this, the headlines that will flash brightly will be those covering the creation of smaller nations via independence movements that are gaining momentum.

Here are just a few:
- Scotland and Wales will leave UK.
- Catalonia from Spain.
- Quebec from Canada.
- Texas and Hawaii and Alaska from the USA.
- Tibet from China.
- Kurdistan from Iraq.
- Palestine from Israel.
- Sicily from Italy.
- Northern Ireland from UK, so as to enable them to join Eire.

There will be more.

The impossible will become very possible.

Life will be wonderfully interesting

B: PEOPLE

1: Jeffrey Archer

Because I'm listing my choices in alphabetical order, Jeffrey Archer gets the number one position, but this is not intended to infer that he is the greatest of them all, interesting though he is.

Nevertheless, it is fair to say that he is a very unusual character and spectacularly successful writer of bestselling novels, so budding authors like me have a lot we can learn from him.

One thing we can learn from Archer is to make sure we stay out of jail.

I first met the legendary author Jeffrey Archer at Ely Cathedral in Cambridgeshire, England, a quarter of a century ago. At that time, I was campaign manager of the cathedral's restoration fund. This beautiful gothic cathedral was fighting centuries of decay to its magnificent facade and millions of pounds were needed to be raised to fix the problem.

Archer joined the restoration team of volunteers in quite extraordinary circumstances.

He had been recently convicted in a London court of a civil offence (involving a lady of somewhat doubtful repute) and the penalty decreed by the judge was that he had to do an extensive period of community service. So, he chose to serve his time on the task of saving Ely Cathedral. I am pleased to report that he made a generous financial gift and actively promoted the campaign. In our brief encounters, we got on well.

Years later, we met again in Australia when he was visiting our shores to promote his latest book (I can't remember its name since he writes one every year). While he was here, we both became involved in a campaign to raise funds to upgrade art and sculpture at Government House (the governor-general's residence in Canberra). We chatted over drinks at one of the promotional functions in Brisbane during which I asked him for advice on how I should go about writing a novel that would become a bestseller.

'Everald, you must become a page turner.'

'What precisely is a page turner, Jeffrey?'

'Your reader must be in bed, really enjoying your book and be so gripped by it that even though he or she is absolutely dead tired, they just cannot resist turning the next page, and the following ones, to find out what happened, until they fall asleep and the book crashes to the floor. Unless you believe you can achieve that, Everald, don't try to become a novelist.'

Most readers of Jeffrey's novels can remember having this page-turning experience on many evenings and know that Archer is correct in defining what constitutes a memorable read.

He subsequently went on to commit a far greater crime than the one that caused his Ely escapade and the judge showed no leniency this time: the crime was perjury. Jeffrey famously served a jail sentence about which he wrote yet another book that also became yet another bestseller.

But I reckon his best literary effort was *The Book of Judas*, written in partnership with a theologian and adopting the style of a traditional book in the Bible.

It is well worth reading as it endeavours to prove in a quite compelling way that Judas was a good guy who was framed by friends to make it appear that he was the one who betrayed Jesus of Nazareth when they all shared the guilt. In other words, he was the 'fall guy'. If you can get a copy, the book certainly is a mind stimulator. Sadly, it sold the least number of copies of any of his books. Theology, quite understandably, is rarely a page turner.

Archer, at one point in his career, became Britain's bestselling author ever, exceeding even the immortal Agatha Christie. However, in more recent years, his quality of writing has declined since he tries too hard to write popular fiction in the manner of his earlier successes, causing readers to believe they have read it before. The result is that he has been surpassed in sales by another British page turner, Ken Follett, whose books I also greatly enjoy.

Despite this, it is an indisputable fact that, although he is a flawed character, Archer once had the rare talent to write bestselling novels that lots of people wanted to read and he has used that talent with considerable success and much good fortune.

A problem we quite often face is that every one of us has a talent to do something special, but too few of us follow the star and make it happen. Sadly, it is likely many of us will die with our music still unplayed.

Be this as it may, remember that it is never too late in life for you and me to start using or reusing whatever talents we were blessed with at birth and make an effort to broaden our life experiences and achievements in an ever-changing world.

No-one can ever accuse Jeffrey Archer of failing to use his literary talents.

As a footnote, since I'm writing about eminent people with whom I crossed paths over my 90 years journey and am doing so in alphabetical order, Archer almost got pipped in the choice to be the first. The fact is that I had former Australian Prime Minister Tony Abbott among my original list of 30 but, on reflection, he didn't make a final cut back to 20, bewildering character though he is.

Many have the belief that you cannot be a memorable writer or artist or musician unless you are a little bit mad.

There is an element of truth in this.

I'm nowhere near the pinnacle of authors, but many people tell me that I'm more than a tad odd. It is a badge I wear with honour.

But, in actual fact, and in whatever profession we may have chosen to follow, few of us really want to be regarded as just ordinary.

Most people do try, maybe unknowingly, to rise above the mediocre and make an impression that is memorable.

This proves we are human.

2:
Joh & Flo Bjelke-Petersen

This one will cause more controversy than any other chapter in the entire book.

But I could not and will not bring myself to leave them out.

Joh and Flo were good friends of mine and I don't ever desert friends.

Whether we personally liked them or not, they created history and did it in an extraordinary way that is worth noting and debating.

I reluctantly left my family home in Toowoomba in 1947 when I was 16 to take up my first full-time job at the Commonwealth Bank at Woolloongabba in Brisbane.

This led me to attend St Andrew's Presbyterian Church in the city where I met Florence Gilmore whose family owned a timber mill out in the western suburbs at Bardon. She was my senior by far more than a decade and one of the leaders of the fellowship group that I attended on Sunday evenings. She was friendly and capable and committed. I liked her and we became good friends — a relationship that lasted a lifetime.

A year later, Florence told us she was marrying a good man from Kingaroy called Joh. We were all a bit stunned as, in that era, any woman who was not married by 30 was dubbed an 'old maid', well and truly 'on the shelf'. We all wished her well

Thus began one of the most memorable and powerful partnerships in the history of Australia.

Joh had been a successful farmer who moved into politics. He and Florence were also prominent members of the Lutheran Church.

Joh became a long serving and highly controversial premier of Queensland, indeed a political legend for both good and bad reasons. Subsequently, Florence served as a senator for Queensland in the Australian Parliament where even her most critical political opponents acknowledged her hard work ethic. Both represented what was then called the Country Party, now the National Party — pointless change that will eventually destroy the party.

Halfway through his term as premier, the National Party under the astute administrative leadership of Sir Robert Sparkes, established the Bjelke-Petersen Foundation as an investment fund to finance Joh's future election campaigns. Sparkes invited me to become fundraising consultant to the foundation and I accepted after agreeing with Joh that every donor would be advised in writing that their gift may entitle them to meetings with him, but he was under no obligation to agree with any requests they made. It would be abundantly clear that he owed them nothing.

Many of Joh's plentiful political opponents publicly questioned my integrity as the organiser of the finances of the foundation but, when the Fitzgerald Commission commenced its investigation into corruption within Joh's government, I personally took all the records of the Foundation to the commission so Fitzgerald could investigate its activities. They found nothing wrong with its operations.

During my time working with Joh, I found no evidence of him being personally involved in any corruption or financial feathering of his own nest.

Nevertheless, I'm certain that some of his political associates were corrupt and there can be no doubt that far too many of his friends benefited from government contracts that they got without going through a public tendering process.

Whenever anyone questioned him about his political and financial relations with his mates, he had the same answer for every question: 'Don't you worry about that.'

Those words became part of a legend that remains alive today.

In considering the legend, it is important to note that Florence was far more than a loving and loyal wife. I was present on several occasions when she told Joh he could not do something, and he heeded her advice

Florence was also an active community worker and a wise political person, as well as being a very proud Queenslander.

And she made magnificent pumpkin scones. I enjoyed many of them!

After Joh left parliament, we kept in touch. Every few months, he would call to have a yarn about what was going on in politics and express his views about what should be done to create prosperity. He would 'instruct' me on how important problems should be fixed and ask me to do what I could to fix them.

My last face-to-face meeting with them, a year before Joh's death, was a sad one. He was in quite poor health and suffering financial hardship as the result of paying legal bills he incurred while defending himself against perjury charges at the Fitzgerald Commission on matters totally different to the fundraising in which we were involved together. He had also made a poor investment in a failed cattle property, the losses of which were huge.

With great humiliation, he and Flo raised much-needed funds by selling his books to the many tourists who visited their legendary home at Bethany, located on a hill near Kingaroy. One book called *Feeding the Chooks* was a bestseller. In Joh's vocabulary, all media people were 'the chooks'.

At our meeting that day, they both greeted me warmly and we happily chatted about old times. He called me 'Flo's Sunday school boyfriend', a title that I regard as an honour.

Joh, once more, warned me 'not to get associated with any more awful socialists'.

He was referring to the fact that Gough Whitlam and Bob Hawke had both been fundraising clients of mine at various times and he knew that I held them both in high regard.

The facts of the matter are that throughout my fundraising career, I have never raised funds directly for any political parties. I raised funds to back the careers of eminent parliamentarians whom I knew personally and reckoned were genuine leaders.

If we have open minds, we will have no problem in finding good guys on all sides of politics whose careers have the potential to serve the nation significantly in a bipartisan fashion.

No-one can deny that, despite all his mistakes and misjudgements, Joh made an enormous contribution to the future of his beloved Queensland. He transformed the state from being an economic backwater into a prosperous economy and, in doing so, his government regularly had budget surpluses.

When Labor's Wayne Goss became premier shortly after Joh had been removed by his own team, he told me that Joh had left him a treasury with a lot of money in the bank.

It should not be overlooked that Joh tried to extend his patriotic contribution beyond the borders of Queensland to the Australian Parliament in Canberra via the ill-fated JOH FOR PM campaign. It was a huge mistake. Not only did it fail, it destroyed John Howard's first attempt to become prime minister.

Flo advised Joh not to launch that campaign but, on this occasion, he failed to take her advice. I have never been able to work out why but all of us have made lots of errors in our lives and we do our utmost to forget them.

However, it will be a long time before the names of Joh and Flo Bjelke-Petersen are forgotten by all their haters and admirers.

Last year, I made another visit to Bethany.

I stayed in one of the cottages built by Joh and Flo's son, John. He rents them out to tourists and they are of good quality and very popular. The cottages are on a hill that gives a splendid view of Kingaroy.

I paid my respects to Joh and Flo at their graves on the property. I felt that I was at a place of significant history from which much can be learned by people with open minds.

Someone once told me that history is made by those who turn up.

Joh and Flo never ever failed to turn up and, on most occasions, their presence was memorable, too often for the wrong reasons.

Nevertheless, they could never be ignored.

3: Charles

Here we look at the man who became the king of England in 2022 when he outlived his mother, Queen Elizabeth, after spending 70 years as the heir apparent. Frail though she was, it's sufficient to say here that she was a dedicated stayer.

I hold the personal view that, if Queen Elizabeth had outlived him, the British people would have missed out on a having a responsible king to reign over them.

Let me make it clear from the outset that I am a staunch advocate of a referendum to change the Australian Constitution by deleting all references to 'The Crown' and replacing them with the words 'The People of Australia' as it is the people with whom the power must lie.

I respect King Charles as a person, but I can find no reason why he should have legal powers that relate in any way to how Australia is governed.

Let me tell you about my meeting with Charles at Exeter Cathedral over three decades ago when he was the Prince of Wales.

The cathedral has a splendid boys choir, one of the finest in the world, and they needed a scholarship fund that would enable them to enlist the best available talent to attend the cathedral school. I was appointed as their fundraising consultant to help them raise the considerable money that was required.

My first recommendation was that they invite Prince Charles to be patron of the scholarship fund. In addition to his prime title of Prince of Wales, he was also Duke of Cornwall, which is the neighbouring county. He has a large estate there. He willingly accepted and made the first gift to the fund, a significantly generous one. We then invited Charles to launch the campaign by attending Evensong at the cathedral where he would read the lesson and then speak at a reception immediately afterwards.

An overflowing crowd attended Evensong and 100 eminent citizens were invited to the reception to enjoy drinks and savouries as they met with Charles. He turned on a splendid performance at both events and, at the reception, he insisted on meeting every attendee personally. He did more than shake hands. He had a short chat with everyone.

When he reached my place in the line, I said a simple, 'Good evening, sir.'

'Ah,' he said, 'the Australian organiser.'

He had done his homework.

He asked me a number of questions about how the campaign was being organised and, confidentially, suggested the names of some possible donors whom we might approach. He then asked a quite notable question.

By way of background, a week or so beforehand, while Charles was representing Queen Elizabeth at a funeral overseas, Diana had gone dining and dancing at a fashionable London club with an eminent and eligible young banker. As was to be expected, she was photographed by a predictable 'cad' who sold the photo to the Murdoch media. They gladly splashed it everywhere and ungraciously commented that, since Charles was such a 'boring chap', Diana had no option but to hit the town whenever she had the chance.

Charles had not been amused, especially as Murdoch was constantly cynically reporting about his life and work. Charles's question was this: 'Have you received a gift to the fund from Rupert Murdoch?'

'Not yet, sir, but negotiations are underway.'

'You have Royal approval to screw Mr Murdoch for as much as you can get.'

'I will do my best, sir.'

'Good luck.'

With a pat on the shoulder, he moved onto the next guest.

Earlier in the day, I had a brief view of another peril that goes with the life of being royalty.

I escorted the chief constable of the county around the cathedral and the cathedral square, helping him to select places where three armed police officers could be placed so to ensure that no-one harmed Charles. I asked the chief constable if there were any particular reasons why anyone would want to shoot Charles.

His response was sharp.

'They don't need a reason. They will do it just to get publicity for some ratbag cause.'

Such is life.

Anyway, in good Australian language, I reckon that Charles is a decent bloke. It is more than a bit sad that he had such a long wait to be king. Queen Elizabeth came from a family that for many generations has excelled at longevity and, frail though she became, she looked as though she would live forever. Her mother made a huge effort to do just that.

Charles is a 1000% better bloke than his younger brother, Andrew, whom the media declare to have been the queen's favourite son.

I met Andrew briefly when he officially opened John Flynn Place at Cloncurry in North-West Queensland, a project of which I was one of the founders. This was back in the days when Andrew was still with Fergie. He appeared to be boringly disinterested, but Fergie stole the show. She was a real player and I thought she added some much-needed and lively zest to the Royals. But in the end, they could not cope with her frequently 'unroyal' behaviour.

Now Andrew has descended to the dark depths of sexual depravity where he was in league with his now deceased friend Jeffrey Epstein. Few now seek his company. Indeed, Andrew faces the threat of many years in an American prison. If he was not a Royal, he may well have been there already.

Let me say that I am pleased that I was wrong in my concerns about the prospects of Charles reaching the throne because of the longevity of his mother. He deserves a go and will be a responsible monarch, with Camilla being a great teammate.

Just a few extra notes.

My wife, Helen, was with me that evening in Exeter and really enjoyed the chat with the Prince of Wales. She was the only woman at church and the reception who didn't wear a hat. After all, why would you wear a hat after 6:30 pm? Well, I don't know, but the Brits seem to think it is important.

Now, you know why I'm an advocate of Australia having one of our own citizens as our own head of state.

Rupert Murdoch did make a gift, but he wasn't as generous as Charles.

The campaign was a success and the choir flourished.

It's tradition in Britain for a Royal to be patron for significant fundraising campaigns.

Charles is involved with one every year.

His sister, Anne, is a tireless charity worker.

When I was fundraising adviser to Worcester Cathedral, Anne worked enthusiastically for the cause. At the events that she attended, she always brought a plate of cakes as a contribution to supper. Her staff told me that she usually made them herself.

So, who really wants to be a Royal?

Going to public events day after day, where you are expected to be nice to everyone, must often get to be a boring routine.

4: The Brothers Costello

The influence of family life on the ultimate destiny of us all is always an interesting study.

In this case, the influence that very committed Christian parents had on the lives of Peter and Tim Costello was huge and it is fascinating that the brothers express their Christian heritage in quite diverse ways.

I found it to be a meaningful experience to know two brothers who have made a significant contribution to Australia while following different pathways in life.

Peter Costello holds the record of being the longest serving treasurer of Australia, delivering 11 annual budgets, an achievement that is unlikely to be beaten any time soon, if ever.

Tim Costello is widely acknowledged as having served as an eminent leader of the Baptist Church, indeed the worldwide Christian community, and World Vision Australia, plus numerous initiatives advocating social change.

I met Peter first when I negotiated with him at Parliament. I met with him quite often over a decade regarding retirement incomes for senior Australians and funding for the Inland Railway. He always gave me a fair hearing.

I only ever managed to obtain occasional small grants from him for the railway as he was a firm believer in only making financial grants to projects that would be financially viable within a short period of time. This was the traditional conservative position on the financing of infrastructure.

However, he was clearly interested in planning how Australia would finance the long-term costs of longevity.

Tim is the older brother of the two. I first met Tim when he spoke at a dinner at the Aspley Uniting Church and stayed overnight at my home where we enjoyed a couple of wee drams of scotch whisky while we chatted for a long while about solving the many social and economic challenges facing humanity. He has a huge social conscience, combined with skill and determination.

It disappointed me greatly that Peter did not become prime minister of Australia. He had the capacity to be a national leader, but it was his own decision to back off on the two occasions when he had a chance to reach the pinnacle of political success. He will always regret it.

The first opportunity was when Peter declined to challenge Howard when it was becoming obvious that John was overstaying his time. Peter didn't have enough votes in his party caucus to win on an initial challenge, but had he made a bid, it would have shaken up the party room. This would have created conditions where it would have been highly possible that he would have won a second challenge, just as Keating had done with Hawke.

The second opportunity was when Howard lost the election of 2007 and Peter declined to run for the leadership of the Liberals. Peter held the view that Rudd would stay in power for at least two terms, and he didn't want to hang around any longer than he had already done in his plan to occupy the Prime Minister's Lodge. He chose to begin a new career in the private sector. This proved to be a significant misjudgement since Rudd didn't even last a full term.

We all make mistakes. I've made plenty. But at least Peter knows that as treasurer he presided over a decade of general prosperity for most Australians.

Tim is not a conservative, politically or theologically. He is a humanitarian. Indeed, the Democrats offered him a senate seat for Victoria, which would have created a situation in which he and Peter would have been political opponents.

Tim declined so he could take up a leadership role at World Vision. This decision gave him the opportunity to travel the world seeking equality and justice and the basics of life for families to overcome poverty. He achieved remarkable things during his long tenure there.

He also took up vital issues within Australia such as his campaign against the social havoc of gambling and drug abuse as well the inhumanity of homelessness and poverty.

Now, both Costello brothers are advancing into their later years, but still enjoying productive but very different lives.

Peter is a merchant banker, a guardian of Australia's Future Fund and chairman of Nine Entertainment, which in recent years took over Fairfax Media. In fact, this makes him the only significant opposition that Rupert Murdoch has in Australia. That is an important role for him and for Australia since Murdoch, an American citizen, has accumulated far too much influence in moulding public opinion.

Tim is now involved in several important leadership roles in community initiatives dealing with social challenges.

The one that I especially follow is his leadership of a challenging think-tank called the Australia We Want.

This is a long overdue initiative because too many of us get around saying we must defend Australian principles, but cannot describe what those principles are, usually declaring that it means we must all be good blokes. Tim is challenging us all to think deeply about what quality of nation we want Australia to become and then work together in a realistic way to achieve that goal. It's a significant initiative.

I run into Peter from time to time in airport lounges and enjoy our chats.

Tim and I talk occasionally by phone and I'm greatly indebted to him for having written the foreword to my book, *The Man on the Twenty Dollar Notes*.

Tim and Peter's books are well worth reading too.

Peter published *The Costello Memoirs*. It's an interesting read about the science of politics, the dynamics of gaining power and the management of the economy.

Tim has written several books. His latest *A Lot With a Little* is hugely inspiring.

So, here we have two great Australians who came from a solid Christian family where they learned to be committed community servants and did something special about it.

This tells us a lot about the social power of a united family.

My experience of the Christian life is that most people who spend their early years in a strongly religious home usually reject their faith in their more mature years.

This has not been the experience of the Costello brothers. Peter continues to hold conservative religious views while Tim embraces a more modern theology.

Personally, I've adopted a more radical view of what it means to be a working partner of Jesus of Nazareth.

One way or another, each and every one of us has the opportunity to come to terms with what our basic values are and how we use them to create a better world.

Working from the power base of a solid Christian family creates a solid framework for a life of achievement.

5:
Zelman Cowen

Our world clearly needs to foster more cohesive societies everywhere, if only to enable people to feel a greater sense of security.

We yearn for leaders who can weld us into a team where we work together to heal our wounds and enjoy a shared good.

Zelman Cowen was one such leader who made an inspirational effort to build a better world.

This chapter of my reminiscences of some of the great and the mighty with whom I worked is devoted to a great man who was my closest friend in public life. He was such an intelligent and decent person and he will not be as well known to you as others who became household names, often because of the controversies that surrounded them.

I first met Zelman Cowen when he was vice chancellor of the University of Queensland. He retained my services as a fundraising consultant to help him establish university colleges in Toowoomba and Cairns, both of which created a basis for new and independent universities to eventually be created in those regions.

When he subsequently became governor-general of Australia, we met again at the official opening of the Good Shepherd hospice in Townsville for which I had helped raise funding. He invited me to arrange a time to meet him privately and this was the beginning of a close friendship that we enjoyed for decades, ending only with his passing in 2011. Our journey together covered a wide range of interests.

I worked with Zelman again at Oriel College at Oxford where he became provost after he completed his term as governor-general. We raised nine million British pounds for the restoration of this famous college that had been founded 1000 years previously.

On Zelman's return from England, we worked together to create a law school at Griffith University in Brisbane and a university college at Buderim in Queensland, which subsequently became the University of the Sunshine Coast.

Then Zelman accepted my invitation to become a director of my fundraising consultancy, Everald Compton International, which enhanced our public stature enormously. His wise counsel was extraordinary.

While these partnerships were very important to me personally, Australia will remember Zelman for three special achievements.

The first was the way Zelman calmly handled the high-profile student riots at the University of Queensland when the campus was a hive of revolutionary activity half a century ago. He showed great dignity under heavy fire. Later, after some of the riotous hotheads had grown up, they became his greatest admirers. Some were hugely apologetic of their outrageous behaviour.

Then, Malcolm Fraser appointed Zelman as governor-general. Parliament was in turmoil and the office of governor-general had been hugely debased in stature following the controversial Whitlam coup. ALP MPs and senators had refused to attend whenever Zelman's predecessor as governor-general, John Kerr, came to Parliament and, since Kerr was often intoxicated, he had ceased to be invited to public functions. So, the commission that Fraser gave to Zelman was that he should heal the nation. A momentous task.

Zelman met often with those angry parliamentarians to discuss their grievances and they agreed to accept and respect him in his role as governor-general. He then travelled around Australia meeting voters to discuss and understand constitutional issues that worried them. He was greeted warmly.

I remember him telling me one day that while a governor-general does have a constitutional power to sack a prime minister, Kerr should never have used it for reasons I outlined in my chapter about Whitlam.

His other great contribution was to outline to Australia the issues relating to making Australia a republic. He was Australia's leading authority on our Constitution and was convinced that Australia could become a republic without insulting Queen Elizabeth or creating political instability. Had Malcolm Turnbull listened to Zelman and involved him in his planning, he would have won the republic referendum in 1999.

Let me finish with three more personal comments.

When Zelman wrote his biography in his later years, I scored three pages about our work together. I'm very proud of that.

At his final meeting with the fellows of Oriel College when Zelman retired as provost of the college and as deputy chancellor of Oxford University, he gained their approval for me to be appointed as an honorary fellow. This entitles me to dine with the fellows whenever I'm in Oxford. I've never taken up the privilege, but I'm very grateful for the honour and proud of it.

When I visited Zelman for the last time a month or so before he died, he had another guest at his home whom he wanted me to meet. It was a family friend, Josh Frydenberg, who, like Zelman, was a respected member of the Melbourne Jewish community. He forecast that, one day, Josh would be prime minister of Australia.

I'm delighted to say that Josh and I have kept in contact ever since and I hope that one day he has the chance to prove he can be a fine prime minister. We would meet regularly for a coffee or a whisky at his parliament office where he had a photograph of Zelman on the wall behind his desk. It constantly reminded Josh that, as a parliamentarian, his prime task is to uphold the law.

Josh lost his seat of Kooyong to an independent in the federal election of 2022, but he'll come back to Parliament again in the not-too-distant future, most probably contesting a different electorate.

Zelman Cowen was a great Australian with a splendid intellect, significant social conscience and had an exceptional ability to explain difficult issues with clarity. He was also a very loyal friend, and my life has been enhanced by our friendship. I'm hugely grateful for it.

Before I close, let me say that Lady Anna Cowen has been a wonderful friend too.

We worked together on the board of directors of National Seniors Australia for several years. It was a happy and productive relationship. Anna is a special person to know and she has written an interesting book on Zelman's term as governor-general that is well worth reading.

I've spent many days of my life searching for and often finding excellent leaders, endeavouring to walk with them on the path to achievement and watching how they handled success, failure and embarrassment.

There are not many genuine leaders to be found these days but Zelman Cowen was one of them. Just like you and me, he had faults and failings, but he had a wonderful mind and a great gift as a communicator.

He could determine quickly the good and bad elements of any situation and make wise decisions on how to react in a manner that would give justice to as many people as possible in as timely a fashion as was possible.

An extraordinary talent. Not many have it. Another governor-general, William Deane, did and he used it when he led the Supreme Court in making the Mabo judgement on First Peoples land rights. I must add that Geoffrey Robertson QC also has a magnificent mind and great communication skills.

I continue to strive to achieve a small fraction of this talent.

6:
Paul Cronin

Paul Cronin was good company and very easy to get on with.

To achieve greatness as one of Australia's most famous television actors and then become the successful founder of a football club is a rare pairing.

He deserves a good round of applause, plus an encore.

The Brisbane Lions Football Club team would not exist today were it not for the dedication of its pioneer, Paul Cronin.

Australian television would also be poorer if not for Paul Cronin having created the legendary Dave Sullivan.

I first met Paul back in the days when I was chairman of National Seniors Australia. He was guest speaker at one of our conferences and we enjoyed a happy lunch together chatting about *The Sullivans* and *Matlock Police* in which he had high-profile acting roles that went on for years, enjoying top ratings. Indeed, there were 1077 episodes of *The Sullivans*.

Years later, when we met for a drink in Melbourne, he told me a delightful tale of a holiday he enjoyed in Ireland where *The Sullivans* was so popular on Irish TV that every episode of it had been shown twice — when the series ended, it was so popular they immediately began replaying the full series.

Paul had once become lost trying to find the home of an Irish relative, so he parked his car in a small village and went to find someone who could give him directions. The farmer to whom he spoke broke out into a broad smile and said, 'My God. Dave Sullivan.'

He then ran around the village yelling his head off and calling out, 'Dave Sullivan is here. Come on out and meet him.'

The entire village quickly turned out in wonderment and refused to allow him to leave until he had shared an Irish whisky with them.

Paul's other great achievement was as founder of the Brisbane Bears, now the Brisbane Lions, after the club eventually merged with the Melbourne team, Fitzroy.

The football club was his brainchild entirely. He did a wonderful job in convincing the hierarchy of the AFL in Melbourne that a club should be established in Brisbane and tenders should be called from interested parties to obtain a licence to run the club.

Paul called to invite me to join his syndicate, which I did happily as I reckoned it would be an interesting experience to work with him. We put in a good submission founded solely on Brisbane-based sponsors. A Melbourne group which was well connected with the AFL also tendered and the AFL board decided to declare them to be the favoured sponsors.

Paul was crestfallen so I studied the AFL rules and found that a new club could not be formed by a decision of the board of directors alone without gaining the approval of a majority of existing AFL clubs.

I suggested to Paul that he go to Melbourne and meet personally with all the clubs to ask them to support him. He did this immediately and every one of them agreed to talk to him. After all, who would knock back the chance to have a drink with Dave Sullivan. He did a wonderful job of selling our vision for a Brisbane team and, when the AFL board called the clubs together to vote, Paul won. Quite easily actually.

Then we had to find some money — four million dollars to pay the AFL to financially secure the licence and another million to organise the establishment of the club.

I arranged for Paul to come with me to see high-profile entrepreneur Christopher Skase and ask him to give us five million in cash up front. This was in the days prior to Skase falling from grace and hiding away from the law on a Spanish island.

Skase agreed to our proposal on the understanding that most matches would be played on the Gold Coast so that his hotel there would be the place where all visiting AFL players and officials stayed.

Skase called the CEO of the ANZ Bank in Melbourne while we listened in. They immediately loaned him five million dollars without even getting his signature or asking for any security. Quite incredible, really.

Then Skase fired me.

He said he wanted his own executive team to work with Paul and he would not tolerate any outsiders on the board other than Paul.

So, it's important for everyone in the world to know that my main claim to fame in life is that I was once sacked by Christopher Skase.

Years later, and just after Skase died, I got a call from the ANZ Bank to say that Skase had never repaid the loan and since I'd been a director of the club on the day the loan was granted, they required me to repay it. I invited them to find my signature on their loan document and send it to me. I heard nothing further. ANZ Bank shareholders copped the loss.

Paul's last few years were not his happiest, but it was great that he lived to see his beloved club win the premiership three times in a row.

The television industry told him that he was too old to be a leading actor anymore and so his highly successful career just faded away.

He then bought a small hardware business in Melbourne that faltered since he had no hope of competing against the Bunnings hardware empire. He deserved a better fate.

We chatted on the phone from time to time when we recalled happier days. He never complained that life was tough. He was quite simply a decent bloke, a quiet achiever. I'm privileged to have shared a friendship with him. The world would be a better place if there were many more Dave Sullivans.

In 2021, the AFL Grand Final was held in Brisbane. It was the first time it was not held at the Melbourne Cricket Ground. I emailed the president and CEO of the Lions to ask if, as a founding director, I could buy two tickets. I did not ask for free ones. They ignored me, despite me making a follow up phone call.

Fame has a short lifespan and can be easily forgotten.

The cold reality of it is that fame isn't worth much at all.

Despite the high regard I had for Paul Cronin's television career, I have now ceased to watch serialised TV shows.

Serials like *Downton Abbey* switch me off — I see them as light-weight entertainment.

I watch only well-researched documentaries on world affairs. I much prefer to read lots of books while I sip my evening whisky.

But I miss *The Sullivans* and *Matlock* and guys like Paul Cronin who came over as people I could relate to, not the light-weight sensationalists who have followed them.

I toast Dave Sullivan.

A good bloke.

7:
Elizabeth II

Queen Elizabeth II was a genuine stayer, and a calm and dignified person, who brought a high degree of commitment and tactful intelligence to her role as British monarch.

We will not see her likes again.

Indeed, her death marks the beginning of the end for Royals worldwide.

They are gradually fading away as an irrelevance in a modern society.

A few short years ago, Prince Harry and his wife Meaghan had a famous and controversial chat with television icon Oprah Winfrey before a worldwide audience of millions. Harry revealed the unfriendly way he felt his fellow Royals had treated Meaghan. He related his strong objection to the manner in which he believed the family had ostracised his mother, Diana, when she officially fell from grace. He also took revenge on the media for their gossiping insinuations that Charles was not his father, meaning that he is not genuinely entitled to be acknowledged officially as a Royal.

This unfortunate episode made life tough for Queen Elizabeth who, at that time, knew that her husband, Prince Philip was in his final year of life.

This added to the critical problem she had to deal with relating to her son Prince Andrew since it was only his Royal status that had prevented him from standing trial on sex charges in USA. As usual, she handled it all with dignity.

I cannot claim to have personally met her, but I have been in a line-up for a royal greeting four times. She simply smiled graciously each time, just as she did with everyone everywhere. She must have grown thoroughly sick of the monotony of it all.

The first occasion was the longest by far.

It happened at Oriel College at Oxford University when I was working with former Australian governor-general, Zelman Cowen in raising funds for the restoration of that ancient college. Zelman had made me an honorary fellow of the Senior Common Room of the college, and this entitled me to a place at the dinner table when the queen came to dine with the fellows.

I watched her public style with interest.

She ate very little of her three-course dinner and only occasionally sipped her wine. This was the way she kept alert and trim after attending several thousand official dinners over many decades. And she made a delightfully short three minute speech that captured the spirit of the occasion. Many politicians would be well advised to take lessons from her if they seriously want to enhance their communication skills.

My other encounters with Queen Elizabeth included her presence at the Centenary of Federation Luncheon in Melbourne in 2001, which I attended along with other recipients of the Centenary Medal that were issued to mark the occasion. I was awarded it for my work in pioneering the Inland Railway.

Then, there were the occasions when she officially opened the Australian Centre for Christianity in Canberra for which I'd helped with fundraising and when she attended Evensong at St John's Cathedral in Brisbane at the time when I was raising funds for its completion.

So, for what it's worth, here is my opinion of her:

> I found her to have considerable grace and presence. She was also astute, intelligent and responsible. Absolutely impeccable behaviour with no evidence of any pompous attitude.

She will be the last queen of Australia just as Charles will be our last king. Not that they can be declared unworthy of the job. It is simply long overdue for Australia to proclaim its independence from Britain. We have grown up. We no longer have any need to shelter in the arms of Mother England in the hope that she will protect us from the evils of the world.

What of the rest of her family?

I haven't met them all, but I did work as organiser on a number of fundraising campaigns in England in which the Royals were patrons.

Other than for Elizabeth herself, in order of seniority, they were the Queen Mother, Margaret, Philip, Charles, Anne, Andrew and Fergie.

I've mentioned in an earlier chapter that Charles is quietly professional and Anne is a committed volunteer. Fergie is a loveable riot. Andrew is the utter opposite of his mother and brothers and Margaret had a considerable problem with alcohol.

However, the Queen Mother — also Elizabeth — was a delightful surprise. She launched a campaign that I organised for the final phase of the rebuilding of Portsmouth Cathedral from wartime damage. She jogged up the steps to the cathedral in her high heels despite being in her tenth decade at the time.

Let me relate to you a happy tale about Prince Harry.

Helen and I enjoyed a holiday on Stewart Island a few years ago. It is the small island just south of Invercargill in New Zealand, a delightfully peaceful place to spend a few days hiding away from the rough and tumble of life. There's no five-star accommodation there, but Helen located a comfortable guesthouse where Harry had stayed a few weeks earlier, so we booked a room there.

On arrival, Helen impishly asked the proprietor if she could sleep in the same bed as Harry had occupied. She was told that protocol demanded that no Royal information could ever be divulged. So she asked if we could have the best and most expensive room in the house as she guessed correctly that this would have been allocated to Harry.

Alas, it had two single beds. I reckon that I got Harry's bed.

My final words relate to Queen Elizabeth's death and funeral. It was one of the most high-profile events of world history and such a shared display of grief by millions.

While I respected her greatly, it was all way over the top and the commentary by media was grossly sentimental. They diminished her with their childish efforts to make us cry.

It would have been fascinating if Elizabeth had written a book in which she spoke frankly about her thoughts on all the great and mighty who came to pay their respects to her over her long reign.

Those who paid their respects were dozens of British prime ministers, countless Commonwealth prime ministers, American presidents, heads of state from around the world and all the other famous people whom she honoured as knights and dames of the realm.

What a story it would have been.

Which Australians would be on her list of memorable leaders?

Robert Menzies would be one. He was our longest serving prime minister who was British to the boot heels and would have met her many times. She's reported to have admired him as a statesman.

I'm unable to distinguish between the stature of the others.

Yet, I'm sure she would have liked to forget Australian Governor-General John Kerr. He caused Elizabeth long-term pain when he dismissed Whitlam as prime minister, and then afterwards indicated in the defence of his actions that he had kept her informed. Kerr's correspondence with Queen Elizabeth has since been verified.

Her thoughts on Malcolm Turnbull would be of interest as he was the humble servant who led the campaign to make Australia a republic.

8:
Tim Fischer

Ever since I caught my first Linville train, I have loved trains.

This is the prime reason why I became heavily involved in the creation of the Inland Railway in Australia.

Along the way I met Tim Fischer, an extraordinary Australian, who was the greatest lover of trains I have ever met. Indeed, he was also a noted historian of trains and railways. He wrote several books about them that made for interesting reading.

I hope that in the great beyond he will find a train beyond his imagination.

'Could we take a short ride in your helicopter, Don? I really would like to visit the remains of an old railway not far from here that served a mine a century ago.'

The question came from Tim Fischer, former deputy prime minister of Australia, and highly probably the most passionate railway advocate that our nation ever produced. He was talking with Don McDonald, a close friend of mine, who is one of Australia's leading graziers.

I was listening in as Tim and I were enjoying breakfast with Don and his family at Devoncourt, south of Cloncurry, the flagship property of the significant McDonald cattle enterprise.

'That old railway is a vital relic in the history of how railways have been the essential life of the mining industry in Australia since the white man arrived,' explained Tim. 'You and Everald and me should leave a message out there in a bottle that some young Australian may find in years to come and be inspired to do something special to contribute to the future of Australia, especially our railways.'

Don readily agreed and flew us in his helicopter into some of the almost impenetrable hills between Cloncurry and Mount Isa.

We found the old railway and walked up its steep incline to the derelict mine. In the last tunnel, we wrote our messages, put them in a large old vegemite bottle and placed it on a ledge. I don't recall what Tim and Don wrote, but my words gave thanks for the pioneering spirit of those who came from the four corners of the globe and found their way out to remote places like this to create that livelihood.

Tim took a selfie of us with the bottle and put the photo among his vast memorabilia of railways.

I remembered my visit to his old home in the Riverina (before he moved to the mountain country of Victoria) and found it to be filled with miniatures and photographs of trains, rolling stock and railway gauges. He loved to chat about them.

We were friends for many years. He helped me enthusiastically with my efforts to get government backing for the Inland Railway.

He also helped Don and me to establish John Flynn Place out at Cloncurry many years ago, and later he launched my book *The Man on the Twenty Dollar Notes* at a function there.

When he was appointed as Australian ambassador to the Vatican (by his political opponent Kevin Rudd), he kept in touch with me via regular emails and phone calls, which I greatly enjoyed. He always signed off with his usual humour by saying, 'The Holy Father sends his personal blessing.'

One of his most memorable emails was the one when he told me that his two autistic sons had gone with him and his wife to be personally blessed by the pope. It was a moving experience for the whole family, as well as the pope. The boys really did cherish the occasion as a special time in their challenging lives.

We talked by phone a couple of weeks before Tim died of cancer. He knew the end was near. It was a positive chat, no self-pity, no fear, but lots of good advice about how to get the Inland Railway built as soon as possible.

Politicians often go through dark days of public criticism for a wide range of issues, such as the unfair status of women in society, the challenge of climate change, the persecution of refugees, corruption and many others. The popularity of politicians is probably as low now as it has ever been in my lifetime.

But in Tim Fischer, we had a good and decent bloke who rarely suffered public anger.

On his last day in Parliament, before he took up his appointment in the Vatican, when he was officially farewelled, the chamber was packed with members from all parties who all paid fine tributes to him. Rarely had Parliament ever seen such goodwill flow. Political ideology was forgotten.

And, on the day of his funeral, it was arranged that his body would be carried on a vintage train to Albury Railway Station. There was standing room only on the platform and thunderous applause as the train pulled into the station. Tears flowed freely.

Here was a man.

A genuine railway man.

A fair-dinkum Aussie.

Someone, somewhere, once said to me, 'Always leave tracks in the sand for others to follow.'

Tim Fischer left many tracks in countless places, especially in the Australian bush.

Many were railway tracks.

And they led to the light on the hill. He always looked upwards and outwards with enthusiasm and the broadest vision of a limitless future.

9: Gerald Ford

Gerald Ford was a rather ordinary guy, but that was his strength.

After the political turmoil caused by the demise of Richard Nixon, the American nation needed a peaceful leader who would restore order in the political establishment, and he did just that.

Lyndon Johnson had once famously and unkindly remarked that 'Gerry can't walk and chew gum at the same time.'

This was a huge misjudgement since he proved to be a quiet person who knew what he wanted to do and did it without flair.

Gerald Ford was the only president of the United States of America I met personally. It happened unplanned in 1976 in a way that was quite extraordinary. Whenever I tell the story, most people think I'm having them on.

Nevertheless, the facts are that I was in Cleveland, Ohio where I had addressed a conference, and heard that, on the following morning, President Ford would speak at an election campaign rally there. So I decided to stay overnight and go along to hear him because he was defending his presidency against a formidable opponent in Jimmy Carter. It was a very tight race that Carter eventually won narrowly.

The venue was packed with a huge audience of Republican Party supporters, and I was one of many who had no option but to stand up for the entire proceedings. My cramped location was right beside the door through which the president would enter. A single rope held back the crowd.

Suddenly, a police officer appeared beside me and began to check out the crowd.

Then said to me, 'Where you from, guy?'

'Australia,' I said.

He proceeded to interview me in depth to find out exactly who I was, why I was there, whether I was involved in politics, and requested identification.

Then he said, 'Because of a dumb organisational stuff up, we don't have enough security guys here right now to protect the president from this crowd. You're big enough for the job and the jacket and tie you are wearing make you look like a security guy. Are you willing to be one for a few minutes?'

'Yes,' I said.

He frisked me from head to toe to make sure I had no guns, knives or bombs, then said, 'Right. Come over to this side of the rope and don't move away from this position. If anyone around here tries to get under the rope or hurl abuse at the president, yell your head off. I won't be far away.'

So I went under the rope and did my best to look important and tough like J Edgar Hoover, the corrupt boss of the FBI.

I was well aware that this whole situation was ridiculous and irresponsible, given that there had already been two failed attempts to assassinate Ford, the only American president who had that happen twice.

After only a few minutes had passed in my career as a presidential guard, Gerald Ford came through the door, so I decided to push my luck and say something.

'Good morning, Mr President.'

I think that my ocker accent intrigued him. He stopped, walked over and we shook hands.

'Your voice tells me you're not an American.'

'Mr President, I'm an Australian. I'm here for a few days on a business trip.'

'I've met your prime minister, Malcolm Fraser. We got on well together.'

'May I wish you well in your campaign for a second term.'

'Thank you. May I ask how a visiting Australian got to be one of my security people.'

I gave him a very brief account of what had happened.

'Well, I figure you may do a better job than some of the guys who are supposed to be looking after me. Travel home safely.'

I got a firm handshake, and he went on his way to make his speech.

My impression was that he was a humble man of basic decency, qualities that are not often found in the political scene.

He eventually defied all assassins by living to the grand old age of 93, passing away in 2006.

He'll go down in American history for two significant reasons, both high-profile constitutional incidents.

The first is that he was the only president who was never elected by the voters of America. Congress, where he had served for many years, voted to appoint him as vice president to Richard Nixon when the elected vice president, Spiro Agnew, was forced to resign after being found guilty of fraud. Then Nixon himself had to resign after the Watergate debacle and Ford was automatically sworn in as president. Because of these accidents of history, he became known as the 'Accidental President'.

The second is the most controversial.

Ford pardoned Nixon since he believed that if Nixon had to go through a trial as a law-breaker, it would take many months of controversy to complete and it was certain that Nixon would spill the beans on many other political figures while dividing the nation. He was probably correct in this assumption, but his decision caused an incredible uproar. It would become a key factor in causing him to lose narrowly to Carter.

Sadly, far too many of the presidents who succeeded Ford adopted the practice of pardoning too many people during their final days in office.

The action of Trump in pardoning scores of quite decadent people only hours before his presidency ended in 2021 has brought many Americans to feel that the right to pardon must be removed from presidential powers. But no law-makers are moving to fix it as yet.

Let me say that all of the above makes me pleased not to be an American.

Democracy in America, in and following the Trump era, has become a corrupt farce and Joe Biden is having a tough time trying to unite a divided nation.

If she is elected to follow Biden as president, Kamala Harris will have the opportunity to become a long overdue reformer of a nation that has ceased to be the world's role model of how democracy should work effectively.

Good guys and gals always find the world of politics to be a more difficult and soul-destroying place than they ever imagined it would be.

So, is there really a place in government for the likes of humble guys such as Gerald Ford?

The short answer is no.

All presidents and prime ministers have to spend at least a quarter of their time watching their backs since they have more enemies on their own side of politics than on the opposition benches.

Then they must spend even more hours defending their family and friends and themselves from constant accusations of invented or actual scandals.

After that begins, there's the ever-dangerous cut and thrust of exercising and surviving political power.

Only a few people want all of that in their lives and only an occasional one has had the ability to handle it successfully.

10:
Julia Gillard

Many conservative voters will never acknowledge that Julia Gillard was worthy of the honour of being the prime minister of Australia or, indeed, was in any way successful when she did get the job.

She had far too many political enemies and they combined, eventually, to bring her down.

However, in my view, she was a fine leader who deserves special acknowledgement for her achievements.

I found Julia Gillard to be a superb one-on-one negotiator, as close to the best as I ever dealt with in politics. Indeed, there was only one other at her level of skill: Bob Hawke, whose personality was considerably different.

Sadly, this did not translate into her public persona. Julia is not a talented public speaker or media performer. She tends to sound like an old aunt who is giving you a lecture, an image that is way out of character.

Except, of course, for her impromptu misogyny speech.

She justifiably and comprehensively tore the hide off opposition leader, Tony Abbott, that day for his crude attitude to women. It will deservedly be remembered as one of the great speeches in the 120 year history of the Australian Parliament.

I met Julia Gillard personally several times for negotiations on seniors' issues and enjoyed the experience. I was given a fair hearing each time and always got answers. Sometimes, I didn't like the answers, but she never failed to give me an answer. The myth that she didn't like seniors because they did not vote for her is political garbage.

Her history as a prime minister will always be regarded as controversial, and somewhat disappointing, as she did make some basic political errors that contributed to her downfall.

For instance, she should not have called an election so soon after removing Kevin Rudd as prime minister in a party room coup. She needed time to establish her credentials as a leader and gain the confidence of the nation. Her campaign was lacklustre and, even though she narrowly survived, she really deserved to lose based on her performance.

She should never have appointed either Kevin Rudd or Bob Carr as her foreign ministers. They were ordinary performers in that role and this diminished the status of her government.

Promising in her election campaign never to introduce a carbon price was wrong too. The nation needed one — it still does, but she didn't handle it well at the time.

Also, her deal with renegade Liberal MP, Peter Slipper, to make him Speaker of the Parliament by ratting on his party just to give her an extra vote on the floor of Parliament was not smart politics.

But she did do a number of great things for which we can all be grateful.

One was to establish the Royal Commission into Institutional Responses to Child Sexual Abuse and to create the NDIS for disabled Australians despite bitter opposition from Abbott on both matters.

Of special note also is that she survived for three years as a minority government, passing over 500 bills while not suffering a single defeat on the floor of the House of Representatives. This was an incredible feat of political discipline.

Independent MP Tony Windsor told me that throughout the three years in which he was one of those whose vote she relied upon for political survival in a hung Parliament, Julia Gillard didn't fail to meet him regularly to discuss her political agenda and debate his concerns.

Tony Abbott did not remove her from office. This is a myth. He failed dismally as he did with most things in his political life.

It was Kevin Rudd who was Julia Gillard's political assassin, and I will believe to my dying day that, had Rudd been banished from the scene for a second time, the subsequent election would have, once more, been Gillard versus Abbott and she would have won again.

So how will we remember her?

Even her most trenchant critics cannot deny her place in history as Australia's first female prime minister. This gives her a permanent place in our folklore. She did make some political blunders but, in my 90 years, I have never known a prime minister who was blameless.

Unlike Abbott, who remained as the 'lethal assassin' of his successor, Malcolm Turnbull, Gillard left Parliament immediately after Rudd beat her in his counter coup. She was gracious in defeat and it is important to note that since leaving Parliament, she is continuing to be a distinguished leader in society.

Her role as chair of Beyond Blue, our nation's most influential mental health advocacy, is vital in the post-COVID-19 world. And we should remember that she was head-hunted for that job by one of her most trenchant political critics, Jeff Kennett, a staunch conservative. He cast politics aside to recognise Gillard's talents as a leader.

Gillard is also chair of two eminent international institutions involved in education and women's rights and she's making a significant impact with both.

Her book *Women and Leadership* is well worth reading.

How will I remember her?

I say simply that it has been a privilege to know her and work with her and I hope that our paths will cross often.

She's a great Australian, no doubt.

I have no doubt that Julia Gillard's short reign as prime minister was brought about by too many males being unable to cope with a society that was led by a woman.

These guys still hold that attitude to this day even though they pretend to be relaxed about female leadership. The undeniable fact is they quietly undermined her and still denigrate her whenever they can. And they will still have their hang-ups when the next female prime minister arrives on the scene.

The bonus to society is that Gillard accepted their obnoxious behaviour with such good grace that it inspired us to hope that an age of enlightenment is not all that far away.

11:
Bob Hawke

Some people are born to be leaders.

Bob Hawke was one of them.

Nevertheless, many years from now, historians will still be struggling to define and describe just what it was that led him to become an unforgettable prime minister.

For the moment, we can acknowledge that he was a rare character who left a lasting impression on Australians.

Bob Hawke had an extraordinary ability to make everyone believe he was their best friend. And he was their best friend until they decided they didn't like him.

I first met Bob Hawke when the Australian Labor Party decided to build John Curtin House in Canberra and retained my services to raise the necessary capital in 1973. He and I got on well and the campaign did well too.

What always intrigued me was that Bob, on every occasion he could, would have a friendly shot at me for being a Presbyterian elder, and subsequently a Uniting Church elder (for 63 years and counting). Bob was the son of a devout minister of the Congregational Church, but had rejected Christianity and often made a public issue of his attitude to religion.

It soon became clear to me as our friendship progressed that he had misgivings about having given it up and would constantly go out of his way to explain why he had done so. No matter where and when we met, he would start a somewhat jocular debate about why I could be so naive as to buy Christianity as a rational belief and a cornerstone of life.

Long after he retired, we would often run into one another at airport lounges, and he would usually call out, 'G'day, you old Christian bastard' in the most jovial tone.

He was trying to square off his memories of his father with justifications of why he had let him down. I reckon that, in his final days of life he was still not quite at peace with the thought of not being a believer. A search for spirituality was certainly a lingering factor in his being.

When I was working with Archbishop Peter Hollingworth on the task of raising funds for the completion of St John's Cathedral in Brisbane, Bob paid a visit to announce a federal grant. It was a building of historic significance, having had its foundation stone laid by the Duke of York in 1910.

I took him on an inspection of the cathedral and we stopped in front of a Lloyd Rees painting that graces one of the walls. He paused for a long time, slowly absorbing its impact.

Then he said, 'You know, Everald, this painting is the most spiritual thing in this building.'

He was still not at peace with the faith of his father.

Now, changing my theme totally, an unforgettable memory of him occurred at the Canberra Rex Hotel in 1974. He invited me and ALP national secretary, David Coombe, to have breakfast with him in his suite at 8:00 am one Sunday to discuss fundraising.

We arrived on time to find him stark naked but quite unperturbed about it.

'Come on in, chaps. Been on the phone since early morning. Haven't had time to dress. Anyway, I've ordered bacon and eggs all round and it will be here in a minute.'

Bob made no attempt to put on any clothes and, when our breakfast arrived, I went to the door to receive the delivery, denying the waitress the unnecessary experience of meeting an unclad Hawke.

He still didn't get dressed and sat down to munch his breakfast as we worked our way through the agenda. Every so often, when some item of business got him agitated, he would get up and walk around the room waving his arms and thumping the furniture.

At one point, David Coombe said, 'Go and put some pants on, Bob.'

The response was swift.

'Your problem, Coombe, is that your life is totally consumed by trivia. You can never see the big picture.'

In the context of the scene of our meeting that day, the words 'big picture' could be interpreted a couple of ways.

When we'd finished breakfast, we could hear the voices of housemaids working in the corridor outside. Hawke's face lit up and he jumped up out of his chair declaring, 'It's time to put these breakfast trays outside.'

I offered to do the job.

'No, Everald, leave it to me. Those girls need something to liven up the boredom of their menial jobs. I always have the welfare of the workers of Australia as a priority of my life.' (Which was true.)

He opened the door and out he went. Screams and running footsteps. Back in came Bob with a grin all over his face.

'The ladies have just enjoyed the most exciting sight of their lives.'

David Coombe was quick with a good response, 'Bullshit, Bob. They're just running late for their morning tea break.'

This ridiculous event was pure Hawke. Absolutely crude and sexist in the extreme, but he saw it as good fun. He was a person who needed always to be the centre of attention and this was just another way of achieving it.

In truth, he was a lonely soul.

His many infamous affairs were not primarily motivated by sex. Childish as it may seem, he just didn't like to be alone at night.

But he was a prime minister of considerable achievement. We have all benefited in one way or another from the economic and social reforms he created.

When Hawke died, two days before 2019 federal election, Bill Shorten stopped campaigning since he reckoned that voters would remember Hawke as a prime example of what a good ALP government could bring to the nation. It was a huge tactical error because Hawke's death simply highlighted to voters the fact that Bill, and most others of his era, were not in the same league as Bob. Indeed, few were.

No-one was like Hawke. He came from a special mould.

May more arrive soon, so long as they keep their pants on.

Australia constantly needs refreshing leadership.

When I was a lad, members of Parliament were expected to be moral bastions of society. Most were not, but they went out of their way to appear to be.

Bob Hawke made an art form of letting everyone know that he was a playboy and was happy to prove it.

He even announced to the nation on television that he was often unfaithful to his wife, Hazel.

He got profoundly drunk in public on far too many occasions.

He used crude language much too profusely.

He was well known publicly as a sexual predator, who didn't ever intend to be abusive, although some of his actions were.

Even so, he won four general elections.

It shows that voters always choose economics above morals.

12:
Edmund Hillary

Every so often we have the good fortune to meet a legend whom we instantly recognise as a genuinely decent person.

Ed Hillary was one worth meeting.

And he was hugely humble as well.

The very quietest among the greatest of achievers.

It was on 29 May 1953 that the news flashed around the world that Edmund Hillary of New Zealand, and Sherpa Tensing Norgay of Nepal had become the first people to climb Mount Everest and return alive.

It was an extraordinary achievement and the people of New Zealand erupted with pride, as did the people of Nepal.

A humble beekeeper who had produced lots of magnificent honey for his fellow citizens to enjoy for many years had become New Zealand's most honoured citizen and famous son. The newly crowned Queen Elizabeth made him a knight of the realm one month later.

I met Sir Edmund in Auckland when we worked together many years ago on a fundraising campaign for the Anglican Diocese of Auckland. I found him to not only be very humble, but enormously shy and thoroughly honourable, as well as being a committed and generous Christian who was a faithful servant of Jesus of Nazareth.

While we were enjoying a coffee after one function that we attended together, I asked him what his immediate thoughts were when he conquered the world's highest mountain.

Very quietly, he said, 'I did not conquer Everest. I conquered myself.'

Think about that.

He was saying that his biggest challenge he had faced was his own lack of confidence. This is emphasised by a high-profile public lecture he once gave titled 'Inferiority, Its Cause and Cure'.

His mother-in-law once told listeners on radio that Hillary had been too frightened to ask her daughter to marry him. He asked his mother-in-law to speak to her daughter on his behalf as the task frightened him more than Everest. Do I have any readers who have had this romantic experience?

After his Everest triumph, Hillary devoted much of his life to improving the economic life of the poverty-stricken Sherpas of Nepal. He established the Himalayan Trust to enable him to do this. His good deeds led him to personal tragedy. His wife, Louise, and their daughter, Belinda, died in a plane crash in Nepal while helping him with his philanthropic work. He grieved quietly, privately and deeply.

Hillary went on to achieve many more memorable things, too many to list here.

Most notable was his walk across the Antarctic continent via the South Pole as well as his journey on foot to the North Pole with the conqueror of the moon, Neil Armstrong. He became the first person ever to stand at both poles.

I happened to be in New Zealand when he died in 2008 and tried to get a seat in the cathedral for his funeral but there were thousands of names on the waiting list.

So, I watched on television.

The crowds around the cathedral and along the route to the crematorium were the largest in the history of his nation. This did not surprise me in the slightest.

After all, he is one of only a few New Zealanders to have his photo on their currency.

The Good Book says, 'The meek shall inherit the Earth.'

I stand in awe of the power of humility, vividly displayed in the life of this humble and achieving human being.

He was always willing to acknowledge that he may not have been the first person to conquer Everest. He said it was possible that Englishman George Mallory may have got there 17 years earlier than him in 1936. Mallory was last seen close to the top but was then covered in heavy cloud and never seen alive again.

In a famous television interview, Ed Hillary was asked, 'Why did you try to climb Mount Everest?'

His answer was bluntly honest: 'Because it was there.'

I ask myself, 'Why is humility so powerful?'

There can be only one answer: 'Because it is so rare.'

13:
Peter Hollingworth

Every one of us makes a significant mistake some time in our lives.

Some, like me, make more than one.

It's what we do to apologise for our sins and make reparations for those errors that finally counts.

I know that Peter Hollingworth is making an inspirational attempt to do exactly that.

I greatly valued a solid working relationship with Peter Hollingworth when he was Anglican archbishop of Brisbane.

We were involved together in undertaking the task of raising funds for and completing Brisbane's St John's Cathedral in the manner that had been planned ever since the foundation stone was laid a century earlier by the Duke of York.

We also worked together in gathering support in Australia for the crusade of Archbishop Desmond Tutu to free South Africa from apartheid.

In both cases, we managed to achieve some success.

We got on well personally. I was a guest at his home for dinner on several occasions and we enjoyed an occasional lunch at the Brisbane Club.

It came as a surprise to me when he accepted John Howard's invitation to become governor-general of Australia. I didn't think that this was his intended vocation in life.

He had always been a crusader for compelling issues of humanity such as homelessness and poverty while he was a distinguished leader of the Brotherhood of St Laurence based in Melbourne. I could not see him being happy in a relatively benign role as a head of state who was required to be always politically and socially neutral.

It is now history that, not long after he settled into the governor-general's residence at Yarralumla in Canberra, he was hit by a tumult of tragic events. Not just for him, but particularly for victims of child abuse.

It was revealed publicly that, during his time as archbishop of Brisbane, there had been several instances of significant child abuse in Anglican schools and parishes that the church had kept under wraps. Peter unfairly copped all the blame for the cover up. It is a proven fact that the Diocesan Council voted unanimously to instruct him not to go public on these matters because any ensuing criminal and civil lawsuits would inflict huge costs on the church.

Additionally, the public risk insurers of the Anglican Church bluntly advised him in writing, and in no uncertain terms, that they would declare the church public risk insurance policies to be null and void if he made any public statement that caused financial payouts to be made to victims.

He reluctantly accepted this advice, and this subsequently proved to be a significant error of judgement for which he paid a huge price of massive personal humiliation.

Because Peter is not a politician, he did not handle the inevitable media flak at all well and was finally hit by an accusation of rape, which led to his resignation as governor-general in 2003.

Above all, a public image developed portraying him as having no compassion for victims of sexual abuse. I know that this vision of him is not true, but the anger of the victims was their personal right to express as human beings who had been grossly violated while in the care of the church.

So ended the significant public life of a community leader who is basically an honourable person.

I gradually lost touch with him for a time. He now lives in Melbourne, and I am in Brisbane.

But we did catch up at the Parliament of the World's Religions in Melbourne in 2009. We were both delegates representing Australia and we shared a meaningful chat over lunch about what we were both trying to do as followers of Jesus of Nazareth to help create a better world. At the conclusion of lunch, I knew with certainty that if he could have his time over again, he would have handled the child abuse tragedy differently. Being wise after an event is a virtue that we all acquire quite often.

He would have ignored his advisers and sought justice for the victims in the same manner as Jesus of Nazareth would have undoubtedly done. Alas, it was all too late. His personal liability cannot be reversed or erased.

Time marches on and the subsequent Royal Commission into Institutional Responses to Child Sexual Abuse has revealed that he was not alone. He was just one of many church leaders who turned a blind eye to the abuse of so many vulnerable people. Those of us who are members of churches all share the blame for not ensuring that our churches acted responsibly.

I was delighted when I received a letter and phone call from him at the time when I was awarded an honour as an Officer of the Order of Australia. We had a pleasant and interesting chat about many things but I was sad to hear his news that, because of the child abuse accusations made against him two decades previous, the Anglican Church had denied him the right to preside at any Eucharist. I hope that by the time this book is published, this appalling injustice will have been reversed.

It really is an act of hypocrisy by those who instructed him to act as he did and then left him to carry the can on their behalf.

It is an injustice to Peter Hollingworth that Cardinal George Pell is able to fully continue his role as a priest of the Roman Catholic Church, but the Anglican Church has denied this privilege to Peter.

I recently visited Peter at his humble Melbourne apartment and, at my request, he shared bread and wine with me as we celebrated the Eucharist together in the tradition of the Uniting Church of which I am an elder.

My personal friendship with Peter does not absolve either him or me from our responsibility as citizens and Christians for the adequate restoration of the lives of the thousands of sexual abuse victims who were betrayed by the churches they had trusted.

This unavoidable responsibility remains with us for the rest of our lives.

14:
Bob Hope

Undoubtedly, the most famous of all the great and the mighty whom I met.

Bob Hope had significant name recognition in every nation on Earth for decades both as a comedian and a movie star.

He was a genuine trouper.

Many decades ago, I boarded a flight from Vancouver to Los Angeles. As I took my seat, I glanced at the guy sitting next to me and reckoned he had a face that looked familiar. Suddenly, it dawned on me who it was. A legend of show business was my travel partner.

Bob Hope.

Since I was not noted for my shyness, I decided to start a conversation.

'Good evening, Mr Hope. My name is Everald Compton and I'm from Australia. It is a great privilege for me to say hello to you.'

'Come again with that goddamn handle of yours. I've never heard anything like it before.'

'It is Everald. My mother discovered it in a book.'

'She actually loved you.'

'Yes. And I loved her.'

'Funny way to show it. But I like Oorstralians. Using your lingo, you are good blokes. Anyway, before this conversation continues one word further, you must answer one important question correctly.'

'I will do my best to get it right.'

'Who is the better golfer, me or Bing Crosby.'

'It is not even a contest, Mr Hope. You win by the length of the straight.'

'My God. You are an astute young guy. You've made a very profound observation and have earned yourself the right to call me Bob.'

We chatted for a while and then he said he needed a nap. This suited me fine as I spend most of my time on planes catching up on a bit of sleep.

When we landed in Los Angeles, we walked together down to the baggage area. I had trouble keeping up with his fast pace even though he was well into his 80s.

I asked him what he felt was the best attitude towards life that anyone can have.

'Know how to leave a dinner without offending people. Too many people think that if you leave early, you'll offend your host so they stay there and wear out their welcome. That is crap. You just need to think of a smart line that gets you out of the place. It's the same on stage. You must walk off when the crowd are howling for you to stay.'

I thanked him for our chat, and we parted happily.

His parting line was, 'Don't let Oorstralia fall off the end of the planet.'

However, the clear message I want to convey in this chapter relates to longevity. Bob Hope was a fine example of how to live actively for a long time.

He achieved this wonderfully well. He died just three months after reaching his century, his last public performance being at age 96.

He had starred in 54 movies, many of them being the Road films with Bing Crosby and Dorothy Lamour, plus countless radio, television and stage appearances. In addition, he went on tours to entertain the American armed services around the world for 50 successive years. The USA Congress, just before he died, passed a special resolution declaring him to be a veteran of the American army.

He hosted the Oscars 19 times. He never won, but the Oscars Academy gave him four honorary Oscars.

I reached 91 in October 2022 and my aim is to join Bob Hope as a centenarian.

The lesson I learned from the great man is that I will only reach this goal if I keep both my body and brain active with the same degree of intensity.

To achieve this, I'm working through a 10-year plan of action and have sorted out a rough plot for each of five more books I plan to write and publish. I also intend to continue to lobby governments about a number of social and constitutional changes that must occur in Australian life sooner rather than later.

My hope is that you will join me in enjoying longevity and exceed my life expectancy by a long way.

Let me finish with Bob Hope's last words to his wife Delores on his death bed when she asked him a practical question. He was an entertainer to the very end.

'Where do you want us to bury you, Bob?'

'Surprise me.'

A stark reality of life is there is no point whatsoever in living a long life unless it's an active and productive one.

Just sitting in a chair and being pampered is selfishly and stupidly pompous and pointless.

Even a person condemned to life in a chair can achieve incredible things if they give it a try.

If this is not possible for me, I've reached an agreement with my family that if I have no option in my life except to be admitted to a nursing home, I want out at that very moment.

I will find some pleasant way to bring on a massive heart seizure.

15: John Howard

As Australia's second longest serving prime minister, John Howard, created as much political controversy as did Julia Gillard, but in reverse.

Voters on the left of Australian politics hated Howard just as much as those on the right hated Gillard.

My experience of Howard is that he was one of the most astute politicians I ever met. He could smell political trouble in the air long before it appeared and usually sorted it out well in advance.

Though political enemies won't agree with me, he gave the nation a general sense of stability, a privilege we have not enjoyed in the decade since he left.

John Howard and I have shared a respectful friendship for four decades. Some of my friends on Facebook and Twitter tell me consistently that they're not impressed by this fact, but their dislike of him has no impact on me. I simply block those who are abusive. He and I get on well, a friendship that began when I worked as a volunteer on Howard's winning campaign in the federal election of 1996 that began the 11 years of his prime ministership after waiting many long years for his victory to come.

I did it, not as a member or supporter of the Liberal Party. Indeed, I was and am neither. I did it because our friendship had begun way back in his long years in the Opposition ranks of the Australian Parliament when we worked together on some issues of mutual interest.

Unlike Scott Morrison, who persistently commented that he was unaware of embarrassing political events, Howard rarely used this excuse. In fact, he felt that it was most unprofessional to do so as a prime minister is supposed to know all that is going on at all times. He had an acute political antenna that enabled him to predict issues before they became problems and he was greatly assisted in this by his politically competent chiefs of staff, Tony Nutt and Arthur Sinodinos, who would never ever fail to inform Howard of even the slightest trivia.

It must firstly be acknowledged that Howard presided over a decade of measurable prosperity for Australia and that decade was relatively peaceful by current standards. Yes, he did make mistakes as all prime ministers do. I did not fail to tell him about them, yet this did not derail our friendship.

The *Tampa* refugee debacle was a major error that I outlined in an earlier chapter.

He ignored a centuries old tradition of the seas that boats must always respond to a distress call from another boat. When the Norwegian freighter rescued refugees from a sinking boat, Australia grossly humiliated them for doing so. It was an awful and inexcusable episode in our history.

Granting franking credits on dividends in cash to people who are not taxpayers, and therefore not paying double taxation, was unjustifiable. It was a crude welfare handout to the middle-class, pure and simple. He made this decision to help win an election, as he did the *Tampa* decision.

Getting involved in pointless wars in Afghanistan and Iraq just to please his friend, George W Bush, and gain better trade terms, was a significant error. Absolutely nothing was achieved by either conflict, while many deaths and much social and economic chaos resulted.

But his achievements far outweigh his sins.

He consistently endeavoured to reduce government debt, a feat that none of the prime ministers who followed him have ever been able to copy, not even remotely closely.

He built the Adelaide-Darwin railway a century after it was first promised as a condition of South Australia joining the Federation of Australian states in 1901. He gained independence for the new nation of East Timor.

Howard also increased compulsory contributions to superannuation and made extra payments available for childcare. He generally caused Australians to feel a little more at peace, a feeling that we don't have at the time of writing this book. There having been four political coups in the decade since he left the scene that destabilised the nation.

So, how will history remember John Howard and his achievements and errors? As a prime minister who stayed on for too long when he could have departed the political scene undefeated? It would have been gracious to give his loyal deputy Peter Costello a go at being prime minister after he'd waited so long.

With some nostalgia, I reckon that even though he rarely expressed visionary ideals, he will be honourably remembered for the prosperity of his long tenure.

Especially, history will note that his courageous tough gun laws implemented after the Port Arthur Massacre were a huge milestone in the perpetuation of a non-violent society in Australia. It showed that we have a more peaceful society than the United States of America has ever been able to enjoy — or even tried to achieve — in their 'world of guns'.

Well, John, keep enjoying your round of golf every week and continue being a cricket tragic for a long time. Despite the everlasting angst of your many critics, you have earned a pleasant retirement.

Critics loved to derisively call John Howard 'Little Johnny'.

He was small in stature, but he had a formidable presence not in the form of loudness but because he was always across the facts even when he

was losing some battles.

It will be a significant footnote of history that he served as Australia's second longest serving prime minister, his 11 years being exceeded only by Robert Menzies.

He achieved this because his long years in the political wilderness gave him time to accumulate experience of how politics really works.

Few people in Parliament ever get to understand it in depth.

Most voters never do.

16: Paul Keating

Never before have I met a politician who was both hated or loved with as much intensity as Paul Keating and who couldn't care less about either.

However, in years to come people will remember him far more than most prime ministers because something of significance always happened regularly throughout his political career.

It has been virtually impossible to ignore him.

Here is Keating at his best:

'Take a look at my friend Everald seated here beside me. He vividly represents the huge ageing problem that Australia has. The old bugger won't die. He doesn't even look like he's going to die anytime soon.

When I planned the legislation that introduced compulsory superannuation, I was reliably advised that most Aussies would die at around eighty, so all my financial calculations were based on that age expectancy.

Now take another look at Everald. He is so bloody obstinate he will live way past ninety and millions of oldies will be motivated to follow his example. This means that all my projections have been shot to pieces by everlasting blokes like Everald.'

This earned me a rousing round of applause from the crowd of 200.

The scene was a Retirement Incomes Forum I chaired in Sydney a few years ago and at which Keating was the keynote speaker. The former prime minister, as usual, did not crack a smile when he described me as a problem and kept on going to spell out the basic truth that retirement incomes in Australia are way short of what many people will need.

Most of us will have exhausted our superannuation capital by our mid-80s and many will become pensioners. Women will be the hardest hit since their capital balances are far below those of men because of the time their motherhood takes them away from the workplace. Keating rightly declared that an urgent superannuation revolution was needed to fix the problem and most people in the crowd agreed with him wholeheartedly, irrespective of whether they were on the political right or left.

Throughout my 25 year role as chairman of National Seniors Australia, I often enjoyed a fair bit of contact with Keating in both of his roles as treasurer and then prime minister.

On one occasion, I attended a briefing at Parliament in Canberra that he gave on his very necessary plan to introduce legislation on franking credits on dividends. He made it bluntly clear that it was being introduced solely to cut out the double taxation that had been occurring in Australia since Federation where a company paid tax on its profits and then its shareholders paid more tax on the dividends that originated from those profits. So, he gave us a credit against our taxation for the tax already paid by the company. In other words, you had to be a current taxpayer before you were eligible for a franking credit.

In my earlier comments on John Howard, I referred to legislation he passed that enabled us to be paid cash for our franking credits whether or not we were taxpayers. This means that the government gets no tax revenue at all from that part of company profits paid as dividends. Howard's action was fundamentally wrong. I strongly opposed it at the time, but lost the battle. It won an election for Howard. It was smart politics that the ALP failed to effectively call out.

Bill Shorten eventually initiated a policy to remove franking credits for non-taxpayers and it lost him an election because he didn't sell it very well and failed to realise that it is difficult to take away a benefit on which many voters have based their retirement in the belief that it was legal to do so. Nevertheless, one day an Australian prime minister as brave as Paul Keating will be compelled to have the courage to change it. It cannot continue: it's a middle-class welfare payment, pure and simple. And I, like many of you, are beneficiaries of it right now.

Those are just a couple of highlights of Keating's volatile career of considerable achievement. He had some lows too, such as 'the recession we had to have' and his admission that his policies could make us a 'banana republic'.

But let me return for a moment to the day of the Retirement Incomes Forum.

I met him down on the footpath when his Commonwealth car arrived. All former prime ministers are entitled to one. He was grumpy.

'I'm having a bad day, Everald, and I'm pissed off about lots of things. I want you to get me on to the platform without having to shake hands or hug anyone. I will talk for about fifteen minutes and then I'm gone.'

I did as I was asked and got him on to the stage in a hurry and with a minimum of human contact as he'd requested. I introduced him and away he went with a highly colourful speech about his favourite topic, offering several visionary solutions to the retirement incomes debacle that has descended upon us.

After half an hour, I decided to respectfully interrupt and remind him that he had another appointment elsewhere.

'Calm down, Everald. Don't interrupt. We are dealing with the difference between prosperity and poverty.'

The fact was that the crowd were cheering him every inch of the way. He was in top form and enjoying it. After a lengthy question time, he whispered, 'Get me out of here in a hurry, Everald.'

I did.

'Out on the footpath,' he said. 'As you well know, Everald, there is only one bloke in Australia who can fix superannuation and you are standing beside him. But those wankers down in Canberra haven't got a bloody clue what to do about it. Totally useless bastards.'

With that he was off and away.

I like Keating as a man as distinct to his politics. His parents came from poor financial circumstances and he had no tertiary education whatsoever. He was totally self-educated and had an incredible ability to cut people down with potent words in one-liners and inject a lot of humour into those words.

It was not smart to make him your political enemy.

His speeches are never dull and three special ones that he made will go down in history as great orations.

The first was his Redfern speech on reconciliation with the First Peoples. Powerful.

Then came his address at the Tomb of the Unknown Soldier in Canberra. Inspirational.

Perhaps the greatest was the one he made at Kokoda in New Guinea to commemorate the 50th anniversary of the battle so valiantly won by outnumbered Australians against fanatical Japanese troops. They saved our nation from invasion. Hardened war veterans had tears in their eyes.

And he is not finished yet.

He was once more superb when he appeared recently for four nights in a row on the ABC *7.30 Report* when it ran a series on the inadequacy of retirement incomes. He cut the government to pieces.

Even so, the cold fact is that he no longer has political power.

And in politics, that is everything.

Paul Keating is a high-profile example of how any person can get to hold the highest office in the land without having a university degree.

He quite simply had extraordinary ability, a magnificent brain and an

incredible will to achieve.

His example means a lot to me because I do not have a university degree.

In 1945, when I was finishing high school, only three students out of my class of 30 were invited to go to university since Queensland had only one small university at that time.

I had no option but to adopt a plan of lifelong learning and make it work for me.

As Keating once said, 'Never cease to learn.'

I won't.

17:
Enid Lyons

Here is an extraordinary person who has an eminent place in the history of Australia.

Enid Lyons' life has been an inspiration to many Australians, especially to women striving to achieve a rightful recognition of their skills.

It was back in the days when the plane most used for regional flights in Australia was a Dutch aircraft, the Fokker F27 Friendship. It was a long and narrow aircraft with quite tight seating.

I was travelling from Melbourne to Devonport in Tasmania and discovered that I was sitting next to a distinguished elderly lady who was short in height and a little stocky in build. As I was an overweight bloke, our seating arrangement was a bit close. I said hello and, as I usually do on short flights, I got out a book to do a bit of reading.

Suddenly, in the same way as had been my good fortune of sitting together with Bob Hope, it dawned on me that my neighbour was a most famous Australian. I decided to start a conversation.

'May I ask if I am correct in assuming that you are Dame Enid Lyons?'

'You can and you are. And who am I speaking with?'

'Everald Compton. I'm not a household name. I come from Queensland.'

'I know who you are. You're the fundraising man.'

'I am. But the important comment I want to make at this moment is that I have had the pleasure of reading your book *Among the Carrion Crows*.'

'Did you enjoy it?'

'Very much.'

So we had a pleasant chat about it, recalling events of her significant life that had made the book so fascinating.

She had been a schoolteacher at Smithton in North-West Tasmania where she met and married another schoolteacher, Joseph Lyons, who was involved in the teachers union. Little did she know that he would soon enter the Tasmanian Parliament as a Labor MP and go on to become state premier.

Nor did she ever imagine that he would then enter federal politics on behalf of the ALP and quickly become prime minister when he broke with the Labor government of James Scullin during the Great Depression to join the conservatives who at that time called themselves the United Australia Party.

Joseph Lyons was quickly elected as their leader and led them to three election victories before he became the first Australian prime minister to die in office, when he had a massive heart attack not long before World War II started. He was succeeded by Robert Menzies.

Enid decided to continue her husband's work and won a seat in Federal Parliament herself. Some years later, she became the first woman to be appointed to the cabinet of an Australian government. Australian voters held her in great respect.

But let us hark back to her time as the wife of a prime minister. A key issue to remember is that she and Joe were very devout Catholics and faithfully followed the edict of their church that they should have many children. Indeed, 12 young Lyons arrived on the scene. When they all lived together in the Prime Minister's Lodge in Canberra during the 1930s, the government didn't allocate any staff to help her. That privilege only began in the 1950s.

So whenever prime minister Joe invited important people to dinner at the Lodge, Enid had to do all the cooking and act as hostess at the dinner itself as well as feed and care for 12 children. It goes without saying that this was an enormous task, especially as guests often included royalty, heads of state, cabinet ministers and state premiers. She survived because she was able to organise her older children into a team to help her. Which they gladly did since they respected their mother.

What a wonderful person.

Having 12 children must have taken a huge toll on her body and raising them all would have been incredibly time-consuming and emotionally draining. I once met one of her daughters who said that Enid spent many hours daily looking after their individual needs and welding them into a close-knit family. Even so, at the end of every day, she still had time to chat quietly with Joe about all of his political problems and offer sound advice, as well as attend countless official functions with him.

I met her again in 1976 a decade after our inflight chat when I invited her to come to Brisbane to launch National Seniors Australia of which I was a founding director, and which grew to have a larger membership than all of Australia's political parties put together. She spoke without notes and made a splendidly human speech about growing old positively. The crowd gave her a wonderful reception.

Afterwards, she joined our board of directors for dinner where, with much encouragement from me, she quietly entertained us with delightful tales of her life journey.

The next day, I drove her to the airport where we enjoyed a coffee as we waited for her flight to depart. Her parting words took me by surprise.

'Everald, I want you to come to my funeral. Your job will be to help make it a very happy event. I know that you will do that well.'

Sadly, I was at Stockholm in Sweden at the time she died and my schedule ahead gave me no time to get back to Australia in time for her funeral so I went to a Lutheran church near my hotel and said a quiet prayer of thanks for her magnificent life and for the privilege of having met her and being able to get to know her just a little.

Years later, when on a business trip to Tasmania, I drove to her old home, which still has its original name of 'Home Hill' and is now recognised as a historic site. An old Tasmanian was taking a look too and his comment to me says it all.

'You know, mate, you would have to travel a bloody long way to find a better sheila than this one.'

Among the Carrion Crows, the book I mentioned earlier, was the tale Dame Enid told of how she enjoyed her life as a parliamentarian after Joe died. She won a place in a parliament in which 98% of MPs and senators were male. It's interesting to note that a carrion crow is a bird that strives to live in isolation. Her parliamentary colleagues treated her with great respect, but at arms-length, never as an equal or an indispensable member of the team. She was not offended by their attitude but quietly lived in hope that one day they would grow up.

I'm not sure that they have matured since female MPs still have to try twice as hard as a male to get to the top in politics.

Enid Lyons did not live to see Julia Gillard become Australia's first female prime minister.

Indeed, I feel sure that she didn't envisage that this tumultuous event would ever happen, but had she been around she would have wept tears of joy.

In Enid's era, women held few executive positions. It was then accepted that females were not destined to hold those jobs. Apparently, God had ordained that their domain was the family home and men heartily endorsed that divine command.

The #MeToo movement had no life at that time and most women of the era would probably have been embarrassed by its presence.

But time has marched on and change marches beside it.

The female revolution is now unstoppable.

It is a tragedy that women have to fight for the equality for which they were entitled at birth.

18: Jenny Macklin

A notable and welcome feature of modern Australian politics is that, as a general rule, female members of Parliament are the creative ones who develop visionary policies and reforms, then work ceaselessly to have them accepted and implemented.

Jenny Macklin was one of those who planned and achieved creatively.

We have all benefited from her positive presence in the politics of Australia.

Members of Parliament who genuinely believe they were elected to care for the needs of Australia and its people are few and far between. Nevertheless, you can find some of these rare people on both sides of Parliament if you're willing to put in time finding them. You will discover that it is also a pleasant exercise that is highly productive in terms of expanding your personal political influence.

So, if you'd set out on this journey before the 2019 federal election when she retired after 23 years in the Australian Parliament, you would have needed to look no further than the office of Jenny Macklin.

I can hear some of my usual critics saying, 'Poor old Everald, he's fallen yet again for another leftie.'

But let me assure you that another set of my critics got quite upset when I recently wrote a piece praising my longstanding conservative mate, John Howard. One actually accused me of fraternising with fascists.

The lesson from this is that if you ever do something that everyone praises, then you can be sure it was a failure.

In a world of politics where the vast majority of politicians seek only power, Jenny always sought to rise above this in serving the people of Australia so she could achieve constructive change and give practical hope to those in need. Importantly, she was a seeker of practical solutions, not an ideologist.

She served in the Federal Parliament in Canberra for many years as the ALP member for the seat of Jagajaga located in the northern suburbs of Melbourne. Her fields of endeavour were pensions and many areas of human need such as disability, childcare, parental leave, First Peoples rights, a fair go for women, and lots of other things.

It's on record that she achieved much, even though she served in a ministry for only six of her years as an MP. Her record shows that she had the genuine ability to negotiate sensibly with the other side of politics, basically because they knew they could trust her.

I met her personally towards the latter part of her parliamentary career and I came to admire her mightily as she is easy to get on with and is a very humble person. Above all, I found that she was always ready to admit her failures.

I remember vividly the many meetings I had with Treasurer Wayne Swan and Jenny in 2008 when I was chairman of National Seniors Australia. We worked together to shepherd a bill through Parliament to achieve the highest increase in the age pension in the century since it was originated in 1908. It was a privileged experience I will not forget.

May I say that Macklin always reminded me of Angela Merkel in her manner of dress and quiet demeanour and her peaceful stubbornness that enhanced her skills as a negotiator.

She rose to be deputy leader of the Labor Party for five years when Kim Beasley was leader, almost becoming deputy prime minister in one election when Beasley received 200,000 more votes than Howard nationwide, but Howard narrowly won more seats. Then when Kevin Rudd subsequently defeated Beasley for the leadership of the ALP, she lost too because she was, unsurprisingly, loyal to her leader.

Jenny is now part of the academic fraternity at the University of Melbourne, where she graduated with a Bachelor of Commerce many years ago, researching and advocating revolutionary plans for better social security for a diverse Australia.

I chat with her from time to time and know that she's still a superb public servant and will be until her days are over. I reckon that she is a wonderful example of what a member of Parliament, who happens to be female, can achieve in a world of where voters fear change and gender equality remains an unresolved issue.

Join me in cheering a great Australian torchbearer, Jenny Macklin.

The political problem that comes with the task of making social changes is that, while voters want change, it is rarely popular because it's not glamorous, just essential.

This means that Jenny Macklin deliberately chose a tough road along which to walk.

Announcing large infrastructure projects gets much applause, as do foreign policy changes and advances in education, but a social services announcement is usually criticised as being either too much or too little or unnecessary.

This did not worry Jenny Macklin. She didn't seek to be a show pony.

However, it should concern you and me that essential reforms to society have such a low priority in the political spectrum.

We can do better.

19: Florence Nightingale

Obviously, I did not meet the great lady personally, but I did say hello to her at her grave.

Many historians say that Florence Nightingale was a very difficult person.

She probably was since she had fierce determination and was a loner. It seems that she had only a few close friends.

But for a woman to achieve great changes in her male dominated era, she had to have the persona of a bulldog.

Let us give thanks that she did.

There's a small village in Hampshire in England called East Wellow, not far from where Lord Louis Mountbatten used to live. There's a small historic church there called St Margaret's. In its grounds is the grave of Florence Nightingale, the Lady with the Lamp.

Many years ago, I received an interesting phone call from the church warden of St Margaret's. He'd heard of my work in raising funds for the restoration of seven of England's most famous cathedrals and asked if I could drop by his church next time I was in England. I did.

Their challenge was a simple one.

The spire of St Margaret's Church was decaying and about to fall down, right on top of Florence Nightingale's tombstone. Considerable funds were needed to fix it. They invited me to organise a campaign to raise the money and I proudly accepted. My sister, Vivienne, was a nurse, and my daughter, Lyndel, is one now, so I took this up as a personal family crusade.

The campaign proved relatively easy to organise. Many people far beyond the village did not want the spire to fall on top of Florence.

Indeed, we appealed to nurses' unions around the world, and none declined to give. Florence was the modern founder of this splendid profession. While women throughout history have nursed the sick and done so magnificently, it was Florence Nightingale who first created a large hospital in Constantinople (now Istanbul) during the Crimean War and was the driving force behind the establishment of larger and better hospitals in England on her return. She organised and supervised the professional training of nurses and her work spread worldwide.

She died in 1910 at age 90, having lived her last 50 years as an invalid in her family home near East Wellow, from where she relentlessly wrote thousands of letters to politicians and newspapers seeking and securing social reforms over a wide range of issues beyond nursing. She never married.

May I relate a humorous incident that delighted the crowd at the launch of the fundraising campaign at St Margaret's?

I had arranged that the local bishop would kick the campaign off at a dinner, followed by Evensong, in the church.

One of our most successful collectors of donations in the village was an old, retired colonel who had a tremendous love of, and huge weakness for, sherry. By the time we got to Evensong, he was well primed. Indeed, he brought a glass of sherry with him into the church just in case he got thirsty if it all dragged on for too long.

The bishop was delivering an inspirational sermon in praise of Florence and, at one point, commented, 'We must never forget that Florence spent a half century of her life in bed.'

To which the colonel loudly called out, 'Who with?'

The bishop managed a wry smile.

Anyway, I'm delighted to report that we raised enough money to fix the spire so that Florence can continue to rest in a well-earned peace.

It's also interesting to note that the BBC, a few years back, ran a nationwide poll to find out who were the top 100 leaders of England throughout its long history.

Winston Churchill topped the poll. Florence achieved the ranking of 52. She deserved a higher ranking than that, but she had the handicap of not being male.

Florence Nightingale defied social prejudice when she took her team of nurses to the Crimean War. High society throughout England publicly labelled her and them as prostitutes. She ignored them. Thousands of wounded and dying soldiers thought she was God as she moved among them night after night with her lamp making sure that everything possible was being done to keep them alive and out of pain.

Vale Florence Nightingale. I hope you noted that I laid a red rose on your grave.

There are a few extra comments I should make.

When Florence died, the prime minister of England declared that she should be buried with the great and the mighty at Westminster Abbey. The nation was stunned when her family graciously declined. Florence had left written instructions that she was to be buried at St Margaret's East Wellow. It was her spiritual home. Her wishes couldn't be overruled, even in death.

In my view, the sherry the colonel loved is an appalling drink that seems to continue to fascinate the somewhat pompous and steadily decadent 'Downton Abbey' high society of England, but not me.

At the launch at St Margaret's, I arranged with the church warden that he should quietly bring me a glass of fine single malt scotch whisky — the nectar of the gods. William Wallace (*Braveheart*) drank several wee drams of it before he belted the hell out of the English army at Bannockburn 1000 years ago. Its spiritual power cannot be underestimated.

It can be safely assumed that if he had partaken of sherry, he would have lost that battle.

I'm baffled by the fact that it took the human race until the 1800s to establish hospitals staffed by a trained nursing profession.

No-one has ever been able to give me an adequate explanation for this gross act of negligence.

Even worse, no-one has ever been able to explain to me why nursing is one of the poorest paid professions in the world. Somehow or other, society has consistently demanded that nurses must prove their commitment to humanity by being willing and able to live and work in poverty.

20: Philip

As you will observe below, I am not a fan of Philip, Duke of Edinburgh.

Nevertheless, it was an impossibility to ignore him.

In 2021 Queen Elizabeth lost her partner, Philip, after 74 years of marriage. Even the harshest of republican advocates had her warmly in their thoughts at that time.

I respectfully remember Philip as I recall the occasions on which I met him even though they were not pleasant.

The first occurred many years ago at Ely Cathedral in Cambridgeshire when I organised a fundraising campaign to restore the fabric of the cathedral after a thousand years of weather had taken its toll. (The same one in which I worked in the company of Jeffrey Archer.)

Philip became patron of the campaign. He wasn't an easy person to work with, but he did have huge influence in circles of money and power which worked to our considerable advantage. However, he did acknowledge my efforts. At a function to conclude the campaign, the Duke of Edinburgh had a few sherries under his belt when he said, 'You know it was that jolly Australian who put this together.'

Years later, I met him again in Australia at a celebration of the restoration of the Brisbane Club building. I'm one of the club's oldest members and Philip was there to declare the club reopened for business. After his speech, I walked over to say hello. We exchanged pleasantries and then he said, 'You fundraisers charge too high a percentage for your services.'

Before I could respond, he moved on to tackle the club's architect and tell him that he also charged too much, then adding a few words of unfounded advice about how the restoration could have been improved.

I decided that I would not let him get away with his untrue comments about my fees. I had never in 50 years as a fundraising consultant ever charged a percentage of funds raised. I simply billed my clients for my time in the same way as an accountant does. I also gave financial guarantees in the event of significant failure.

So, I went home and sent a personal handwritten letter to the duke at his Buckingham Palace address enclosing a copy of my contract with Ely Cathedral after underlining the paragraph that stated my fees. I told him bluntly that he owed me an apology.

To his credit, he did reply some months later.

More accurately, his private secretary replied at his command to say that His Royal Highness had read my letter and contract with interest and noted with pleasure that the fundraising campaign had been a great success. But no apology.

But enough of my occasional escapades with one of the most famous men in the world.

It is of note that the social media regularly raked up several scandals surrounding the Duke of Edinburgh and some women in his life.

One headline made this comment on the relationship of the Royal couple: 'They have been cheating on one another.'

In the case of Philip, the accusations are probably correct.

In the case of Elizabeth, I'm absolutely confident they are wrong. It would have been out of character.

The social media also accused Philip of forcing Charles into his disastrous marriage with Diana. That also is probably true, but I give thanks that he did. The world would have been a sadder place without Diana. She had class.

Closer to home, we should note that Philip unwittingly helped to bring down an Australian prime minister. When Tony Abbott recklessly awarded him an Australian knighthood in a 'captain's call', this gave Abbott's political enemies the excuse they needed to launch a coup.

In closing, let me say that Philip did leave the queen and Boris Johnson with a huge problem.

The Poms have magnificent skills in organising splendid funerals. How would they do this when Britain was in a COVID-19 lockdown? They had to be very careful not to stage a superspreader event, but I reckon that it was all handled with a simplicity, even though Philip rarely acted in a simple manner.

And Prince Harry was made welcome, if only temporarily.

A pleasant piece of family bonding.

Anyway, vale Philip.

Protocol demanded that Philip always had to walk two paces behind Queen Elizabeth at all public functions.

He appeared to do this quite happily.

I must say that I would have found this to be quite humiliating. There is no way I would have been able to carry this out.

But that would have been quite crass.

Men, like me, have been embarrassing women since time began.

So, it is appropriate that, in an era of level playing fields when change is now in the air permanently, guys like me need to be humbled more than a bit.

Meeting More of the Greats

Now that I've entered my 90s in the numerical counting of age, I don't meet face to face with as many leaders as I used to in my earlier days, even though I still get to chat to many by phone.

However, I continue to enjoy catching up with some leaders once every year.

Let me comment on three whom I am certain will make a mark in future years.

All are valued friends of mine and I name them in alphabetical order.

First in line is one who will be prime minister of Australia in the not-too-distant future. *Jim Chalmers*, currently the federal treasurer of Australia. He is the most promising political leader I have come across for decades. He will become a visionary statesman of great quality because he represents positive, progressive, intelligent change.

His potential rival in the leadership stakes is *Josh Frydenberg*, former treasurer of Australia who is Jim Chalmers' political opposite. Josh is Liberal. Jim is Labor. Josh, who has natural leadership qualities, lost his seat in Parliament in the 2022 election, but I hope he plans to return in a new seat as soon as possible. However, he will face a huge challenge in tackling the need to create a new conservative party as the Liberals appear to be in their death throes.

Beyond politics is *Holly Ransom*. She's an author, and the creator of many leaders of change, who works from Melbourne in reaching out to the whole world to find those who have the capacity to change it. Her book *The Leading Edge* is a classic that I recommend you read (if only because it has a few pages in it about me). We need more leaders like Holly because the world is very short of inspirational role models.

There are others too who, sadly I have never met. Such as former tennis champ *Ash Barty* and feminist *Grace Tame*.

We live in a world fuelled by hope.

C: PLACES

1: Kyoto

Spirituality is a valued cornerstone of my life and I'm sure that many of my readers will think likewise.

Japan is a nation where spirituality is embedded into many aspects of daily life.

I found Kyoto to be a focal point for a meaningful exploration of the depths of spirituality.

A few years back, I travelled to Japan with Helen. It was one of several pleasant journeys we have made there, but this one was planned to specifically visit the ancient city of Kyoto.

I was fascinated by its long history as the original capital city of Japan for more than a thousand years before a political decision was made by their emperor to move to Tokyo. A pointless decision that demeaned spirituality to enhance politics.

Especially, Helen and I were determined to visit some of its many spectacular Buddhist and Shinto temples.

Our accommodation was located in an ancient style hotel of quaint Japanese architecture on the pleasant banks of a river in the outer suburbs of the city. We had our own private garden for meditation. It proved to be an excellent choice.

I asked the concierge at the hotel to arrange for us to retain the services of an English-speaking limousine driver who could take us on a private tour of the city to visit the temples and he assured us that he knew a very experienced one.

Our driver arrived in an upmarket limo, explaining that his more modest car was being serviced so we were enjoying a fine car at a bargain price. He spoke splendid English (more precise than mine) and had a considerable knowledge of religion, architecture and history, treating us to a delightful day of fascinating learning.

During the course of our tour, he took us to a quite famous and revered Buddhist garden, the name of which I now cannot remember — put it down to old age.

We took in the peace and beauty of the garden while keeping our conversation very soft, which is quite difficult for me. He told us that he had driven American philanthropist Bill Gates to and from the garden on several occasions.

On one trip, Gates had spent three days there in quiet meditation, and on that particular visit had, during those quite peaceful hours, decided to establish the Bill & Melinda Gates Foundation and endow it with an initial gift of 50 billion dollars to fund social projects of significant international impact.

Despite his enormous wealth, this was a significant moment in his life and in the world of philanthropy, as there have been few charitable gifts larger than this in the history of humanity. Indeed, we would have to go back a century to find a gift that was relatively larger. It was made by the richest man who ever lived, John D Rockefeller.

Gates has regularly topped up the capital of the foundation so it could continue to make large grants to health programs in underdeveloped nations. One such program will eventually eradicate malaria from our planet. An extraordinary achievement.

Gates has in recent times fallen from grace due to his highly publicised divorce from Melinda and his forced resignation from the board of

Microsoft, the technology company he founded. This followed the revelation of a longstanding affair with a junior staff member, but there can be no denying that his contribution to technology and philanthropy has been an extraordinary personal achievement.

He still visits the Buddhist garden in Kyoto every year so he can spend more hours in quiet meditation.

Our limo driver also took us to a memorable Shinto shrine and explained that many millions of Japanese people accept and participate in both the Buddhist and Shinto faiths. They find that elements of both faiths combine to give them greater spiritual strength.

This impressed me and set me wondering if I could add elements of other faiths to my life as a committed working partner of Jesus of Nazareth.

The fact is that I can. I have read widely about other faiths and there are some core beliefs of the Muslim, Jewish, Buddhist, Hindu, Sikh and Mormon faiths that are similar to my Christian beliefs or, in some cases, are a more enlightened version of them that is worth adopting,

This indicates that the interfaith movement in which I participate in Brisbane is important in my life and adds spiritual strength to my being.

Other elements of Japanese life appeal to me.

They are more disciplined in their lifestyle than most other nations, have high standards of hygiene and a strong family culture that is not declining as significantly as it is has done in the Western world.

We were pleased to find that Kyoto, despite now being a large city, has no slum suburbs and has a basic quality of housing in poorer areas. Their transport system is far more efficient and comfortable than that of my home city of Brisbane and their local cuisine is superb. We avoided all European style restaurants as they pale in comparison.

These memories of Japan endorse my view that an expanding trade and cultural and spiritual relationship with Japan is important to Australia. They are a stable nation with whom we can establish trust in developing a reliable long-term partnership of genuine value.

As we flew out of Kyoto to continue our journey to China, I remembered my first visit to Tokyo decades earlier.

I had taken a taxi from the airport to downtown Tokyo and wondered if my middle-aged taxi driver had been a Japanese soldier who may have beheaded Australians in their infamous prisoner of war camps. I did not find out, but I raised the matter with our Kyoto guide.

He didn't take offence. He explained that my Tokyo driver most probably was a former military man, but then went on to explain that the political faction that started the war and masterminded its brutality represented not more than 5% of the population of Japan and had controlled the hearts and minds of the Japanese people totally and ruthlessly. Any dissenters were shot. The guide personally remembered the war years as 'dark days of national shame' and meditated on it often.

He assured us that, during the war, and despite it, the Buddhist garden had, as always, been a place of infinite peace.

I have lived a life in which I have always been impatient to achieve things, visit more and more of the world and learn new things.

While I spend a lot of time planning projects and researching books, I have rarely spent time contemplating my spiritual values except for an hour at church on most Sundays.

My visit to Kyoto made me change that more than a little.

I now set aside a few minutes every evening to honestly contemplate the state of my life and my relationship with humanity. I reflect on what I did right and wrong each day and what I can do better the next day.

Miniscule serenity, really, but it has improved my capacity to think about my interaction with others and my capacity to generate goodwill on a level that is above the superficial.

I'm slowly leaving the treadmill and quietly entering a world of greater calm.

And I'm enjoying the experience.

2:
The Great Wall of China

China is a huge nation both in population, land and the sheer scale of its government.

I've been there three times and have seen only a tiny fraction of it.

But what I did see was enough to convince me that it is an undeniably powerful nation that has the capacity and the will to eventually dominate the world.

History is littered with naive attempts to isolate nations or communities or religious zealots from the rest of the world and it's important to note that every such endeavour has consistently failed.

A prime example of this is the decision to build the Great Wall of China, a spectacular event that had its birth many centuries ago in a serious endeavour to keep out the Mongols, Manchus and others who had regularly invaded China since the beginning of time.

Strangely, its builders didn't even remotely consider the possibility that the day would come when invaders would find a way to make it obsolete. It would have been unimaginable to them that it would eventually be possible to lob shells over their wall or fly over it or fire nuclear rockets across it, thereby negating the purpose of its existence.

China's many emperors also failed to plan for the possibility that invaders would come predominately by sea, but that is how the British, French, Portuguese, Germans and Japanese occupied significant tracts of their land from time to time without those invaders even being aware that the wall existed.

This tremendous wall, which is hundreds of kilometres long, is now nothing but a relic of history, albeit a spectacular one.

I visited it only once and it was a memorable experience.

I now regret that I only walked along the top of it for just a couple of kilometres. It is worth far greater inspection, but it was enough to comprehend the immensity of it and consider how many thousands of slaves must have died in building it and how many millions of tons of rock were mined and transported there to enable it to be constructed.

I sat down on one of its many stairs and contemplated the sheer enormity of it. But then I realised that everything about China is enormous.

Its population is 1.5 billion souls so far. When I was born in 1931 there were only 300 million people in China and I considered that to be a huge number. This all changed when Mao took power in 1948. He ordered the Chinese people to have large families because he needed lots of people to help defend China in the years ahead. He believed that either Russia or America would invade one day and he would beat them by throwing millions of people into the task of defending it.

Now, it seems that Chinese leaders believe the only way to effectively control such a large population and efficiently harness the nation's resources is to have a totalitarian government such as they have now achieved. But can that decision survive inevitable internal rebellions as more people decide that they need more democratic institutions? Can control be maintained in reality in the long term? After all, India is operating as an effective democracy with a similar population.

I doubt it. The Chinese Red Army is enormous, and its weapons are capable of waging very significant wars, internal and external, if China chooses to do so. But a day of reckoning will come eventually. Everything about China is beyond what the world would call normal.

The major cities of China are massive. Several of them have 50 million people in each and I can say with certainty that I would never ever choose to live in a city of that size. It would be a horrible life in which it would be difficult to have any identity or purpose. Public hygiene in such large cities would not be effective either.

Despite this enormity, China is not yet the largest economy in the world, nor is it the largest military power. The USA has that honour even though it may well lose it to China within a decade or so.

The advantage that China has with both its internal government and international presence is that President Xi has far more political power than President Biden. Xi can make a decision on any matter and know it will be implemented by his highly centralised power structure. However, every decision made by Biden must be ratified by Congress and that is a tough and time-consuming task that has frustrated all American presidents.

So, the Great Wall is now irrelevant except as a significant earner of tourist dollars for China. And this it certainly is.

It was designed to keep the world out of China, but now China clearly wants to create a situation where its power will be the major influence in the world. A total reversal.

I won't be around when China reaches its zenith, but it surely will occur, and the consequences will be long lasting.

We can only hope that Australia handles it wisely and that it will occur peacefully.

Keep smiling. All will be well.

There was an era just 500 years ago when China had the world's largest economy. It also led the world in many skills such as pottery, painting and weapons and so on.

And the religion of Confucius eventually came to be regarded

internationally as one of great enlightenment.

Now China has made a comeback in its economic growth because the rest of the world underestimated and ignored it.

An unwise error.

We have created a colossus.

3:
Taj Mahal

It is pointless to try to make up for a loveless relationship after death has intervened.

How often has it occurred in our lives that we regretted not having mended our relationships with people before they died?

The Taj Mahal is a constant reminder of human frailty and insincerity.

The fascinating tale of the Taj Mahal of India represents one of the most romantic frauds of history.

It began in the year 1632 when a Mughal emperor, Shah Jahan, who had ruled his kingdom ruthlessly for 30 years, lost in childbirth one of his many wives, Mumtaz. He declared her to be the only one of his wives he truly loved and he mourned her loss with hugely overdone public grief.

To make sure that no-one doubted his grief, he built the Taj Mahal in her honour and memory. It cost a fortune to build with ivory white marble, but he reckoned it was worth it as a first step in his grand design to permanently glorify himself.

Such is its architectural beauty that it was declared at the time to be one of the Seven Wonders of the World. Centuries later, in 1983, this opinion was verified by UNESCO when it declared the incredible building to be a World Heritage Site as the splendid Jewel of Muslim Art.

This contradicts the generally held belief of tourists that the Taj is a sacred Hindu site. Down the centuries, Hindu leaders tried to claim it as predominantly a Hindu museum, but were never able to gain acceptance. It is clearly Muslim.

But this is a minor part of the controversy that has always surrounded this magnificent building.

Historians soon discovered that Shah Jahan did not love Mumtaz. Indeed, he treated her badly, often brutally, as he did with all the many women in his life. He had created a myth that he was a loving man because he wanted to generate public affection towards himself so his people would want to build a larger version of the Taj Mahal just across the river in his honour after his death. He had plans drawn up for it that would make the original Taj Mahal look like an outhouse.

However, his allies as well as his servants knew what a hypocritical brute he was and so, after his death, they did nothing to honour him. So it is that the land across the river remains empty to this day.

As most of you may know, the Taj Mahal is located just outside the Indian city of Agra, a few hours train journey south from Delhi.

I visited it 40 years ago, just for one day. I was in India on a business trip and did not want to miss seeing one of the wonders of the world. It was worth the time and the cost. An incredible sight to behold.

Unfortunately, it was crowded with tourists plus many beggars trying to get money from those visitors, and so I have sad memories of ragged people pushing deformed children at me and weeping as they asked over and over again for money. I knew that, if I gave money to any one of them, a bloody riot would have erupted as the crowd of beggars fought for possession of whatever was my gift.

This remains as one of my disturbing memories of India after having made several visits there to be a guest speaker at conferences. There is far too much filth, poverty, hunger, homelessness and loss of hope without very much being done about it. In many cities, the air smells all day long.

This is a tragedy of humanity that should not ever have been allowed to happen.

British rule of India for three centuries was a great example of the sheer plunder of a land with huge economic potential. There was no real effort by the colonists to raise the standard of living of the ordinary Indian and give them a basic education. This situation has vastly improved after 75 years of independence, but is still well below par.

I cheered in 1947 when Mahatma Gandhi won independence for his people.

I regard him as one of the greatest people who ever lived. When he was assassinated shortly after independence, his successors did little to organise family planning in the nation in any disciplined way, and so the population has since multiplied five times and caused every social and economic problem we can possibly imagine.

It is just so sad. India has a fine culture and had a proud history before the British arrived. However, its people now face huge challenges if its 1.4 billion people are ever to enjoy a good life.

We in Australia have an enormous opportunity to form a greater relationship with India in the same manner as we do with China.

India is easier to trade with because it still observes British common law as its legal framework. Not like China that regularly changes its laws to suit current convenience.

It's time to work diligently at this partnership right now. India constitutes the largest market in the world, just a little smaller than China's market.

It's not smart to ignore. Our relationship with India is more important to Australia than our traditional relationship with the UK and the USA, both of which simply patronise us.

That India, despite its massive social, religious and economic issues, has been able to stand on its own feet after being raped and pillaged by Britain for centuries is an incredible feat.

What the world must now demand is that the European nations — Britain, France, Germany, Netherlands, Italy, Spain, Portugal — that plundered their colonies across the planet and never apologised must stand condemned for their greed and absence of compassion.

An apology and financial recompense are long overdue and should be delayed no longer.

Sadly, it will.

4: Victoria Falls

There are few sights more magnificent than a waterfall in a wet season and no continent more physically spectacular than Africa.

Sadly, Victoria Falls is part of a nation that is a scene of social and economic tragedy.

Helen and I stood on the viewing platform of the magnificent Victoria Falls in Zimbabwe and watched in awe as the mighty Zambezi River roared over the broadest of waterfalls in the world, creating an enormous spray that looked like smoke.

This is why the locals call it the 'smoke that thunders'.

Nearby is a statue of British explorer David Livingstone, which has a plaque that says that he 'discovered' the falls in 1854.

Our native Zimbabwean guide, who proved to be an interesting character, said, 'Actually, our boys discovered it about 50,000 years before him.'

This superb comment highlights the arrogance that European colonial powers represented all around the world. In Australia, an Englishman claimed to have 'discovered' Uluru. He was 65,000 years late.

In both Zimbabwe and Australia, the land was stolen from its rightful owners by European colonists.

Now we have yet another tragedy. The majesty of Victoria Falls is in steady decline due to a lack of water.

Climate change, among other issues of neglect and irresponsibility, has caused Africa to have ever increasing droughts and advancing deserts, while upstream, many people plunder more and more water from the once mighty Zambezi. For a few months in 2021 only a trickle of water was dropping over the falls for the first time in memory, but deniers still assure us that climate change is a myth even though its once mighty flow has not yet been restored.

'There are none so blind as those who will not see.'

But to be more cheerful, the Victoria Falls Hotel, located not far from the falls, is really something. Built in 1904 in honour of the infamous mining magnate, Cecil Rhodes, at a time that the colony was called Rhodesia, it is one of the jewels of African tourism. We had a magnificent dinner there at the lowest price I have ever paid for a first-class meal.

We chose to have their set menu. Their splendid menu offered us pre-dinner drinks of top-quality single malt scotch whisky and many canapes served by Zimbabweans wearing old colonial tiger shooter hats and the colourful uniforms of British officers. Then followed soup, entrée, main, dessert, cheese, coffee, biscuits and chocolates all washed down with magnificent white and red wines plus liqueurs from the splendid vineyards of Stellenbosch in South Africa.

Mugabe was still in power as president of Zimbabwe at that time and he had destroyed the economy and devastated the Zimbabwe currency.

When I paid the bill with a credit card, I took a deep breath. It was more than 2000 Zimbabwe dollars, the largest dinner bill for two people I had ever paid in my life. When I arrived home and looked anxiously at my bank statement, I discovered that it had cost me just 21 Australian dollars.

This is a sad commentary on the inequality that dominates humanity.

The former Rhodesia was prosperous, even though the British settlers sent their fortunes home to British banks. They had presided over the development of the most magnificent farming and grazing land I had ever seen at the time. I visited in the dying days of the colonial regime around the time that Mugabe brutally took over. He destroyed the country's productivity in one of the most devastating wastes of wealth I've ever witnessed in my life.

At the time, I was working on a fundraising campaign for the Presbyterian Church of Southern Africa and met the last white prime minister of Rhodesia, Ian Smith, at a Presbyterian church in the city that was then called Salisbury, now Harare.

Over coffee one Sunday, Smith forecast the demise of the emerging nation, but said to me, 'It is our fault. Britain took over this nation totally. We did not ever try to share it with its original owners. We used them as servants and never tried to train them to run a stable and efficient government. It has been appalling arrogance.'

This rang a bell with me. The British carried out the same style of takeover when they stole Australia from our continent's First Peoples but with far better economic and social results than Zimbabwe. Nevertheless, we have yet to pay the financial and social price of that plunder of heritage, solely because Australia has far more whites than First Peoples.

So there it is.

Zimbabwe is a massive tragedy.

Mugabe has gone but his successors are no better. I weep for the people. They've not had the chance to re-create a prosperous and cohesive nation, but I live in hope that one day the sun will shine for them.

Let me share with you a happy tale of one reason why I will never forget the people of that nation.

While working for the Presbyterian Church of Southern Africa, I spent some time at one small church just outside of Bulawayo in southern Zimbabwe. The people there are Zulus, but are called Matabeles, and they really are fine physical specimens who had the ability to crush me into little pieces if they ever chose to do so. I managed to help them reorganise their finances so their church could have a future.

They were very grateful and their chief wanted to honour me with the highest quality gift he could make. He told me quite sincerely that, by ancient tradition of reward for valour, I was entitled to choose six wives from the maidens of his tribe at any time in the years ahead. Of course, he was sure that I would never be able to take up the offer, but it delighted him to be able to tell me that I had earned it.

Egotist though I am, I must admit that I could not survive with six wives (nor could they). Besides, I had a wonderful one back home. So, I gratefully and graciously declined. Nevertheless, he assured me I could come back and claim my right.

It is still possible — I'm only 91 and quite a romantic.

Zimbabwe, undeniably, has the potential once more to become a prosperous and enlightened nation just as soon as it is possible to elect competent leadership.

The land is as magnificent as you and I could discover anywhere on the planet. It awaits care by skilled people who seek only to enhance it.

I fondly remember the scene when I once addressed a conference at the Troutbeck Inn at the wonderful Rhodes Matopos National Park in the far east of Zimbabwe near its border with Mozambique.

It is a delightful British inn, with the architecture of a quaint pub in an English village, right beside a lovely stream in which you can catch very healthy trout if you have the necessary skills.

All of this is a reminder of what may have been saved and enhanced if its British conquerors had ever acquired the slightest concept of justice and equality for its colonial subjects whose wealth they consistently stole for centuries without ever experiencing a shred of guilt.

5:
The Nile

How did a nation that was once the most powerful in the world fall from grace so mightily and irreparably?

How did the mighty river Nile that gives Egypt its life become so polluted?

When I first visited Cairo decades ago, I stayed at the world-famous Shepheard Hotel and dined with an Australian diplomat at its splendid rooftop restaurant. It gives a grand vista of the Nile, one of the greatest rivers on the planet, without which Egypt would be a miserable expanse of never-ending desert able only to sustain a fraction of its current population.

I chatted with my host about memories of Egypt that had an influence on my life.

In my Sunday school days, I was thrilled by the legend of Moses leading his people out of Egypt and performing a miracle through which the soldiers of the pharaohs were drowned in the Red Sea. The drowning story was mythical, of course, but it reminds us what a great leader and nation-builder Moses was.

I also was captivated by the way that Joseph and Mary fled as refugees to Egypt taking Jesus to safety from the tyranny of King Herod, then later returned to their homeland. I didn't know it then, but I'm now grateful that Egypt did not have any offshore detention camps such as Australia so disgracefully and brutally established for refugees 2000 years later.

Back in my early years, I also was, and still am, a huge fan of Agatha Christie and enjoyed more than 50 of her hugely successful novels. One is *Death on the Nile*, a cracker of a murder yarn.

So, I made up my mind that one day I would travel there and take time to journey up the Nile and into the realms of ancient history.

Many years after my initial business visit, I led a National Seniors tour of Egypt at the time when I was chairman of that significant advocacy group that sought reforms on all issues relating to longevity.

It was in the year just before Egypt's long-time dictator, Mubarak, lost power in a revolution. This revolt did not surprise me. The nation was obviously descending into chaos with small rebellions breaking out everywhere about a wide range of important issues. Discontent was made even more obvious by the filth and smell of the Nile, which was causing significantly increasing health problems and regular failures of agriculture. This was a tragedy as, at its source, the Nile is fed by some of the purest water in the world.

The Upper Nile is a place that must be visited, not only in terms of history, but to see the enormity of the Aswan Dam, one of the largest in the world.

The tombs of the Pharaohs are incredible and the messages written on the walls are fascinating. I became aware that at one point in history this was the world's great power, a huge centre of learning and a cradle of religion, especially since the pharaohs themselves were worshipped as gods in their own lifetime.

But let me comment on some of the more vivid memories I have of Egypt.

The pyramids are an incredible feat of engineering. It is difficult to comprehend how, without modern equipment, they were able to cut the stones so precisely and have slaves carry them up such great heights to put them in place in a manner that would never allow a pyramid to collapse. Obviously, those ancient Egyptians were engineers of quality.

The current politics of Egypt are a divisive disgrace of brutal control, a message that was clearly expressed to me by Australian journalist, Peter Greste, when I attended a lunch that he addressed in Brisbane to outline his illegal and brutal imprisonment in Egypt.

Expressed in the simplest of political terms, there are four clearly identifiable opposing forces.

The Muslim Brotherhood are fundamentalist Muslims who made a briefly successful bid for power when Mubarak fell, but failed because of their religious extremism and are now victims of heavy persecution and long-term imprisonment.

Moderate Muslims are now the majority, but are tame, powerless and afraid.

The Egyptian army represents a small faction of thugs who have grabbed power, exercised it ruthlessly, and will remain in power for a long time to come, especially as they have, unlike other Arab nations, managed to perpetuate a peaceful relationship with Israel that gives them some vital international credibility.

Fourth are 10 million Coptic Christians, the largest Christian church in the Middle East, who practise their faith quite differently to Christians of the Western world. They are tolerated by the military, but suffer regular economic and physical persecution from Muslim extremists.

I have a very sad memory of my meeting with some of the Coptic Christians.

On one of the days of my National Seniors tour, I took our group to visit a beautiful, simply designed Coptic church out in the countryside not far from Cairo. Their priest was a devoutly humble man who spoke clearly understandable English.

He told us how his church had been established in Alexandria by St Mark 50 years after the crucifixion of Jesus. They developed their own bible and distinctive theology but were now a minority religion in a dominant Muslim nation. I was hugely impressed by the depth of his personal faith and his graceful tolerance of, and clear answers to, my many questions. He shared tea with us and conveyed a moving expression of love of humanity no matter what differences we may have in our beliefs.

A couple of months after I left Egypt, a crude mob of Muslim fanatics attacked the priest's church. He was murdered along with dozens of his people. The news upset me greatly, but there was nothing I could do about it from Australia.

I will never forget his parting words to me when our visit came to a close.

'Travel safely, my brother. Follow with sincerity the road you have chosen in serving God. May it bring you much happiness.'

It has. It is helped by the fact that I live in a far more democratic nation than my friend did.

Nevertheless, I'm constantly reminded that religion, in all of its many faiths and extreme divisions, has regularly throughout history been the source of much hatred and violence. Clearly, we have all fallen short of the mark in inadequate efforts to create a world of peace and justice.

It is long overdue for us to do some critical thinking about our negligence.

The kingdom of the pharaohs lasted for a thousand years, and like the Roman Empire it just faded into irrelevance.

None of the great powers of history have been able to maintain their influence through to our modern era. Power always disappears into the mist with a whisper.

Of them all, only Jesus, Muhammad and Confucius still influence human behaviour in any meaningful way.

It seems inevitable that, one day, religion will also fade away.

None of us can accurately forecast what will replace it.

But humanity needs a cornerstone of values.

6: Jerusalem

I fondly recall my year in Sunday school when I told my teacher that 'one day I will go to the land where Jesus was born and find out all about him'.

It took me a long time to achieve this aim but I eventually made four visits.

One of them was quite dramatic.

The other three were simply fascinating.

'Don't run away, Everald. That will convince them you're frightened and they will chase you all day. Just ignore them, walk slowly and look unconcerned.'

The speaker was an American, an Anglican priest from St George's Cathedral in Jerusalem, who had befriended me and was walking with me along the disputed road that separates East and West Jerusalem.

Muslims live on one side of the road and Jews on the other. In good Aussie lingo, it is truthful to say that they hate one another's guts.

The fact that my friend was obviously American in looks, speech and attire had drawn the attention of these young Muslims who wanted to blame all their problems on the USA. One of them spoke reasonable English and he kept calling us 'American murderers'. He and his friends were throwing stones at us.

It was a bit hard to take my friend's advice to remain calm as one stone hit a glancing blow on my head and another stung my arm. I accepted his advice and they eventually lost interest in us.

He then made a comment I won't ever forget.

'This incident is a tiny reminder to us of a major issue that the world must resolve. There will be no peace in the Middle East until the United Nations votes to make Jerusalem an independent international city like Singapore, free from both Israel and Palestine, in which Muslims, Jews and Christians can live together in peace, and they invite every religion in the world, such as Hindus, Buddhists, etcetera, to send their brightest people to live here and work together with them. This will enable Jerusalem to eventually become the world centre of religion and peace.'

I expressed the hope that I may live to see the day when it happens, but commented that I would not bet my house on it.

Years later, and after I'd made a couple more business visits to Jerusalem, Helen and I had an enjoyably interesting journey to Israel at the conclusion of a holiday in Egypt and Jordan. Before leaving Australia, I had retained, at some cost, the professional services of a professor of religion from Tel Aviv University, arranging with him to drive us around Jerusalem for three days. He spoke excellent English and was a respected academic in the history of three religions, Christianity, Islam and Jewish.

As I mentioned briefly in an earlier chapter, when he arrived to pick us up at our hotel in Jerusalem, I was chatting with Helen in the foyer, surrounded by tourists from everywhere. He picked my Australian accent and walked over to say, 'You must be Everald. My name is Moses.'

To which I happily replied, 'Delighted to meet you, Moses. I have been wanting to make your acquaintance ever since my Sunday school days when I was fascinated by the story of how you were hidden in the bullrushes.'

In our three days together, we drove to the more famous religious places, especially those around the Sea of Galilee, in his black Mercedes that had tinted bulletproof windows and windscreen. He informed us that the terrorist group Hamas had a habit of shooting at tourist buses so we would be a little safer in his car. Nevertheless, we did a lot of walking too and, fortunately for us, no-one abused or attacked us.

He made it clear to us that the tourist industry had distorted the location of religious sites to suit their commercial and logistical needs. For example, the place on the Jordan where Jesus was baptised by John the Baptist had been conveniently moved two kilometres away because buses couldn't get access to the real site. The same distortion applies to moving the location from where Jesus preached the Sermon on the Mount.

On our last day, we were walking along the Via Dolorosa, the road along which Jesus carried the cross 2000 years ago.

Moses said to us, 'There is little in the scriptures of the three religions that dominate this city that can be believed as verifiable facts or truths. They are sincere recordings of legends handed down the centuries and, in the passing of words, many things have been distorted or simply not understood. Anyone who adopts a fundamentalist acceptance of any of the religious scriptures is simply a very weak believer whose fragile faith needs propping up. We are only true believers when we acknowledge that we can't prove any written words about our faith as fact but are pleased to say "I believe."

In other words, you've either got the faith or you haven't. You just know that you are empowered by it in the most peaceful way. You neither need nor want any written evidence.'

We agreed and shook hands on it.

Despite my comment above, I still have a concern that no-one has ever found or even tried to find a piece of paper or papers on which Jesus wrote words about his life and beliefs. We only know what others have said about him. It would be fascinating to read Jesus' own words.

So it is that, as the result of these and other visits to the Holy Land, I have joined with my friend, Bishop George Browning, to work actively for the cause of Palestine being granted its freedom from Israel.

It is a just cause that George has advocated relentlessly for years and the facts are on his side.

When the Jews were driven out of the Holy Land in 300 AD, the people of Palestine occupied the land for 1600 years until the United Nations created the nation of Israel 70 years ago. The land clearly belongs to Palestinians by right of long-term possession. They'll never be able to get it all back but they can get to control at least some of it. Both nations can show some common sense and agree that there will be two independent states with justifiable boundaries and they can sign a legitimate peace treaty that is guaranteed by the United Nations.

In addition to this much-needed breakthrough, I continue to work for the recognition of Jerusalem as an independent city. What a wonderful international meeting place it could be for all who have a spiritual dimension to their lives.

As the Bible rightly says, 'A city that is set upon a hill cannot be hid.'

It is fascinating to ponder this crucial question: if Jesus of Nazareth physically returned to the Holy Land today, whose side would he be on in the land battle? Israel, Palestine, both or neither?

I haven't the slightest doubt that he would say Palestine. Simply because he stands for justice and Israel has not treated Palestine with anything resembling justice and is never likely to do so for a multitude of reasons.

And he would make it known that Jerusalem is the spiritual capital of the world, not Mecca, nor the Vatican.

It is the place where all religions can meet, break bread together and strive to live in peace while working together to create a better world.

7: Malta

Back in my days in Linville, I enjoyed seeing a Humphrey Bogart movie at the community hall. It was The Maltese Falcon, so I decided it would be a good idea to learn something about the history of Malta.

I found it to be fascinating.

It was quite extraordinary that this small island has been able to dominate the history of the Mediterranean for centuries.

I decided that it would be worth a visit one day.

And I made it happen and enjoyed it immensely.

As World War II raged on, I came to hugely admire the people of Malta.

This small nation of 500,000 people, an archipelago surrounding one large island, is located in the centre of the Mediterranean just 80 kilometres south of Sicily. Both Mussolini and Hitler tried to invade Malta several times, failing dismally at each attempt. Then, they tried to bomb Malta out of existence, but the Maltese would never surrender. They were absolutely defiant.

The opportunity for me to visit Malta arose 25 years ago as I sought to discover what gave them such tenacity. An important element of my interest in them was fostered by my religious education as a follower of Jesus of Nazareth. This had made me aware that St Paul — the great evangelist – had been shipwrecked there while on his way to Rome as a prisoner facing execution.

Helen travelled with me and we booked into an apartment at St Paul's Bay right near the spot where St Paul was almost drowned.

We visited the small underground jail where St Paul was once held captive and where he converted his jailer to the Christian faith. The converted jailer then arranged for him to meet the Roman governor whom Paul eventually converted also. Paul sold the faith so extraordinarily well because, despite regular invasions by Muslim nations, the Maltese Christian community has survived strongly. Today, Malta has more churches per square kilometre than any other nation in the world.

This confirms what a superb salesman Paul was. He got long-term results. I enjoyed writing an essay about him when I did my studies to become a certified practising marketer (CPM) at age 25. In it, I declared St Paul to be the greatest salesman in the history of the world and I am of the same opinion today. I was delighted to win a prize for it.

I became particularly interested in learning about the Knights of Malta, otherwise known the Order of St John of Jerusalem, as we have several strong Maltese communities in Australia. It came to be recognised as a great honour to be declared a Knight of Malta since they had an enormous influence on the history of the Mediterranean for valour and service to the faith. They were the only ones who defeated Suleiman the Magnificent when he tried to conquer all the nations of the Mediterranean.

I have met a number of eminent Australians who have been inducted as Knights of Malta for service to our nation and humanity. They regard it as the highest honour it is possible to get.

So it is that I have fond memories of Malta. Its architecture is unique, reminiscent of every nation and culture and faith that has occupied the island since its first settlers arrived there in 6000 BC. Its food is excellent and they produce unique wine, which I enjoyed more than that of France and Italy.

They eventually won their freedom from their colonial masters in Britain in 1964 without firing a shot and have enjoyed stable government ever since.

Helen and I have one special memory of our visit to Malta.

We visited a large Catholic church not far from St Paul's Bay and discovered that, during the war, while a crowded congregation was celebrating Mass, a German bomb hit the dome and crashed down into the church onto a spot right beside the altar. It did not explode. The congregation believe then and now that they were saved by an act of God. We could debate this belief forever but Helen and I paused at the spot where it had landed, bowed our heads and gave thanks that we live in a nation that, except for Darwin, mostly escaped the war.

However, above all, whenever I recall our visit to Malta, I think of St Paul.

If Christians today had his conviction, zeal and communication skills, our mainline churches would not be steadily dying. Believers like me have, for far too long, made the significant mistake of trying to be part of an exclusive society that talks only to ourselves.

Paul talked to the world and got its long-term attention.

This act can be repeated.

Whenever I think of St Paul and his introduction of the Christian faith to Malta, I find it noteworthy that he did not tell them to build a church.

They chose to do that all by themselves, just as Christians did all over the world.

It will eventually prove to have been a huge mistake to base the faith around beautiful buildings.

One day, Christians will decide to change our convenient thinking to a level somewhere near to that of St Paul and begin a new reformation that is long overdue.

8:
The Vatican

The home of the popes has always been a great mystery to me.

Why does the leader of the world's Catholics have any need whatsoever to live in such a palatial place?

My early practice of religion in the Methodist/Presbyterian theology stressed that we must be humble in our lifestyle because Jesus was a man who had no possessions.

Thankfully, Pope Francis broke centuries of tradition by choosing not to live in splendour in the papal apartments but in a modest apartment within the Vatican.

We can but hope that his example becomes a tradition.

There is only one nation in the world that is exclusively the headquarters of a church.

The Vatican has this honour.

It claims to operate spiritually, not politically, which of course is a fabrication of the truth. It uses its power to influence world affairs as it has constantly done century after century. Many popes have caused wars to begin and millions have been killed by their commands. While doing this, they accumulated great wealth and, until recent times, few popes were ever celibate even though they demanded their priests to be so. Their history is neither honourable nor enlightened nor a worthy example to humanity.

Having said this, the Vatican cannot be ignored as a focal point of religion and politics even though Catholics worldwide are slowly and steadily ignoring the authority of a church that once dominated their lives.

Nevertheless, it's important for all who embrace the Christian faith that we, at least once, should visit this fascinating place of history and religion to ponder what it could have been as a reforming spiritual power had it tried to faithfully represent Jesus of Nazareth instead of just being a religious power base.

Helen and I enjoyed our visit there a decade ago and, as a result, more clearly understand the basis of our lifelong calling to follow a man called Jesus.

It's impossible to go into St Peter's Basilica and not be moved by its tremendous history as a bastion of the faith or to stand before the statue of the great man and not revere him. We noted how smooth and small his feet now are after having been touched by millions of the faithful over so many centuries. We can hope that they will have gained spiritual strength from the experience.

Nor is it possible to visit the Sistine Chapel and view the magnificent art created by Michelangelo in the year 1512 without being entranced by it and being fascinated by how he achieved it in four years while lying on his back on elevated planks. Was it spiritual strength that drove him on, or the promise that the pope would pay him well, or both? Or was it just a passionate love of art and a pursuit of excellence in its creation? I reckon it was the latter.

It also stimulated our minds to stand in the square where millions have often gathered to listen to the pope speaking from a window in his apartment to give them a blessing. The experience has greatly influenced the lives and thoughts of millions who seek to strengthen their faith.

There is no sense of spiritual depth in the Vatican.

We did feel a sense of spiritual depth when we stood in the square at Avignon in France to which, long ago, the popes moved the Vatican for a century when there was a rebellion against Rome led by French Catholics. We cannot avoid the fact that the two founders of Christianity, Peter and Paul, were murdered in Rome.

Like all great empires throughout history, the power of the Church of Rome will fade away and die. Its future is limited. The faithful steadily reject its credibility despite the presence of Pope Francis, the most spiritual and sincere pope of my lifetime. Sadly, his words and deeds are always immediately smothered by the Roman Curia who exist to exercise power.

What has actually happened to the Catholic Church? And to many Protestant and other religious movements?

They have focused their entire being on the exercise of power and forgotten their origins in the life and work and spiritual strength of Jesus.

As a famous Catholic priest, Richard Rohr, once said, 'We worshipped Jesus instead of following him. We made Jesus into a religion instead of a journey to God and life. We went to church to believe and belong instead of becoming transformers of society.'

Those words hit the nail squarely on the head and open our minds to consider this inevitable question:

Is it too late to save the Vatican?

Yes.

Can there be another Reformation?

Yes.

Emphatically yes.

Jesus of Nazareth is a man with whom any one of us can become a working partner.

We live with faith, hope, love and charity as we work together to make the world a better place.

Whether or not we recognise it, every one of us has a need to have a role model in our lives.

After a long and searching spiritual journey, I have chosen as mine Jesus the Man, not the Jesus Christ created by the church.

I regard his spiritual power as essential to the creation of a world of compassion.

My journey with him is more compelling and productive as I walk through my tenth decade.

Not because I have any fear of death. Indeed, I have none whatsoever.

I am simply running out of years in which I can achieve things that are worthwhile for humanity.

9:
St Petersburg

I found Russia to be quite unlike the rest of Europe.

Its history, culture, religion and politics are clearly different, yet the USA persistently endeavours to convince the Russian people that the American way of life is the best.

In doing so, they widen the gap between the two countries.

The advent of the war in Ukraine emphasises the difference in their own view of the world that will remain even when they lose that war.

Nevertheless, St Petersburg is a gem in its own right.

'I cannot buy any tickets for you to the Kirov Theatre, but I can advise you how to get them from the mafia.'

This somewhat surprising advice was given to me by the concierge at the hotel in Saint Petersburg where Helen and I were staying. It goes without saying that I was not overjoyed at the prospect of doing business with the mafia.

'Please tell me how I do that.'

'Go to the theatre this morning and speak to the receptionist on duty. Tell her you want tickets for tonight. She will say it is booked out. You express your disappointment, then stand aside for a few moments. A man will emerge from a corridor nearby and say he can get you excellent seats so long as you pay him in cash in American dollars. You pay whatever price he asks. Do not argue. He does not have a sense of humour. But you will get the tickets you want.'

We walked a few blocks to the Kirov Theatre (now the Mariinsky Theatre), one of the great theatres of the world. I carried out the instructions that had been recommended. The scene occurred exactly as predicted. I departed from the script slightly to ask if I could pay in roubles since I had lots of the local currency that no-one in Russia ever wanted to take from me. The mafia guy was not impressed. He said in halting English, 'No. Worthless. Dollars please.'

So, at some extravagant expense, we got to see a performance at the Kirov, a place of legend in the splendid history of the arts.

On most occasions the Kirov is used for the wonderful ballet productions. But it was the opera season. We enjoyed *Carmen*, a Spanish opera, sung in French in a Russian theatre where it was viewed by Aussies.

We sat in beautiful lounge chairs on a spacious balcony box that had permanently been reserved a century earlier for sole use by the Romanov tsar and tsarina. The Russian mafia really look after you (at a price). They even gave us vodka (apparently the brand the tsar liked). I pretended to enjoy it, but it really is tasteless rubbish. No wonder the Romanovs got tossed out in a revolution. It would never have happened if they had been genuine whisky lovers who had enjoyed its admirable mind-expanding benefits.

But Russia is an intriguing place. It has a totally different culture and lifestyle to ours even though the communists have now (supposedly) gone.

We were there when Boris Yeltsin had just come to power after organising the political demise of Gorbachev. The entire nation was in economic and social chaos. Yeltsin was a drunken fool who led a corrupt government whose gross incompetence ensured that everything was in short supply and at high cost.

You will not believe me when I tell you we had cabbage for breakfast every morning. The streets were filthy, as was public transport.

Nevertheless, we were fascinated throughout our time in both Moscow and St Petersburg. The latter is the better city by far. Its waterways rival Venice and we enjoyed them by arranging transport through yet another mafia guy, a poorer one this time. He organised a gondola that would row us around the canals for an afternoon for only 15 US dollars to view splendid architecture that was in obvious need of restoration.

And we discovered that the Hermitage in St Petersburg has the finest collection of art on the planet. A truly magnificent place that should be on everyone's bucket list.

St Petersburg is a relatively young city by Russian standards. St Petersburg was founded by Peter the Great in 1703 and developed by Catherine the Great. It was their intent to make it the finest centre of culture in the world and they went close to achieving that. They also repeated the exercise in Kvoi (Kiev) in Ukraine.

Much of St Petersburg was destroyed during World War II when Russia defiantly held on to it after a long and bloody siege by the Germans. At that time, the Russians had renamed it Leningrad but soon saw the light and went back to its original name as they steadily restore the city. In recent times, they have let it decline and decay once more. However, I understand that Putin has now begun a further renewal.

Currently, it has a population of five million and, until the recent Russia-Ukraine War sanctions, it was visited by 15 million tourists annually.

As we all know, Putin's Russia is very different to the era of Yeltsin and Gorbachev and those who came before them. The former communists are now largely irrelevant but have been replaced by brutal totalitarian political thugs who enjoy a prosperous partnership with the mafia and oligarchs at the expense of 99% of the nation.

Putin himself is alleged to be worth 50 billion US dollars.

Be this as it may, we can but live in hope that one day the thoughts of

Dr Zhivago will be realised in the words of the Lara theme song 'Somewhere, My Love':

'Somewhere, my love, there will be songs to sing.'

The invasion of Ukraine has hugely diminished the status of Russia on the world scene.

No matter how that war is finally resolved, Russia will remain a pariah nation and Putin will, if he survives, be a despised leader.

Of most concern is the Putin view that Ukraine is fundamentally part of Russia via its history and culture.

He has affirmed that it is essential that it be returned to its motherland.

In some respects, this is true, but by the same rationale, Belarus, the Baltic States and Georgia must be on his list for the restoration of his empire.

However, the reality is that it is all about power and greed.

And those two scourges of humanity are not the sole preserve of Russia.

We can add to our concern the fact that political cults on every continent hold similar views to those of Putin.

Be this as it may, there is one more undeniable factor at play.

Putin feels personally humiliated by the break-up of the Soviet Union that occurred during the Gorbachev era before he came to power. He staunchly believes that the world, led by the USA, is laughing and joking about it still.

He wants to reach a point where all of the world apologises for rejoicing about its demise or face the consequences.

We won't.

10: Iceland

The remote island nation of Iceland is often avoided by many tourists because they presume it is covered in ice.

The truth is that even in the most frigid of winters it does not ever become totally covered in ice. The volcanoes and geysers make sure this does not happen.

Nevertheless, I hope Iceland never reaches a point when is overrun by tourists.

It is an environmental treasure that must have everlasting protection.

I was always a keen student of geography at school and this caused me to develop a zealous interest in travel at an early age, even though I didn't think I would ever get enough money to do much of it since in those days travel was the realm of the wealthy. My dad was a labourer, earning just the basic wage, which was barely enough to enable us to live through the Great Depression and a world war.

Whenever I looked at a map of the world, I reckoned that Iceland was about as far away from Australia as it is possible to get. So, I decided that I would visit it one day if only to find out how people were able to spend their lives on an island that must be freezing cold, which it is occasionally.

My interest was greatly heightened when my schoolteacher asked me to read a book, written in the middle of the 19th century by the great French author, Jules Verne, called *Journey to the Centre of the Earth* and write an essay about it.

I was gripped from the opening pages as I read about the journey that began in Iceland where a professor of geology and one of his students discover a cave near one of the volcanoes. This leads them down and down and down to many hair-raising experiences. They finally come out of their incredible adventure in the middle of the Sahara Desert.

I vividly described this in my essay, so much so that it won an award as the best in my small school class. My teacher gave me a boiled lolly as a prize and I declared to my fellow students that one day I would go to Iceland, find that hole, and go all the way down to the depths.

It took me almost nine decades until I finally made it there in 2019 to attempt to fulfil my commitment. Helen and I greatly enjoyed our visit when we were accompanied by our daughter, Lyndel, who lives in England.

Iceland turned out to be a magnificent country with more spectacular vistas to see and enjoy than could ever be found anywhere else on the planet — volcanoes, glaciers, waterfalls, geysers, rugged mountains and dramatic coastlines, plus green fields.

In addition to all of that, Iceland breeds the finest lambs you will ever have for dinner, and has air that is as pure as you will find anywhere on the planet, plus clean communities with no evident poverty. And they catch and cook splendid fish that are quite different to what we enjoy here in Australia.

We only saw a fraction of it all in a week, but I made sure we got to Snaefels, the volcano where Jules Verne said the professor had found the hole. To my surprise and delight, I discovered that some crafty young Icelanders had cashed in on the Jules Verne story. They had discovered a narrow crater in the mountain where they set themselves up in the tourist trade, operating a venture where they take you down in groups of 20 and for a reasonable price.

Lyndel and I signed up. Helen remained in our car ready to text a message to the world that we had not returned and were on our way to the Sahara.

The team gave us special shoes to wear, a jacket to save us from freezing and a light to put on our heads. Off we went into the black hole, down a spiral staircase of about 150 steps that led to a long sloping lava tube that took us further down while holding onto a rope. After about 20 minutes, we hit the bottom. There, the guide asked us to put out our lights and, in pitch black and below zero temperature, recounted to us the Jules Verne story.

It was a wonderful experience even though the trip back, upwards and out, was a bit tough for an old guy like me, but I made it with Lyndel's help by just putting one foot after the other. Helen breathed a sigh of relief when we reappeared

We needed to celebrate, so we went to the local inn.

I asked the barman for a genuine Iceland brew that was the closest they had to a whisky. I wanted to toast my journey to the centre of the Earth. He said they had a powerful local nip they called *The Black Death* — we signed up. I am compelled to tell you that you just need only one glass of this dynamite. When I finished after sipping it very slowly, I really did believe that I had made it to the Sahara.

But let us get back to the history of Iceland for a moment or two. It is an incredible tale.

They established the first democracy in the world, 400 years before the Americans did. We visited their ancient open-air parliament in the centre of the island. The stone seats are still embedded in the ground, unused now since the modern parliament no longer meets there. The chiefs of their many tribes had gathered there regularly for centuries to argue and agree on how they could survive and prosper together.

Their homegrown democracy worked well until the Vikings and the Danes took over their island for no justifiable reason other than the usual disgraceful plundering that European nations practised worldwide for too many centuries. Now, the Icelanders are finally rid of them and have a stable parliament that governs their 300,000 citizens well. Their MPs are predominantly female — something Australia should note and copy.

I'm now too old to go back again as I am running out of years. Also, I have too many other places on my urgent bucket list like Greenland, the Shetlands, the Galapagos Islands, Tibet, the Volga River, Mongolia and Antarctica.

Let me finish by saluting Jules Verne and his vivid imagination.

He wrote two other famous books I immensely enjoyed. *Twenty Thousand Leagues Under the Sea* and *Around the World in 80 Days*. All three are classics that are among the bestsellers of all time. Indeed, they still sell well today. As a budding author, I can only dream that people will read my books 200 years from now.

One other piece of advice.

Only go to Iceland during their summer — June, July, August.

During our visit in July the maximum temperature was 19°C. This was higher than usual due to global warming. Its normal summer temperature is 17°C.

Iceland hit the media in the headlines during the Global Financial Crisis that engulfed the world in 2007.

Their previously sedate local banks had entrusted their management to a team of hot-shot bankers from the United States who expanded their outreach to much of Europe via a superb marketing campaign that successfully sold a variety of high-yield financial products that soon crashed mightily.

The Icelandic government fell as the result of authorising this stupidity.

The new prime minister was a competent and fearless woman who fired the decadent bankers and re-created an internal banking system that is now small but solid.

Iceland is now a stable nation with a sustainable future.

This experience has created the view that small nations are the best place to live in rather than surviving among giants of no conscience.

Small breakaway nations will soon be created and grow in every part of the world.

This will be a good thing for humanity.

11
The Isle of Islay

My mother, Thelma, was a fundamentalist Christian. Her parents were even more fundamentalist, being descendants of devout Lutheran missionaries.

They sternly informed me at a very early age that I was headed for the hell fires if I ever touched 'the demon drink'.

My dad liked to have a beer and Mum carefully explained that it was the least sinful drink since it didn't have much alcohol in it. But, she emphasised, whisky was the greatest evil of all booze. It has lots of alcohol in it and is so expensive that only the wicked wealthy could afford it. Indeed, the Lord had a very dim view of whisky.

I made a mental note that it would be a good idea to have a real good look at this famous evil and find out why it upset the Lord so much.

It will not surprise you when I confess that I found it to be a pleasant experience about which the Lord was mistaken.

My Mum had missed out on something rather special.

In the enlightened realm of whisky lovers, the Isle of Islay in Scotland is the equivalent of what the Vatican is to Roman Catholics.

If you study a map of Scotland, you'll discover Islay to be the most southerly of the Western Isles of Scotland, offshore from Glasgow with easy access by ferry from Oban. Only a short journey for what to me was a religious pilgrimage.

In reality, it's just a huge lump of peat that has been maturing out in the Atlantic Ocean for a few billion years, but it is a delightful place to visit and Helen and I did 20 years ago.

It has nine whisky distilleries that produce world-famous single malts. Lagavulin, Ardbeg, Laphraoig and Bowmore are strongly peated, while Caol Ila, Bunnahabhain, Bruichladdich, Inchmoan and Port Ellen are mildly peated with a strong aroma of the sea. I've sampled them all and can enthusiastically report that they are the nectar of the gods.

We loved our few days on this quaint little Isle, finding that it also produced magnificent cheese.

We visited an old church that is completely round, built that way 'so there are no corners where the devil can hide'. This tells us how ancient a civilisation Islay really is.

One delightful evening we went to a pleasant restaurant in an abandoned school. They had haggis on the menu. Remembering the traditional Robbie Burns dinner that we often attended at Scots Church at Clayfield in Brisbane where they made a big show of 'piping in the haggis' on a smoking shovel, I said to the very friendly and courteous waitress who was decked out in an imposing tartan,

'I want your finest haggis brought to me on a shovel that is smothered in smoking peat and I will wash it down with a generous glass of Lagavulin.'

'Sir, my apologies. I will have to speak to the chef.'

She returned a few moments later and said quite gravely, 'May I beg your pardon, sir, but the chef says they only do that sort of thing out in the colonies.'

So, even though I'm a proud colonial rebel with a disdain for the British aristocracy, I recommend you visit Islay soon and stay where we did at the tiny Bowmore Hotel which has only six rooms that all look out over the bay with a great view of other distilleries across the water. It has a quality restaurant with a splendid bar that has a huge range of choices of fine whisky. Admirably, it is right next door to the Bowmore distillery and both are painted a spotless white to emphasise the purity of single malt whisky.

Allow me to interrupt at this point of this reverent tale to share my list of the 10 finest single malt whiskies in the world, only three of which are to be found on Islay.

Just remember that you read this treasured information here first. They are listed in order of my version of quality:

- Lagavulin (Islay)
- Caol Ila (Islay)
- Talisker (Skye)
- Springbank (Mull of Kintyre)
- Highland Park (Orkneys)
- Glenrothes (Speyside)
- Hellyers Road (Tasmania)
- Bladnoch (Highlands)
- Bruichladdich (Islay)
- Iniquity (South Australia)

I urge you to sample them all (and slowly) and enjoy this unique experience while reading a good book (preferably one of mine).

And don't ever contaminate your whisky with ginger ale or coke under any circumstances. Nor drink any blended whiskies that are made with smooth texture to satisfy the simple desires of non-believers. They are miserable by comparison.

And remember that whisky exports from Scotland make up 5% of the GDP of UK. If Scotland becomes independent, it will make a dent in the British economy since whisky sales are spiralling upwards.

This is due to the Chinese having just commenced putting it in their tea and declaring it to be more mind-expanding than opium ever was.

A final word on my number one choice — Lagavulin.

I must admit that I first discovered it years ago while reading a murder yarn.

The villain of this tale had finally been found guilty and sentenced to death. He was strapped in an electric chair, waiting to be sent to the hell fires.

He was asked if he had one last wish.

'Yes. I would like very much to enjoy a wee dram of a whisky called Lagavulin.'

The executioner was a refined soul and had a bottle of this magnificent whisky locked away in a cupboard in his office. He sent a cop to get it and gave the prisoner a small nip of it. The doomed man sipped it slowly and tenderly for several minutes, then uttered very profound words as his very last, 'This is bloody near perfection.'

He had a broad smile of contentment on his face as they flicked the switch.

Salut!

Such is the expansion of the whisky market in China, there are 1.5 billion souls who can potentially become addicts. The popularity of whisky has caused the Chinese government to announce that they are establishing their own distillery on Islay.

They have employed distinguished Scottish distillers for a decade to train their own team of Chinese nationals to become experts at the trade.

This is yet another example of the relentless expansion of Chinese influence around the planet. Many people worry about that but it's no worse than America's current domination of the world or the original spread of the British Empire relentlessly to all parts of the world centuries ago.

Eventually, history will once more reveal that all conquerors fade away.

So, enjoy your wee dram with contentment. It will survive them all.

12:
Tarrant Monkton

I've been quietly polling my friends for many years to find out how many have traced their ancestors back to their origins. I found that most of my friends have made no attempt to do so.

Many couldn't tell me of any ancestor beyond their grandparents.

They have missed out on something really special since it is an experience that I found fascinating and informative.

I am a proud descendant of a British convict who was in 1831 transported to Australia for life for the horrendous crime of stealing a bed worth three pounds. He was my great great grandfather and his name was Stephen Compton, born in a tiny village called Tarrant Monkton in Dorset not far from Blandford Forum.

I discovered him decades ago when I began researching the history of my family for a book that I wrote and called *Shadows and Sunlight*.

So it was that I visited his birthplace during one of my many visits to UK back in the days when I was heavily involved in organising major fundraising campaigns for the restoration of nine splendid British cathedrals.

Helen drove with me as we carefully navigated our way down narrow country lanes to find Tarrant Monkton and discover that it was indeed still a small village, about the same size as it was when Stephen's mother and father, Robert and Martha, were married there in 1789 in a tiny Norman church that had its origins in 1310.

We stood together at the altar while studying a book containing the ancient wording that was used for their wedding ceremony and then went to the font where Stephen was baptised in 1795 by a vicar who had served there for 60 years. Little did his parents know that 36 years later, Stephen would spend the rest of his life in Australia after arriving there as a convicted criminal.

His transportation to Australia was an event I feel that caused me to become a committed advocate of Australia's independence from Britain. The treatment that Stephen and all other convicts received from British colonists was barbaric. Locked up for six months in a cramped filthy cabin in a boat where only slush was served for food and then forced to work as slaves for years after arriving in Australia is not the way that any civilised nation should treat its people.

I now regard the foul treatment of convicts as very similar to the way the British brutally abused, dispossessed and killed the First Peoples. The British have never ever apologised for either atrocity.

Stephen married his wife Betty in 1822 and they lived in quite poor circumstances with their five sons in Brighton in southern England until Stephen was convicted. After his forced departure, Betty lived in poverty and survived only because she, believing that Stephen would never return, took in a male partner who provided her and her sons with food and lodging for nine years, during which time they also had a son.

So it was that, after Stephen finished his slavery in Australia and was pardoned, the Colonial Government of NSW arranged for Betty and the boys to come out to Australia to live with him free of any charge for the boat fare. When Stephen counted six boys coming off the boat with Betty instead of five, there was a bit of explaining to be done but it all worked out well. He was wise enough to recognise that he now had a family only because of her courage and self-sacrifice.

When Stephen died at age 83, he owned five houses in Maitland, New South Wales after years of hard work and constant saving, and all of his family were well established in homes and jobs. Had they not been sent to Australia, they would have lived in misery in England and died at an early age.

Now there are over 2000 Comptons in Australia descended from Stephen and Betty. Forty years ago, I organised a Compton gathering in Sydney to meet as many as I could. Two hundred and fifty attended and it was a happy and proud day for us all.

Just a few years ago, Helen and I went back to Tarrant Monkton for a second visit and enjoyed a lunch of wild boar sausages at the local pub called the Langton Arms. Our guest at the lunch was a member of the village church who was an enthusiastic amateur historian with lots of information to tell us about what life had been like at Tarrant Monkton in feudal England.

It made me realise how easy life has been for Helen and I compared to the days when Stephen and Betty Compton made their way through brutal times to establish themselves in a new land. I hope that the tenacity they passed on to me has enabled me in a small way to repay Australia for all the opportunities that have come my way.

I will never forget that tiny Dorset village.

I've named my family company, Tarrant Monkton Pty Ltd, in honour and memory of a faraway community that gave all of Australia's Comptons our start in life.

Other interesting notes on my family heritage worth recording include:

My mother's ancestors were German Lutheran missionaries who were sent to Australia in 1880 with a specific charter to remove all sin from the continent. Despite the huge effort they made to honour the terms of their sacred mission, I think we can reliably report that they significantly failed in their battle against sin. Their surnames were Guhr and Pukallus.

Nevertheless, my mother's family arrived in Australia about 40 years after Stephen Compton and created circumstances that led to me being a mixture of British criminality and German aggression. This explains many strange attributes that my friends may have noticed!

The records of the convict boat that brought Stephen to Australia reveal that he was the tallest man on the boat at 5 ft 5 inches. We all seem to have grown a bit since then. An Irishman who was chained up next to him was sent out for life for stealing a pair of scissors. This tells us that the 'break and enter guys' here in Australia get off very easily today.

My family research revealed that I'm a distant relative of the legendary English cricketer, Dennis Compton. He made two centuries against Don Bradman's Invincibles in the Ashes Tests in England in 1948. I tried and failed to inherit his skills.

Any search on Google reveals a large number or ways and resources that can help you and me to trace our ancestry.

Many are free of charge for basic research, but if you decide to take it seriously, you can spend as much money as you choose to in paying search fees for documents about births deaths and marriages.

For example, I decided to find the transcript of the trial of Stephen Compton in Brighton when he was convicted of stealing the infamous bed. Getting it cost me 50 British pounds but it proved to be a good investment.

I found that in sentencing Stephen the magistrate took into account a previous conviction for the theft of a number of small items worth about one pound.

Nevertheless, life imprisonment in a distant colony for stealing a bed and a few trade tools was severe punishment.

To this day, I believe that the magistrate's wife must have been in the bed that he stole.

13: Cathedrals

Cathedrals are magnificent places of worship that were built by the wealthy and the powerful in effort to sufficiently please God so their place in heaven would be assured.

Most of them would have inevitably suffered massive disappointment.

Nevertheless, now that we have so many cathedrals on every continent in the world, we have a great opportunity to use their incredible presence in far more meaningful ways than we now do.

This is a difficult chapter for me to write.

I love ancient architecture, especially cathedrals, but I have come to believe that an hour in my local church every Sunday is not now the key focal point of my life as a working partner of Jesus of Nazareth. It is a time of spiritual reflection and motivation to help me in my major commitment to serve humanity in the world beyond the church.

I'm certain that the hour would be more appropriately inspirational if I spent it with other followers of Jesus in reflection out under the trees in a nice park. That setting was the one chosen by the great evangelist John

Wesley who preached many more sermons outside of church buildings than in them.

My personal ministry is now not confined to any church building, it is out in the world sharing time and money and compassion with people who are doing it tough. Church buildings as such are not a crucial necessity for me anymore.

Nevertheless, this leads me to now make a personal confession that will make me look like a chameleon.

The most memorable moments in my long fundraising career have been spent organising to raise the funds needed to restore splendid cathedrals suffering the decay of old age. I firmly believe that, even if people in the years ahead ceased going to worship, those beautiful buildings must be preserved and used for some other noble purpose.

My first cathedral restoration campaign was to save St David's in Hobart.

St David's Cathedral was built by convicts shortly after the first penal colony was established in Tasmania 200 years ago and can claim to be Australia's oldest cathedral as, at that time, Sydney had built a church but not a cathedral. The chains on the walls that were used to tie up convicts when they were marched to worship every Sunday can still be seen there today.

I organised more fundraising campaigns to complete partially built cathedrals in Newcastle, Adelaide and Brisbane and to rebuild Darwin's Christ Church Anglican Cathedral after a cyclone had destroyed the original one.

Subsequently, I heard that Ely Cathedral in Cambridgeshire in England was in need of restoration. I wanted to work on that campaign because the BBC had declared it to be the most beautiful cathedral in the British Commonwealth and number two in the entire world. They decided that Chartres in France was number one. So I went to England, sought a meeting with the dean of Ely and was appointed to raise the funds that we needed.

It was a successful venture and led to other significant assignments for the splendid cathedrals at Gloucester, Worcester, Winchester, Bath, Exeter, Chichester, Portsmouth, Blackburn and Norwich, plus the abbey at Tewkesbury.

There followed my involvement in more international cathedral campaigns in Edinburgh (Scotland), Limerick (Ireland), Jerusalem (Israel), Victoria (Canada), plus Wellington and Auckland (New Zealand).

Throughout all of those years, and in my spare moments, I would spend time walking around each cathedral to study the paintings, statues, coffins and plaques and learn of the ancient history and religious turmoil and human tragedy that occurred within those holy walls that were often anything but holy.

And I would sit in a pew in the twilight to take in the beauty of each building and reflect in peace, often enjoying splendid music and singing as the organist and choir carried out their regular practice.

Sometime later, I read and enjoyed Ken Follett's great novel *The Pillars of the Earth* that tells the saga of the building of a magnificent cathedral in a fictitious English town in the year 1100.

It vividly reminded me of the many reasons why costly cathedrals were built and how much painstaking work was done by so many talented people, and how so many lives were lost in their long years of completion, to make these such magnificent sentinels.

There it is. An important segment of my life.

My age and a constantly reforming personal faith now prevent me from working on more cathedral projects like any of those I mentioned, but I'll never forget the meaningful experiences. At the time, I sincerely felt that I was keeping history alive and reminding the world of what a significant role religion has had in the creation of society as we know it today, too often in its destruction.

It's now a challenge of my life to ensure that spirituality continues in more relevant and renewed ways in the future of an enlightened society.

Some cathedrals are now used as centres for the arts in all aspects or as places where history and culture can be interpreted to all those who want to study it.

Secular usage of cathedrals will grow, I'm sure.

The engineering skills required to build cathedrals are astonishing and they always required the heavy lifting of building materials when the only lifting power was human effort, much like the incredible construction of the pyramids of Egypt.

The inspirational impact of cathedrals lives to this day despite changes to the way in which people view Christianity.

Notre-Dame cathedral in Paris, one of the most famous cathedrals in the world, was partially destroyed in 2019 by a huge fire.

Notre-Dame was saved because one man was nearby to the fire who knew exactly how it had been built and was able to tell firemen where to direct water to save several crucial structures that would have caused the entire cathedral to collapse if the fire had reached there.

Incredibly, donations came in large amounts from all around the world to be used for its restoration, most of it coming from people with no religious background or conviction whatsoever.

Astonishingly, the French parliament instantly granted an immense sum of money to be used as soon as possible in its restoration without there being any dissent from atheists in their ranks or any public political backlash.

The mystique of beautiful buildings is a science in itself, stretching far beyond the realms of religion.

14: Quebec

*Canada is a nation sharply divided by heritage and culture —
British, French, indigenous.*

However, they manage to handle their diversity quite well.

Quebec is a prime example of how this is done.

It's a splendid place to visit.

Helen and I had just taken our seats at an upmarket sidewalk French restaurant in the old sector of the very French Quebec City in Eastern Canada. There are lots of top-quality French restaurants to be enjoyed in this historic city.

A young waiter greeted us warmly in French and I made a weak attempt to respond in the same language which, of course, is the predominant dialect of Quebec province.

'Parlez vous Anglais?'

'Sure do, mate.'

Our waiter was an Aussie who'd chosen to finish his studies at a Canadian university.

He gave us splendid service of delightful food and told us that, while he would forever remain a proud Aussie, he loved the French culture, cuisine and language of Quebec much better than if he was in France itself. This was an interesting comment since we discovered that many citizens of Quebec were happy to be thought of as more French than the French.

Unlike Australia, both English and French are the official languages of Canada and steps have been taken to, eventually, embrace a third language: the one spoken by American Indians who were the original and rightful owners of the land. This decision would be a huge step forward in the recognition of indigenous languages worldwide.

Australia could easily have become French — the same situation as Quebec. The French sailor, La Perouse, was only a few days behind Arthur Phillip in reaching Botany Bay. It earned him the honour of having a Sydney suburb named after him and he may have more readily embraced the culture of the First Peoples than the British ever thought of doing.

So it was that Helen and I spent several happy days walking around Quebec and enjoying the experience immensely. We explored the cliffs and fields where British general Wolfe defeated French general Montcalm to claim all of Canada for his king, but the stubborn French civilians did not and would not leave. The French won the peace, and they continue their affinity for the culture and language of France to this day.

The Party Quebecois, established by French speaking people, wins almost all the seats in Quebec province at every national and provincial election and one day they will declare independence from the rest of Canada as a separate nation without ever considering the possibility of becoming an overseas province of France itself — as Tahiti and New Caledonia now, sadly, are.

This will not be an oddity, as this issue of sovereignty for small breakaway nations is gaining pace and recognition worldwide.

I believe that within the next few decades Scotland and Wales will separate from England, and Northern Ireland will unite with Eire. Catalonia will secede from Spain and so will the Basques. Parts of Greece and Bulgaria will join Macedonia, while Hawaii, Alaska and Texas will leave USA. West Papua will gain independence from Indonesia, and Western Australia will secede from the Commonwealth of Australia. May I also predict that

Cantonese China will secede from Mandarin China. This would be a huge event that could really shake up the world.

Even more interesting will be the long-term fate of Canada's St Lawrence River through which much the USA trade to and from the Great Lakes goes out and back to the world. An independent Quebec nation would almost certainly use their control of it as the basis for negotiating beneficial trade deals with the USA that will ensure their long-term economic prosperity.

And the St Lawrence River really is a mighty river, one of the greatest in the world. Helen and I went on a day cruise on it from Quebec and were staggered by the huge volume of freight traffic that it carries 24 hours every day.

So it is that we live in a fascinating world that constantly changes and Quebec is a role model for the way in which change can be made beneficial.

I loved Quebec and, as I enjoyed eating their snails and frog legs, I recalled my happy school days in the Aussie bush, eating tripe and brains. I have survived it all.

Viva la France. (This rallying call needs a revival after Australia ratted on its French submarine contract for no valid reason.)

Canada and Australia are members of the British Commonwealth of Nations and we retain our constitutional links with the British Crown while ignoring the fact that two-thirds of the other members of the Commonwealth, including India, Pakistan and South Africa, are republics and have been for a long time. Even tiny Barbados has severed their legal relationship with the monarchy and Jamaica has signalled its intention to do likewise.

Nevertheless, those republics still welcome the British Royals as honoured visitors. Queen Elizabeth visited India three times after it became a republic.

So, it is time that Australia and Canada grew up and stopped hanging onto mother's apron strings by having a British king as our head of state.

Neither nation belongs to Britain (nor France).

15: Philadelphia

Philadelphia is the historic city where democracy was born in the United States of America.

If the Founding Fathers of the United States were able to return to see how their beloved new democracy was faring in Washington at this moment in history, they would be appalled.

It would be a struggle for them to understand why their vision of a great nation has fallen into a collection of divided factions in Congress that do their utmost to tear the constitutional fabric apart.

The Liberty Bell in Philadelphia is an iconic symbol that reminds us of how the United States of America gained its independence from British rule and formed its own government elected by the people.

Due to a defect in its production, the bell has acquired a crack, but no attempt has ever been made to repair it. The crack symbolises how easy it is to fracture the basic principles of democracy if it is not cared for with honesty and tenderness. The bell is located at the historic Independence Hall where the Declaration of Independence and the subsequent Constitution were drafted, adopted and signed.

As a proud Australian who wants to sever our constitutional, but not social, ties with the British in far more peaceful ways than happened in USA, it was an important mission of my later life to visit the hallowed place where Americans chose to part company with an oppressive colonial England. I travelled to Philadelphia a decade ago and happily roamed through this icon of American heritage for a few days.

Sitting in Independence Hall, I could almost hear the impassioned voices of Thomas Jefferson, Alexander Hamilton, Benjamin Franklin, John Adams, James Madison and George Washington echoing around the walls as they spelled out the cause of freedom.

I read the account of the British declaration that they were all traitors who should die for their arrogant disloyalty to the Crown, and I enjoyed reading Benjamin Franklin's famous comment when the representatives of various states disagreed on how to handle a vital issue:

'Look, we must all hang together on this or we will hang individually.'

It is undeniable that the Founding Fathers launched a huge exercise to practise and record the principles of democracy that would become the role model for emerging nations everywhere. Unfortunately, this grand vision has gradually decayed and today the USA is nothing like that which its eminent and valiant Founding Fathers planned it to be.

What caused this? What put the crack in the Liberty Bell?

There are endless viewpoints on it, so let me start a debate about it.

I hold the view that the world's most famous Constitution has a fatal flaw.

By creating the office of president, constitutionally separate from the Congress, it means that too many presidents have been stopped from carrying out their stated agendas because they faced Congress dominated by an opposite and often hostile political party.

Alternatively, the Westminster system of government that Australia adopted has a prime minister who is in the parliament, not separate from it, and they can only be prime minister for any length of time if they command a majority of votes in parliament or can reliably get things done if they establish a sound working relationship with independent members. This means that a government can function responsibly.

The American presidential system, therefore, has inevitably created stumbling blocks in the pathway by which the nation can be governed well.

The USA also had a tumultuous civil war in 1860 when much blood was spilt. The civil war was fought over the inhumanity of slavery. When the South lost, they fostered a resentment of their defeat and that has prevailed ever since. They still treat African Americans as second-class citizens, continuing to go to extreme lengths to stop them from voting. No nation can have any quality of life or prosperity while those blatant racist divisions exist.

Religion too has, unfortunately, dominated politics and life for far too long, and caused excessive bigotry and hatred, not just between liberal and conservative citizens, but between Christians and other faiths, especially Muslims. It has torn society apart, an event that Jesus of Nazareth would never have tolerated.

The military establishment dominates American life and thrives on continued involvement of America in wars, either directly or remotely. Huge amounts of money are spent on armaments to the detriment of society as a whole, especially causing an under-investment in the basic infrastructure of roads, railways, ports, water and energy supplies and so on, all of which is now in a state of decay.

The clause in the Constitution that gives Americans the right to bear arms has been misinterpreted. It was intended to give every citizen the right to defend themselves against British invaders. It has no place in any civilised society. While I'm not deterred by it, I feel less safe when I'm in the USA than in any other democratic nation that I visit.

The passion for personal freedom, which in principle is admirable, is not matched by any similar fervour for a responsibility to society as a whole that must exist for freedom ever to be exercised.

There are many more troubling factors in play in American society, but let me just comment on two things in closing.

Any nation that has as its citizens 70 million people who voted twice in successive elections for someone so dangerously decadent and irresponsible as Donald Trump is a nation in deep trouble. They should hang their heads in shame.

Added to this, and to their eternal disgrace, the USA is a nation that has never elected a woman as president and this clearly indicates that our American friends are a long way behind the rest of the world on fundamental issues of humanity.

Having said this, I'm acutely aware that Australia also has too many considerable defects in its nationhood that we must work on changing with urgency. This means that we are really not in a position to overly criticise Americans, but I will continue to do so while I have life and breath since America dominates the world far more than we do.

The vital issue is this:

The world needs the USA as a vibrant and progressive nation, but it is not.

I hope that leaders will emerge who can take it back up to the heights that the Founding Fathers dreamed of and put their lives on the line to do so.

The crack in the Liberty Bell can be repaired.

Indeed, it must be.

Those who planned and organised the placement of the Liberty Bell in Philadelphia were leaders with great vision, courage and considerable political skill.

When by force they drove the British out of their land they did not say 'Let's put America first' as Trump said so often to his far too many millions of admirers.

They went out of their way to continue to trade with Britain and create close links with France and the rest of Europe. Isolation was not on their agenda. They simply wanted independence.

As migrants poured into America from all over the world right from

its first days of independence, close links were naturally forged with the nations from which they came.

In today's world of instant communication, it would be an enormous task to become the hermit kingdom that Trump tried, and almost succeeded, to create.

16: America by Motorhome

We went in search of the soul of America and yet we struggled to work out why we could not find it or understand its reason for being.

Nevertheless, a trip across America was a wonderful experience from which we learned much about the many differences between the USA and Australia.

Our daughter Wendy went to Chicago for a year as a Rotary exchange student 45 years ago. So, Helen and I decided that we should join her there for a family reunion.

We flew to San Francisco with our children, Robyn, Paul and Lyndel, rented a large self-contained Winnebago motorhome and drove across America to meet Wendy in Chicago, then went south to Miami, westward along the Mexican border and north to our starting point. We reckon there are not too many Aussie families who have driven a motorhome across the USA and back again.

We enjoyed our quest to discover what made America tick.

What did we find?

First, the visual impressions — the Rocky Mountains are magnificent.

Seeing the influential Mormon community in Salt Lake City is a fascinating experience in learning how a powerful religion can be successfully established.

- The prairies are an enormous food bowl that boggle the mind.
- Australia would be a much more productive continent if we had an inland sea like the Great Lakes.
- Disney World and Disneyland are wonderful places for any family to spend delightful days together.
- New Orleans is an interesting reminder of how close France came to establishing a permanent colony in the American South.
- Everything in Texas is huge, as were the massive steaks we ate there.
- Las Vegas is a splendid example of how easy it is to relieve people of their money.
- The Grand Canyon is an incredible picture of nature at work.
- Yosemite is a wonderful example of how every nation needs more national parks of that quality.

Now, the key human impression:

- America is huge and powerful, innovative and wealthy (especially for the privileged), but it fails to relate to the rest of the world with any sincerity or conviction.

Then and now (we have been back many times since), we look with both amazement and concern at the ever-growing social chasms, such as the stark gaps between:

- Rich and poor
- Men and women
- Whites, blacks, Latinos and Asians
- American Indians alienated from society by the depletion of their ancient lands by their plundering conquerors
- LGBTIQ people and the rest of society
- Republicans and Democrats
- Christians and those of other faiths or no faith

- Those who have guns and those who want them banned
- Both sides of the abortion debate

Refreshingly, we often met wonderful Americans who went out of their way to make sure we enjoyed our visit. While we appreciated their generous welcome, we were pleased to come back to Australia because it is our home.

For all its faults, Australia has more opportunities than the USA for people to achieve their dreams in a cohesive society.

Far too many Americans have never left their national shores to explore the world. More than half of the population don't have a passport and have no desire ever to get one. This is why Donald Trump's constant AMERICA FIRST slogan won him so many votes in two presidential elections. Millions of voters have experience of only one nation. Their own. The rest of the world does not exist to them.

This self-imposed desire for isolation was indelibly impressed on us when our children wrote these words on a mud covered back window of our motorhome:

WE ARE FROM AUSTRALIA.

Everywhere we went that day people asked us, 'What state is Australia in?'

In an earlier chapter of this book, I talked about a memorable visit that Helen and I had made many years later to Philadelphia to see the Liberty Bell and Independence Hall where the American Constitution was written and approved.

Whenever I think of the Liberty Bell, I keep asking myself, 'Why is there no-one who is trying to close the symbolic gap in the Liberty Bell?'

I will always ponder the question and I hope it will constantly create lively debate. The failure of democracy in the United States will change the future history of humanity.

It will be a tumultuous event.

Inevitably, it will happen.

Nevertheless, we enjoyed our visit to a nation that once was great. It was an incredible experience that we have never regretted.

Abraham Lincoln showed the world how democracy should be exercised for the benefit of the people, not its politicians.

He is the only president of the United States who invited his most powerful political enemies to accept appointments to his Cabinet even though they had gone to extreme lengths to stop him being elected.

They were called a Team of Rivals and not one of them was a personal friend of Lincoln at the time he appointed them.

Lincoln welded them into a team of patriots who kept the Union together through a bitter civil war.

He was a committed proponent of justice and an extraordinary human being of incredible humility.

Whenever I think of America, I think of Lincoln with enormous respect.

He was the human soul of the Liberty Bell.

The ringing of the bell is a heart-stirring sound he sent across America and which caused us to drive our motorhome to Springfield, Illinois to visit the place where his legal and political careers began. Here, Lincoln found the calling to serve his fellow Americans at the expense of his own life.

It was a spiritual experience of huge dimensions.

Indeed, our entire motorhome journey was a never-ending experience of learning.

The experience fired us up, wanting to create a better Australia.

Significantly, it gave Wendy, Robyn, Paul and Lyndel a healthy fascination of the world beyond Australia. Paul now lives in the USA and Lyndel in England, but all four became regular travellers around the world.

17: Recoleta

A century ago, Argentina was the wealthiest nation in the world, per head of population.

It produced more cattle and better cattle than Australia and was much closer to the European market.

Somehow, it lost its way and has never recovered its former glory.

A prime reason is that it has never had a leader of stature, intelligence and skill.

In 2008, I travelled with Helen to Buenos Aires, enjoying a brief visit there on our way to Patagonia in Southern Argentina.

On our first day in Buenos Aires, I asked the doorman at our hotel if he could get a taxi to take us to the cemetery at Recoleta where Eva Peron — politician, activist and actress — is buried.

'Sir, may I recommend that you do not go there. Our government discourages any public recognition of Peron.'

'We still want to go.'

Reluctantly, he waved over a cab.

When we reached Recoleta, the guard on duty asked, in halting English, which grave we wanted to visit. He shook his head when I said Peron. So, I got a bit aggressive and repeated in a loud voice 'Peron' and walked quickly towards the entrance. He finally got the message and led us to her tiny tomb in a narrow corridor of a remote part of the cemetery.

We were alone. There were no other visitors. We were stunned.

In a very confined place, where only two people can comfortably gather at any time, lies Eva Peron, the most famous person in the history of Argentina. Indeed, she was the most photographed woman in the world in the years before her death from cancer in 1952 at the age of just 33. The only person in the world who has exceeded her photography record was Diana, one time Princess of Wales.

Why did Eva Peron fall from grace?

Eva was born into poverty in a small town out in the Pampas of Argentina. She tried to launch a career as an actress but failed and became a sex worker for upmarket clients with wealth, fame and power.

One night she found herself in the bed of General Juan Peron who had ambitions beyond his ability to become president of Argentina.

She sensed a huge opportunity and decided to become his indispensable friend. He soon worked out that she could be a genuine political asset. Which she was. Helped by Eva's popular campaigning, Juan Peron became president.

She set up the Eva Peron Foundation to finance projects to lift people out of poverty and also to champion the fundamental right of women to vote.

She became a legend and toured the world, drawing huge crowds wherever she went. She even had a private audience in Rome with the pope. This gave her aspirations to replace her husband as president.

However, while she was planning her ascent to power, Juan Peron was removed as president in a swift coup, caused by valid accusations of corruption. Predictably, he was replaced by a politician who was just as corrupt as he was.

At the same time, an aggressive cancer struck down Eva, and she died quickly.

On the day of Eva's death, 2000 people were injured and admitted to hospitals after being trampled by the huge crowds who tried to view her body as it lay in state.

Juan Peron's successors sent her remains to Spain for preservation and kept them there for 23 years as the new junta feared that regular Peronist uprisings would occur if she was buried as a saint in Argentina. So it was that she finally came home to her tiny grave at Recoleta in 1975. Few Argentinians now publicly mourn her passing.

Years later, a highly successful musical called *Evita* was produced and performed around the world. It is still on the theatre circuit. We enjoyed a performance of it one New Year's Eve in London's West End.

If you have not seen it, you should, as it is magnificent.

The opening words of the theme song 'Don't Cry for Me Argentina' of the musical tell it all:

'Don't cry for me, Argentina.

For in truth, I never left you.'

Such is fame and power. Both are fleeting assets.

May I comment that our journey to Patagonia, which occupies magnificent mountains lakes and rivers of both Argentina and Chile proved to be one of the most beautiful places we have visited on the planet.

And it has a strong Celtic culture. The poorly paid and downtrodden coalminers of Wales fled there in large numbers a century or more ago seeking a better life. They found it in Patagonia. It proved to be an excellent choice. Their presence is still evident.

You can learn how it happened by reading a book called *Up the Singing Mountain*. It's the sequel to Richard Llewellyn's great novel *How Green Was My Valley*, which magnificently tells the cruel saga of the disgraceful coal mines of Wales. I read it again last year and it once more stirred my soul. As did the movie that was based on it and which I enjoyed seeing in the Linville Hall 75 years ago.

Why did Argentina fall from its position as the wealthiest nation on Earth and lapse into a continuous state of recession?

The answer is simple. Corruption throughout society aided by incompetent government and violent politics.

Can it ever recover?

I hope so, but I doubt it.

Argentina has no worthy leaders and never has had. This is because even the finest leadership prospect would have great difficulty fighting their way through the disgusting web of dishonest and corrupt powerbrokers who smother the nation with the aid of the military.

It's such a huge tragedy.

It is a nation of enormous potential that has everything going for it, except hope and competence.

Sadly, South America is littered with nations that have never ever achieved a stature that is anywhere near their real potential. A prime example is Brazil, which should be a world power not a corrupt basket case.

18: Waitangi

Britain intended that New Zealand would join its six colonies in Australia to create a new nation.

New Zealand wanted that to happen but Australia stupidly stuffed it up by insisting on a pointless racist agenda.

The Bay of Islands, hidden away in the far north of New Zealand, is a delightful place to enjoy an interesting holiday.

Helen and I have enjoyed two holidays there and, back in my days as a fundraising consultant, I organised successful campaigns in the community for the Anglican Church there and the local sports stadium.

Importantly, on every occasion that I visited, I paid my respects to Waitangi, the place of history in the Bay of Islands where the British and the Māoris signed a treaty in 1840 that recognised the Māori people as British citizens and, eventually, as citizens of New Zealand with the same rights as whites.

It was a genuine experience to read the words of the Treaty. I believe it rivals the Magna Carta and the United States Declaration of Independence as a meaningful statement of a merging of cultures.

As white men have always done so persistently and disgracefully all around the world since the beginning of time, the British manipulated the

Treaty so as to enable them to gradually steal considerable tracts of land from the Māoris, but in recent times New Zealand governments have respected the basis of the Treaty by progressively restoring at least some of the land to its rightful original owners.

The Treaty of 1840 eventually came to have a huge impact on Australia, which has steadfastly and arrogantly refused to give its indigenous people any more rights than are absolutely necessary. Significantly, the First Peoples were not given any voice in the negotiations to create the Australian nation in 1901, were not recognised as citizens in the Constitution and were not given the right to vote until 1967. It really is quite disgraceful.

This racist attitude caused New Zealand to withdraw from the merger negotiations for it to become the seventh state of Australia when the Federation of Australia took place in 1901. They quite rightly requested that the First Peoples be given the same citizenship status as Māoris were given in 1840 since there was no way they could have a different status. When all six Australian states refused to accept this quite reasonable and justifiable request, the New Zealanders did the only thing they could do. They withdrew from federation negotiations and went home. Rightly so. It would not have been honourable to do anything else.

All of this is tragic, but there is bit more history to the Bay of Islands.

One of the islands contains a small but significant village called Russell that has earned its place in history as the first capital city of New Zealand. Russell was originally a prosperous centre for the whaling, fishing and timber industries and was a much warmer place to live than the communities to the south.

We enjoyed dinner there one pleasant evening at its old colonial hotel that recalls the grand old days of its power. It was served with the antique crockery and cutlery from the 1840s and the waiters looked like the pompous toffs from *Downton Abbey*. A fascinating portrait of an age that's gone forever. What was delightful was that the chef on the night we were there was a Māori.

All of this begs some questions.

What style of nation would now dominate the South Pacific if New Zealand and Australia had merged in 1901?

It would have been a genuine nation of the Pacific, not a big brother that handed out occasional gifts. Eventually, many island nations would have sought to join the Federation.

What name would it have been given? Good question.

It would not have been Australia.

Would it have harmed Australia if our First Peoples had been given the same status as the Māoris?

No. It would have enhanced our culture.

Is it too late for Australia to have its own Treaty of Waitangi?

No.

Any treaty with the First Peoples should be signed at Uluru by representatives of every First Peoples tribe and of every one of the 100 nations from whom citizens of Australia have come, plus some descendants of the convicts. The document must then become an addendum to the Constitution as a permanent acknowledgement of the heritage of Australia.

I plan to live to the day when it happens and will be honoured to be a representative of the convicts. I am a proud descendant of one, and angry about the brutality with which the British treated him.

I am privileged to be a reforming Australian who seeks to honour the intent of Waitangi.

I envy the way in which New Zealanders govern themselves.

They have no states and therefore no state governments to cause divisions and parochial jealousy.

They have only one house of parliament. No upper house where a few prima donnas can block progress as happens too often in the Australian Senate.

They practise proportional representation.

Most MPs are chosen by electorates of roughly equal population,

similar to those in Australia.

But a significant number are also elected on the percentage of votes that their party receives nationally.

This gives minor parties the chance to win seats and cause negotiated democracy to come into play.

It's a huge improvement on the undemocratic way that Australia sometimes governs itself.

19: The Great Barrier Reef

What a magnificent asset Australia has in the Great Barrier Reef.

It's absolutely priceless and it is our responsibility to preserve and protect it.

However, it is now a tragedy of neglect.

Why have we done our best to destroy it?

The Great Barrier Reef first came to my attention during history lessons at primary school when I learned how in 1770 the great mariner Captain James Cook almost sank his boat *Endeavour* by accidentally hitting the reef near what we now call Cooktown in far north Queensland.

I didn't get to see any part of the reef until I arranged to go for a holiday there when I was just 18 years of age, a mere 73 years ago, a blink in time for a reef that has existed for billions of years. I remember how I marvelled at the beautiful clear colour of the tropical sea and the vibrant majesty of the coral.

I've gone back there every few years of my life, the last time being just before COVID-19 hit us. Now the sea is looking a bit darker and the reef is appearing to be somewhat tired.

What has happened?

The short answer is that Australia has persistently neglected its duty as the defender, preserver and enhancer of the reef. We have every reason to feel guilt. The restoration task is massive, but we are a wealthy nation that can easily meet the cost of getting it right. We just lack the will to restore it. We hope the problem will naturally fix itself. It won't, even though the reef does have a long-term restorative capacity.

It's time to look at what a challenge this really is for us.

The Great Barrier Reef is one of the wonders of the world and, as such, is a World Heritage Site and a UNESCO site that consists of 2900 reefs and 900 islands. Those reefs have a combined length of 2300 kilometres and an area of 344,000 square kilometres. It is the world's largest coral reef system, but currently suffers from bleaching and warming temperatures. Both of these problems are steadily worsening.

Much of the damage is caused by the run-off from pesticides and chemicals that flow down our river systems from mines, farms and riverside communities, as well as contamination from shipping waste and accidents.

So, what can we do about it? We can decide on a plan to save the reef within a decade. We must pay the price.

Australia has the money. We can do it quite simply by allocating every year the same amount of money as is spent by Aussies on gambling.

We do have in our community the necessary skills in science — international quality skills — so we have no excuses.

All we lack is political drive, organisation and vision. This attitude is fostered by selfish Aussies who appear to have an inbuilt desire to help ourselves rather than the environment.

But I live in hope, fondly remembering wonderful holidays and day visits on enchanting reef islands — South Molle, Daydream, Hamilton, Hayman, Lindeman, Magnetic, Green and Heron plus lots of refreshing walks on long, white sandy beaches and spectacular viewing of incredibly magnificent coral through glass bottom boats.

I hope I didn't personally contaminate the reef in any way during my visits, but I fear that I probably did.

This means that I am planning to spend the tenth decade of my life getting involved in the fight to get it right and keeping it right.

At least I can report that I'm a regular contributor to not-for-profit organisations that do great work restoring the reef.

But, honestly, this really is quite nominal.

This all means that I also have an obligation as a responsible citizen to make an effort to confront politicians with the need for significant investment in the protection and restoration of the Great Barrier Reef.

A significant number of Australians believe that human beings, especially themselves, do not pollute the world or harm the environment in any way.

All the talk about saving the Great Barrier Reef and combating climate change is, in their view, just political propaganda fostered by radical 'lefties and money-making scientists' and they are not likely to be persuaded differently.

Nevertheless, may I affirm that I am not a leftie. Never have been. Never will be.

Nor am I a scientist. Nor a member or supporter of any political parties on the right (or the left).

I have never joined a political party and never will.

People who do should occasionally ask themselves whether or not their ideology causes them to have closed minds.

I regard myself as a reforming conservative.

This means that as a responsible citizen I have obligations to the environment that I cannot avoid.

Anyone of any political colour who doesn't accept this obligation is a millstone around the neck of all humanity.

20: Uluru

Is it possible for a continent have a soul?

Yes, it is. Indeed, it needs one, and Uluru is the prime home for such a soul.

Australia will be a greater nation in every way when we find our soul and make it the cornerstone of our lives.

If you have not yet made a personal visit to Uluru, may I suggest that you do so as soon as circumstances allow it to happen. It awaits the spiritual presence of every Australian who cherishes the values of life.

All political and cultural indicators tell us that from this point in our history, Uluru will gradually change from being a popular tourist destination to becoming a sacred place where the people of Australia, no matter their ethnic or religious backgrounds, will come to reunite in spirit, hope, purpose and achievement.

I'm reluctant to admit that I've been there only twice in my 90 years, but will make up for this in my next decade. It is important for me personally to experience once more the atmosphere that gives our nation such a spiritual heart.

The first time I went there, it was called Ayers Rock (yet another insensitive and pointless title arrogantly determined by white men) and I tried to climb it along with lots of other tourists. Foolishly, I had worn the wrong type of shoes, slipped not long after starting my climb and did a bit of damage to my ankle. So, I proceeded no further and sat down for a while to ponder that it could have been a message 'from above'.

As I sat there nursing my wounds, I wondered why so many tourists like me were climbing this awesome sandstone rock that scientists say began its formation 550 million years ago. Most of us were doing it just to enjoy the view from the top. Few sit down to ponder the significant place of the rock and the land in our lives.

Now, and at last, the climbing of Uluru is banned.

So, on my second visit, I walked the land around it and pondered how it would be possible for Uluru to become a spiritual force that inspires and unites all Australians to become a more inclusive, cohesive and compassionate society.

It is still a prominent thought in my mind and always will be. I deliberately create positive dialogue on the matter, hoping that it may lead to a progress in our spirituality. Most of the responses I receive are positive but too many are quite racist.

As a passionate working partner of Jesus of Nazareth, it's clear to me that an important part of my mission in life must be to participate actively in respecting, preserving and enhancing our land, air, water, flora and fauna as part of the responsible livelihood of our humanity and the quality of our values as a nation that seeks to reduce pollution and land overuse and degradation from our continent.

This debate has livened up in recent years with the result of the publication of the 'Uluru Statement from the Heart'. It is a magnificent document, even if somewhat impractical in political terms, and potentially divisive.

The tragedy is that it is unlikely to gain in totality the approval of our parliaments, or our voters in a referendum, since it's widely regarded as more political than spiritual and has not sought to include the thoughts of a majority of those from over 100 nations, in addition to the First Peoples who call Australia home.

So, we have a calling to start again, using the Uluru Statement as a basic document of spirituality, and ask every ethnic grouping in Australia to confer regularly at Uluru on what values they cherish and observe proudly as a meaningful contribution to the beliefs on which our nation aspires and exists.

This cannot be forged in churches or mosques or temples or town halls or ancient caves or parliaments.

However, it can have its birth and its life at Uluru, located at the geographical centre of our vast continent, surrounded on all sides by the very heart and soul of our nation in communion with the spirit of our ancestors and the many faiths and ideologies that are now the core of our lives as genuine Australians.

We will walk together one day soon.

So long as we undertake a lot of constructive, respectful and visionary action in the meantime, we will be able to gain inspiration from our journey together.

My early life at school was spent, not only in Linville, but also for two years at an even smaller village further up the Brisbane River called Monsildale, another timber town.

At both schools, I established a solid friendship with two First Peoples children, Jackie and Kathleen Dumbleton. We enjoyed our time at school, played together and visited each other's homes.

Their dad, Fred Dumbleton, worked beside my father at the timber mill. He was a hard worker, a very reliable bloke.

We parted when the Monsildale mill closed. They went to North Queensland and my family moved to Toowoomba.

We didn't meet again and that is a missing gap in my life.

What I've never forgotten is the way, quite naturally, that they taught me, by their actions not their words, the love of the land and its prime place as the treasured lifeblood of humanity.

I am forever grateful for their contribution to my life. It is a spiritual treasure, and it forever reminds me that there is a power beyond my personal being that forever leads me to cherish the highest values of life.

Bucket List

I guess that most of my readers will have drawn up a list of places they really do want to visit before they die. I certainly have a list even though my physical ability to travel is steadily diminishing.

At the top of the list is the *Galapagos Islands*. I want to study what Charles Darwin discovered there and how he turned traditional Christianity view of a creator God on its ear.

Hotly following is the *Volga River*. This remote river in Russia, one of the longest in the world, has fascinated me ever since we used to sing 'The Song of the Volga Boatmen' at school.

Then *Greenland*. It is the last bastion in stopping the ravages of climate change. If the ice at Greenland melts, we are in big trouble.

And *Tibet*. Its remoteness mystifies me greatly.

Siberia. A train journey across the north of Asia would unravel an awesome vastness.

The *Shetlands*, lying in the Arctic Ocean between Scotland and Iceland have always fascinated me by their isolation and their Gaelic traditions.

There are more, but I must be a bit practical in terms of time and energy. Nevertheless, I firmly intend to visit one special place.

The island of *Iona*, one of the smallest of the Western Isles of Scotland.

It is a unique spiritual community established in 1950 by George MacLeod, a giant of the Christian faith, who invited the world, no matter what their religion to come to Iona to reflect on how we can grow our spirituality and take it out into the world with the mission of meeting the needs of humanity in crisis.

This is a wonderful mission.

D: NOSTALGIA

1: Great Books

Books are the finest invention in the history of humanity.

What quality of life would I have experienced without them?

Indeed, a very ordinary existence.

As a young lad in Linville, the first book I read was *Treasure Island*, that famous tale of adventure written by the incomparable Scottish author, Robert Louis Stevenson. For what seemed a long time, it was the only book I had, but I enjoyed it while my family struggled through the Great Depression. Then someone gave me another great Stevenson book, *Kidnapped*. Those two splendid tales kindled my interest in books and opened doors to a life that has thrived on reading and writing.

They also led me, 70 years later, to travel to Samoa to make a pilgrimage to Stevenson's old home from where he wrote most of his finest work after coming there from Scotland, hoping, without success, that a warmer climate would cure his severe health issues.

Early in life, I made the wise decision to read two books at a time, a chapter of each every day. This helped me to develop a good memory since it forced me to remember the characters and plot of the first book when I returned to it after reading a chapter of the second, and vice versa.

A decade ago, I expanded this to reading five books at a time, a pleasure that lasts for about three hours on most days and does help to keep my memory up to scratch. The five are usually based on history, politics, money and religion, plus an escapist novel. I enjoy this pastime immensely as it fuels my brain with thoughtful inputs for books and articles I write regularly.

So, which books have been the highlights of my life? Tough choice as I reckon I've read more than 2000 books during my 90 years.

Let me comment on a few special books.

My journey through life has been hugely influenced by two books written by a revered American Lutheran pastor a century ago. His name was Lloyd Douglas and the books were *The Magnificent Obsession* and *The Robe*, both of which sold millions of copies.

The former is based on the life of a man who believed that when you regularly give away a significant portion of your wealth, whether you be rich or poor, and seek no thanks or recognition of the gifts, nor any rewards, a spiritual power comes into your life that enables you to achieve great things for humanity that would not otherwise have occurred. From time to time, I have personally proven this belief and now regret that I did not take it up more seriously and persistently.

The second tells the challenging tale of the life of a Roman tribune who was in charge of the crucifixion of Jesus and given the robe that Jesus wore on the cross. Its presence utterly changed the tribune's life, which ends when Caesar has him killed for spreading the faith. This book convinced me that life is pointless unless it is based on a cornerstone of either religion or morals or ethics or ideology or all of the above.

A third book had a similar influence. It was written by a fine Scottish author, A J Cronin. It bears the title *The Keys of the Kingdom* and is the story of an enthusiastic young Catholic priest from Scotland who is sent as a missionary to a remote part of China in the 19th century in an attempt to convert the locals to his faith. He discovers how difficult it is to find a way of selling a traditional Celtic faith in a meaningful way to people of a foreign culture that has survived for thousands of years. How can Christianity become relevant to their lives and culture right there and then?

I think of this book often as I wonder why churches still try, and fail, to sell ancient dogmas and rigid creeds instead of inviting people to encounter Jesus of Nazareth right here and now and adopt him as their role model.

As you would expect, there were many other books that influenced me greatly, too many to list here but I will mention a few.

How Green Was My Valley. I have mentioned this briefly in an earlier chapter. It is Richard Llewellyn's powerful story of the way in which the beautiful valleys of Wales were raped and pillaged by ruthless coalminers consumed by greed. The Welsh people were callously committed to lives of poverty, filth, contamination and lung disease from coal dust. Reading this magnificent book led me to despise rampant capitalism and become a passionate advocate of a common good that will enable every person to have equal opportunity to advance personal skills on a level and clean playing field.

The Tyranny of Distance. Geoffrey Blainey's great book is about the isolation of Australia from the rest of the world and especially the way in which Australia has never ever tried to conquer the costly expense that rural producers face in getting their products to our capital cities and then to the world. Its message eventually led me to partner with my valued friend Don McDonald in pioneering the Inland Railway as a means of solving this impediment to rural prosperity.

We of the Never Never by Jeannie Gunn — I really did enjoy this great Australian story based in northern Australia as well as the bushranger thriller *Robbery Under Arms* by Rolf Bolderwood, and the powerful book on convicts *For the Term of His Natural Life* by Marcus Clarke.

All of the above probably amount to just enough comment about special books, but a few comments about books in general may be of interest.

I never took to Shakespeare or the great poets. They switched me off. But I reckon Charles Dickens' book *A Tale of Two Cities* is one of the great ones, especially the opening line. 'It was the best of days and the worst of days.'

This is the experience of every life.

I loved reading Banjo Patterson and Henry Lawson plus the books written by Winston Churchill and other fine historians such as American James McCullough, English Barbara Tuchman and Australians Geoffrey Blainey and Grantlee Kieza.

I devoured all the books I could find about powerful characters from history whose lives fascinate me. These included Cicero, Cleopatra, St Francis of Assisi, William Wallace, James Cook, Abraham Lincoln, William Wilberforce, the Pankhurst sisters, Theodore Roosevelt, Harry Truman, Martin Luther King, Nelson Mandela and Angela Merkel plus many others.

Great novelists of the mould of Mark Twain, Morris West, Daphne du Maurier, Ken Follett, John Buchan, Margaret Attwood, Dan Brown, Peter Fitzsimons and Edward Rutherford are treasures of my life, as are thriller writers David Baldacci, John Grisham, Frederick Forsyth and Jeffrey Archer.

Finally, I must admit to reading and enjoying all of the many Agatha Christie's murder yarns. They were often a great way to finish a difficult day by trying to work out whether it was the vicar or the colonel or the maid who did the dirty deed.

My best wishes to you for fascinating reading, especially if you are reading my own books:

The Man on the Twenty Dollar Notes

Dinner With the Founding Fathers

A Beautiful Sunset

The Power Gift

In the meantime, I will keep reading. I'm just starting to learn what life is all about and I'm running out of time to devour more knowledge.

I have as my constant travel companion a Kindle, which has many ebooks on it, but I still prefer to read a printed book.

The smell and feel of a book make me feel as if I am present at the scene of the story.

Indeed, when I write my books, I do my utmost to encourage my readers to feel that the book was written especially for them.

I don't always succeed but I'm seriously working at it.

One day, I will get it right.

2: Fine Movies

The Saturday matinee at the local movie theatre in Toowoomba was a happy core of my youthful life.

It helped me to understand and forever be fascinated by what a great wide world there is out there in which I could try to find a happy and meaningful place.

I have fond memories of the excitement of going to the movies in Linville in my youthful years.

There was a business called Paget's Pictures that had a movie projector they took around the Brisbane River valley, showing films in the community halls of most towns. They usually came to Linville once a month.

I now can't remember many of the movies we saw at that time but I do recall enjoying Australia's high-profile actor Errol Flynn famously take the role of Robin Hood and give the wicked Sheriff of Nottingham a real hiding.

Then we went to live in the tiny timber village of Monsildale, but sadly Pagets did not visit there so we had a couple of barren years with no movies.

Nevertheless, good times came when Dad got a job at the bacon factory in Toowoomba, a city that had four cinemas, so we went to the matinees regularly and this started a lifelong pattern of regular relaxation at the movies (or now at home with Netflix).

So, I have given some careful thought as to what, in my view, are the 10 best movies of my 90 years.

Here are my choices, in alphabetical order:

Casablanca. Humphrey Bogart and Ingrid Bergman at their best. It had a memorable theme song 'As Time Goes By' with the lyrics, 'It's still the same old story, a fight for love and glory.'

Chariots of Fire. The inspiring story of Scotland's Eric Liddell winning a gold medal at the Paris Olympics of 1924 before going to China as a Christian missionary where he was killed by the Japanese army.

Dr Zhivago. A passionate account of the Russian Revolution and a magnificent romance. 'Somewhere my love there will be songs to sing.'

Gone With the Wind. The longest movie of my lifetime. A huge saga of four hours about the American Civil War. It has a wonderful final line when Clark Gable (Rhett Butler) says to Vivien Leigh (Scarlett O'Hara) as he leaves her forever, 'Frankly, my dear, I don't give a damn.'

Lawrence of Arabia. He was a huge figure of the history of British involvement in the Middle East and Peter O'Toole acted him superbly. Omar Sharif had a powerful role too, just as he did in *Dr Zhivago.*

Mrs Miniver. The most human story of World War II. Greer Garson and Walter Pidgeon brought it to life, just as they did together in several other great movies such as *Blossoms in the Dust* and *Madam Curie.*

Philomena. A powerful story of how the Roman Catholic Church in Ireland cruelly destroyed the lives of unmarried women who had children. A very moving performance from Judi Dench (as always). She quietly highlighted the determined strength of one woman who went on a relentless pursuit to find the son the church brutally took from her.

The Dam Busters. Richard Todd at his finest in acting Guy Gibson who led the greatest bombing raid on the great dams of Germany in World War II. The theme song is still popular today.

The Longest Day. Just huge and powerful. The day in which the greatest armada in the history of the world invaded France on 6 June 1944, and began the final destruction of Adolph Hitler and his murdering regime. A top-quality cast led by Robert Mitchum, John Wayne and Peter Lawford.

To Kill a Mockingbird. The record-breaking film of Harper Lee's great novel. The courtroom speech by Gregory Peck defending an innocent black man before an all-white jury is one of the finest orations I've ever heard.

So, which was Number 1? *Dr Zhivago*!

I also have a list of five best actors in any movies I've enjoyed, again alphabetically by first names:

Cate Blanchett. A great Australian actor. I have not ever seen her put in anything less than a superb performance. She was tremendous as Queen Elizabeth I.

Clint Eastwood. He has had huge success as actor, director and producer. Few have excelled at all three.

Judi Dench. She is simply magnificent with great ability to take on many varied roles.

Laurence Olivier. An incredible talent.

Sidney Poitier. He gave hope to African Americans in films like *Guess Who's Coming to Dinner* and *To Sir, with Love*.

My Number 1 actor is Judi Dench.

Let me share a couple of extra thoughts.

No comment on movies in my lifetime is complete without mentioning James Bond and Alfred Hitchcock.

The latter was a master of suspense and Helen and I saw every one of his films and enjoyed them all. The most memorable was *Psycho*, especially the scene where Janet Leigh is murdered in the bath and all you see is increasing volumes of blood going down the plug hole while she screams her life away.

Bond was always memorable, particularly when Sean Connery acted him. The others were pale imitations. What upset me was that in all my constant travels, never once have I experienced the pleasure of having girls climb through my hotel room window in the moonlight, but Bond enjoyed it three or four times in every movie. Totally unfair, but such is life.

Finally, the best Australian movie I enjoyed:

Light Between the Oceans. A powerful, tender and mind-opening movie. All about a tragic series of human events. I was greatly moved by it. I went to the sites at Stanley in Tasmania where it was filmed. They are now popular tourist attractions.

But let me add that the grand old authentic Aussie bushman of my youth, Chips Rafferty, was memorable in the wartime movie *The Overlanders*, the story of how the cattlemen of the Northern Territory drove their herds south-east to escape what they were certain would be a Japanese invasion.

That is it.

I just wish Netflix and all its competitors would provide a better selection of home movies than the rubbish they trot out now. I always need to allow an hour to select a movie worth watching, plus a stiff whisky to calm me down.

I do hope that my local cinema survives. Whenever we've gone there during the ongoing COVID-19 world, the audience has never been more than a dozen people.

This is quite simply sad.

If the local cinema does close, it would be the end of a cherished element of my lifetime.

Far too often, after I went to the cinema and enjoyed a movie that greatly impressed me, I would buy the book so as to quietly absorb the impact of the story.

On every occasion, the book has differed considerably from the film, and usually the book has been much a much better depiction of the story.

Why producers and directors of films have the ego to destroy great books is beyond me.

They are 'cultural peasants', but their ranks are growing.

3:
Fabulous Theatre

A huge change occurred in theatre over my lifetime.

The ability to change scenery, colour and sound by extraordinary electronics has been tremendous and it's greatly improved the impact of stage performances.

Nevertheless, talented actors will always mesmerise an audience, simply by their presence and their command of the scene and the language, with or without electronics.

I will always enjoy a relaxing night at the cinema, but the finest entertainment experience is to be found with live theatre.

Let's talk about my experience of musicals first.

Great composers have been producing words and music throughout my lifetime and yours and will keep on doing so forever.

May I list my top 10 in order of my personal rating of them.

Phantom of the Opera. Simply powerful. Helen and I enjoyed it several times, especially on one occasion on a visit to China (where it was sung in English). The song 'All I Ask of You' tells us very important things about life.

Les Misérables. The French Revolution, bloody though it was, has always been to me an immensely powerful landmark of history since it was the first step in a long journey to reduce the power of the privileged and wealthy, particularly those who claim the privilege of royalty and nobility. I love to sing the lyrics, 'Do you hear the people sing, singing the songs of angry men.' It fires me up when I prepare for my regular meetings with politicians.

My Fair Lady. A delightful story with top-quality music. When Eliza Doolittle sings the lyrics, 'All I want is a room somewhere' it sustains my lifelong crusade to narrow the gap in the great divide between the rich and poor.

Jesus Christ Superstar. I love anything that stirs debate about Christianity and this one hit fundamentalist Christians right between the eyes. It got me thinking positively about new ways to tell the world about Jesus the Man as distinct to the Jesus of ancient church dogma.

South Pacific. The character of Bloody Mary is magnificent. This musical did create a real sense of some enchanted evening and I found the song 'This Nearly Was Mine' to be very moving.

The Wizard of Oz. I saw and heard this performed live in a few local theatres and really enjoyed it, but in this rare case the film was better because it was the finest performance of Judy Garland's tragic career.

The Sound of Music. As happy a show as I have ever seen. I worked out 'how we solve a problem like Maria' and, more importantly, how to 'climb every mountain'.

Guys and Dolls. The most delightful line is when the great lover bets his mates that he can seduce any woman to whom they introduce him anywhere in the world and they point to a young lady singing outside the pub in the Salvation Army band trying to save their souls and say, 'This one.'

Annie Get Your Gun. The wild west at its best. Out in the bush where I grew up, the boys declared Annie Oakley to be a 'great sheila'.

Lili Marleen. Many years ago, I was in Melbourne for business and having lunch with a friend. He told me that he had a ticket to see Marlene Dietrich who was making her last performance in Australia but he could not attend.

He asked if I would like to go in his place. I said I would. The theatre was packed and a large crowd waited outside, trying to get a glimpse of her. She sang all the great songs of her long career, including the ones from her wartime years in Germany. Many wept as she sang 'Underneath the lamplight, oer the barricades, darling you remember the way we used to sing'. A memorable evening.

There were many others, too many to describe, but I cherish the evenings when I enjoyed great shows like these: *The King and I*, *Oklahoma*, *Cats*, *West Side Story*, *Grease*, *The Book of Mormon*, *Godspell*, *Maid of the Mountains*, *Frozen*, *The Pirates of Penzance*, *Chicago*, *Wicked* and *Showboat*.

May there be many more, especially those whose hit songs are sung at all the Pops Concerts we have enjoyed for years and years.

Let me also comment on just five theatre plays we enjoyed:

The Lady in the Van. I had the good fortune to see this in London where the incomparable Maggie Smith had the lead role as a grubby old lady who declared Margaret Thatcher to be a communist and, in protest, parked the decrepit van in which she lived right in the middle of an upmarket street in Mayfair. That evening, Smith got one of the longest and loudest standing ovations I have ever experienced.

The Mouse Trap. This is Agatha Christie's famous play that has been performed in the West End of London for more than half a century. As usual, I failed to pick who the murderer was, but it didn't really matter. It was a superb thriller.

Blythe Spirit. I enjoyed this play at the famous Pitlochry Theatre in the highlands of Scotland. A hugely entertaining yarn written by Noel Coward about a philandering husband whose wife dies and then returns as a ghost to haunt him and his many lady friends.

Michael Parkinson. Recently, Michael Parkinson made a farewell tour of Australia to appear in *An Evening With Michael Parkinson*. This was a wonderful couple of hours spent as Parkinson told fascinating tales about the great and the mighty who appeared with him on television for decades.

The Gospel According to Paul. An incredible performance by Jonathan Biggins in writing and acting. It is a tale about the life of Paul Keating. Helen, who is a conservative person, laughed happily throughout the evening and then declared she may have made a profound mistake in not ever voting for Keating.

May I also say that we got great satisfaction watching the many fine plays written by Australian playwright David Williamson. A superb talent.

I won't comment at length on opera and ballet since they're not my favourite scene, but I attend them occasionally in loyalty to Helen who enjoys both.

However, may I say that I did enjoy *Swan Lake* when we saw it at the State Theatre in Moscow. The Russians have magnificent dancers. I also thought highly of *Carmen* at the Kirov Theatre in St Petersburg where it was sung in French.

While in a state of nostalgia, it is always possible to forget the unforgettable, as I have certainly done here as I review and edit this book.

I just remembered a thoughtful evening when I enjoyed a 90 minute solo chat at Brisbane's Lyric Theatre by that fine Canadian author, Margaret Attwood, who talked to us about her career and her life. It was wonderful theatre and it encouraged me to read more of her fine books.

Then there was an extraordinary evening at a tiny theatre in Pitt Street in Sydney that was once an old church. Only 100 of us could fit in the place as we watched a group of amateur actors present a play based on the famous English novel A Passage to India. It was just splendid and reminded us that amateur theatre is the place where great actors are born.

By the time this book is printed, I will have remembered more such delightful occasions of great theatre.

Sufficient now to say how important it is to be taken away, as often as possible, from the mundane things of life and transported into a world apart.

The stage provides that magic journey.

I yearn for more.

4: Magical Media

Nothing has changed more in my lifetime than the role that media — public and social — has in moulding the thoughts of society 24/7.

It will continue to change with alarming speed, but probably not for the better.

When I lived ever so happily in the bush in the 1930s, our only regular contact with the world was via our radio, which was tuned to only one station, ABC. I naively presumed that our national broadcaster conveyed only the truth to its many listeners and it took me a long while to work out that the media, in all its facets, rarely tells the truth. They give versions of the truth, mostly biased, but now I come to think of it, this is exactly what we do ourselves personally. The truth is in the eye of the beholder.

Gradually, the world entered a time of commercial radio but it didn't ever sound quite as authentic as the ABC.

Occasionally, my dad bought the *Brisbane Courier Mail*. His basic wage did not stretch to daily readership. It was a fine conservative newspaper back in those days, utterly different to its modern edition, which like most newspapers is now in terminal decline since it solely highlights the sensational in even more sensational style.

Today, you and I live in a world of relentless news coverage, reaching out to us via a host of variable media sources that were unimaginable in the days of my youth and I have significant doubt that their presence has improved my existence. Nevertheless, I have some nostalgic memories of a few giants of the media.

I remember listening to many delightful years of radio episodes of *Blue Hills* written by the prolific storyteller, Gwen Meredith, who was a wonderful communicator of the values of human decency. Similarly, there were never-ending episodes of *Dad and Dave* that were based on Steele Rudd's legendary characters. And wonderful comedy guys too like Roy Rene as Mo McCackie, plus his mate Spencer the Garbage Man. And I won't ever forget Jack Davey, the grand host of many popular radio shows.

Eventually, we were able to connect to the BBC and I always listened with fascination whenever I heard the words, 'This is London calling. Here is the news from the BBC.' It took me to a world beyond the scope of the Linville train in Australia.

Then came television in the 1950s and I recall watching the first TV news broadcast in Brisbane read by Hugh Cornish who years later became a valued friend.

While my current television usage is restricted mainly to the evening news, preferably on SBS, which is now the quality channel of Australia, I fondly remember TV in the golden era of Graham Kennedy, Bert Newton, Jeannie Little, Jackie Weaver, Edna Everage and many other long-term legends like Richie Benaud bringing the cricket into our homes, plus the unforgettable *Steptoe and Son* from England and Ed Sullivan from USA.

Now the internet has consumed us and I have taken up an enjoyable presence on both Twitter and Facebook that enables me to constantly harass and terrorise politicians, financiers and religious fakes. But I am very aware of the dark side of social media use by too many undesirable people of very limited intelligence and unsavoury intent.

This brings to mind the fact that you and I live in a world where privacy exists no longer. However, in the end, who really cares? We can do little about it.

Be this as it may, let me get back to more nostalgia.

The Syme and Fairfax families have had a huge impact as giants of the media in Australia for generations, as have the Murdochs, the former having made a far more responsible contribution while Rupert Murdoch has generated an army of haters.

Ita Buttrose has had a memorable presence in the publication of magazines and now I enjoy the feature articles written by interesting people like Annabel Crabb, Katharine Murphy, Paul Bongiorno and Laura Tingle. I have good memories of Laurie Oakes too. Plus, the incomparable Kerry O'Brien of ABC current affairs.

Of course, Alan Jones was a large presence in our lives on both radio and television. He has interviewed me several times on both and has treated me kindly, but I know that this was not the experience of many. I did score an invitation to a dinner party at his impressive Sydney home where he entertained us with tales about the great and the mighty that even he would have restrained from stating in public.

John Laws dominated radio for a long time, but my favourite radio presenter is Brisbane's Greg Cary, who was a superb interviewer and also now a valued friend, who has embarked on a new career as a writer of interesting books.

Overseas, I enjoyed the greatest of all newsreaders, Walter Cronkite, while Richard Dimbleby was superb in London, as was David Attenborough whose powerful presentation of the world of nature is unforgettable and still continues even though he is older than me.

Never to be forgotten is that magnificent cricket writer Neville Cardus whose incredible talent with words and enormous knowledge of the English language brought cricket alive. He could bring the most boring cricket match to a state of splendour and make you believe that it had created vibrance for the entire world. He was also a superb critic of theatre, an odd combination, but I think he regarded cricket as theatre.

There is much more I could say, but I may finish with three vital questions:
- Can we live without the media? No.
- Are we compelled to allow it to dominate our lives? No.
- Can we try to use it for good? Absolutely.

Forever optimistic.

Nothing in life is certain.

This is what makes life exciting.

Too many people believe that the impact of the mainstream media decides who wins and loses elections.

This is a total untruth.

Far too many politicians foster this belief so they can use it to hide their inability to reveal any campaigning skills.

Social media influences many more people than mainstream media but, in the final analysis, the success of any election winner is determined by how many people they meet face to face on the campaign trail and how many volunteers they are able to enlist to personally spread the message to their friends and contacts.

Most election media advertising is largely a waste of money. Only a few vulnerable or gullible people take any notice of it. Its main impact is to create images in our minds rather that give us digestible facts.

But media does have a huge role in influencing what we buy and sell even though many of us are blithely unaware of it.

5: Memorable Sport

I was born in the days when a majority of players in most sports were dedicated amateurs playing for glory, not money.

Now, very few do that.

Very little happens without money smothering the sporting scene.

Unfortunately, money takes the spirituality out of the human endeavour but I doubt that we can change this since glory does not put three meals a day on the table.

When I was a lad, I was absolutely certain that my destiny was to play cricket and table tennis for Australia. It is one of the great tragedies in the history of humanity that the selectors of sporting teams did not recognise my obvious talents.

Despite this massive setback to my ego, until in recent years, I remained an avid follower and observer of all major sports. I have now lost interest in professional sport today. It doesn't have the quality of participants that amateur sport had in my era, nor does it have the decency and dignity and goodwill that went with it. Sadly, it will decline even further as greed advances as a prime motivator behind sports.

Nevertheless, I still enjoy giving much thought to my experiences as a competitor and fan of sporting endeavours and have come up with my choice of the five greatest sporting memories of my 90 years. Here they are, listed in the order in which they happened.

Don Bradman's Last Innings. It was the fifth and final test match of the 1948 tour of England by the finest team that Australia has ever put into the field in the history of cricket, then and now — they were called the Invincibles. Australia had already won the Ashes with victories in the four earlier Tests and Don Bradman had announced that this was his farewell match at the end of a magnificent career.

A huge crowd had assembled at the Oval in London to witness a great moment of sporting legend. As he came out to bat, the crowd gave Bradman a loud and long sustained ovation. I very much doubt that anyone has ever received such an accolade at a cricket match or any other sporting event. It may be that he was overcome with emotion, but he misjudged a somewhat tame ball from a veteran spin bowler, Eric Hollies, that he would normally have hit to the boundary and was bowled for a duck. He left the field to an even greater ovation.

The statistical tragedy was that this rare failure meant Bradman's average innings of his long career in Test Cricket was 99.6 runs. If he had managed to hit just one four, his career average would have been 100.

I listened by radio and was crestfallen. I felt immensely sorry for him. Life can be cruel.

But that near miss statistic has been often discussed by cricket lovers ever since, much more avidly than if he had achieved the statistical 100. Nevertheless, no-one else in cricket history worldwide has achieved an average of 99.6 and I don't think anyone ever will.

Melbourne Olympics of 1956. At that point in time, it was the greatest sporting event in Australia's history, staged a decade after the end of World War II.

Never before had we hosted an event in which all the world participated. Huge national interest was generated when Australia was selected to be the host nation having beaten Buenos Aires for the honour by just one vote at a meeting of the world body that organised the Olympics.

It would be the first Olympics ever held in the Southern Hemisphere.

The Melbourne Cricket Ground was the focal point, and it hosted the largest crowds ever assembled for the Olympics anywhere in the world. It was a wonderful sight when our world champion long-distance runner, Ron Clarke, lit the Olympic flame and much excitement when the Duke of Edinburgh officially opened the Olympic Games.

Australia did well, especially in the swimming. We won a total of 13 gold medals, 35 medals in all.

Significantly, and long overdue, the Olympic Games generated a movement to have our own national anthem to replace the British anthem.

At the medal ceremonies, whenever an Australian won, 'God Save the Queen' was played just as it was when there was a British or New Zealand winner. It really was humiliating as other nations were astonished that we were without our own anthem. They presumed that we were still a British colony. Indeed, they still think we are since in 2022 we remain a nominal colony with King Charles as our head of state and the British Union Jack still part of our flag.

It took us a while, but we eventually agreed on 'Advance Australia Fair' as our anthem. I disagreed strongly with the choice, and still do, as we should have put new words to 'Waltzing Matilda'. But, as expected, no-one took much notice of me.

As we all well know, Australia again had the honour of holding the Olympics in Sydney in 2000 but, great as they were, they did not have the magic of 1956, which was really the first occasion when most of the world recognised that Australia existed, hidden as we are down at the bottom of the globe.

We look forward to 2032 in Brisbane.

Cathy Freeman. I will not spend time describing the dramatic race in which Cathy Freeman won her gold medal in the 400 metres at the Sydney

Olympics. The media has already described it 1000 times. Ninety-nine percent of Aussies watched it. She won it splendidly and convincingly and it was well deserved.

The highlight of it all was that she won it for Australia. Only a primitive few in the media and community made the patronising error of saying that it was a great victory for the First Peoples. She was an Aussie and this was all that mattered.

Nevertheless, she took the nation a huge step forward along the pathway to reconciling the unnecessary political, social, cultural and financial gaps that have divided Australians for far too long.

There is still a long way to go, but Freeman created a very significant milestone. May we achieve more bonding with increasing regularity, using the Uluru Statement as our benchmark for a referendum on the matter.

The Greatest. It was at the Atlanta Olympic Games in 1996 that Muhammad Ali made one of his last but, in my view, his finest public appearances.

He was suffering badly from Parkinson's disease and could barely reach the podium to light the Olympic flame, but he did so gallantly and the whole world responded most positively to acknowledge a controversial but magnificent life that lives on in legend.

He rose from poverty to win a gold medal at boxing at the Rome Olympics in 1960 and moved on to become world heavyweight boxing champion several times, drawing huge crowds and enormous television audiences.

In doing so, he made a dramatic change to his life in accepting the Muslim faith, bravely and dangerously rejecting the draft for military service in the pointless war in Vietnam.

Many regard him as the greatest natural athlete the world has ever seen in any sport. I endorse that view.

And, with it, he had a superb ability to convey his verbal messages to the world via witty one-line comments that we all still remember.

Above all, he gave racism a great punch in the face.

I now cheer a great life and billions join me in doing so.

Ride Like a Girl. Michelle Payne was the first woman to ride to victory in the Melbourne Cup and she did it in 2015 with the help of her disabled brother, Stevie, who was the strapper, and a gallant horse, Prince of Penzance, at odds which at one point peaked at 100-to-1.

As a result, Payne broke down a century of prejudice against female jockeys and the millions of women who valiantly seek the equality that is their right in any profession.

I really enjoyed the splendid movie *Ride like a Girl* that featured her achievement. The book of the same name was a great read too.

Just like Cathy Freeman and Muhammad Ali, Payne conquered a world of privilege without ever complaining about her struggle. She simply achieved.

As did Stevie who acted himself really well in the movie.

Other Great Sporting Moments. In selecting my five greatest sporting memories, I had a hard time leaving out the fabulous tied Test Cricket in Brisbane between Australia and the West Indies back in the 1960. It was a nail biter. My fingers have never recovered.

Equally difficult to omit was Australia's great yachting victory in the America's Cup at Newport, Rhode Island, a triumph for the mercurial entrepreneur, Alan Bond, before he crashed into financial and social oblivion.

Evonne Goolagong's tremendous tennis victory at Wimbledon was unforgettable, as was the valiant triumph of First Peoples boxer, Lionel Rose, who became a humble world champion.

I have no doubt that in years to come, many more such heroes will continue to inspire us all to reach for the stars.

Let me add this: if you asked me to name the sporting personality whom I have most admired, I would, without hesitation, select Roger Federer. He is a sublime artist with a tennis racquet and a fine human being whose retirement in 2022 was a sad moment.

These are the rambling thoughts of an old fast bowler from Linville who was not a bad table tennis player either, and who now plays nine holes of golf every week to stop arthritis from taking over his old frame. I enjoy that even though my skill is far below that of Tiger Woods.

Most people need a 'God' in their lives, someone to believe in and trust.

A role model?

An inspirational figure?

As humans have steadily and persistently moved away from religious gods, they began to believe in sporting gods, mostly footballers like Pele and Maradona, or football teams like Manchester United.

This human need will continue.

Is it a good thing?

Yes, indeed.

It is infinitely better than believing in nothing.

More Dreams

Memories, thankfully, never die.

Nostalgia remains with us always.

What also remains with us is the need to enjoy our treasured thoughts and beliefs.

Even my golf is a delightful challenge, as I strive to hit the finest golf shot of my life sometime during my tenth decade.

I intend to spend as many years as possible enjoying reading lots of top strata books, and viewing films, theatre, media and sport.

My hope is to find ever-improving quality of content, but I fear for the way in which the sensational has ever increasing popularity at the cost of excellence.

I hope that my contribution to the creation of nostalgia in the minds of many will be achieved through writing more books. I'm very aware that if each one is not an improvement on my previous efforts and makes no attempt to try to be ranked among the greatest, then I thoroughly deserve to fail.

My focus is on proving that I'm still toiling hard enough with my limited skills to reach for the stars in my tenth decade.

And, hopefully, beyond.

E: ME

1: St Andrew's Hospital

When I finished my full-time education and sought challenging employment, an extension of my early travels on the Linville train initially took me to work in Toowoomba and then Nyngan in western New South Wales before choosing Brisbane as my home base.

It led me to change my intention to be a high-profile public accountant.

I decided instead to become a project organiser.

It was a career that would lead me a long way from Linville in conditions that enabled me to observe world events and have a role in a few of them.

In this initial assignment at St Andrew's Hospital, I was able to witness firsthand the way in which public health is just as reliant on philanthropy as it is on governments.

Now, COVID-19 has shown us that governments and communities have massively underinvested in health.

It was a life changing moment in 1956.

The landlady of the boarding house at Clayfield in Brisbane, which in my days as a bachelor was my humble abode, tapped on my door to say that there was a call for me on her landline phone from Dr Harold Crawford. I hastened to her tiny office.

'Good evening, Everald. My name is Harold Crawford, Chairman of the Committee of the Presbyterian Church responsible for the establishment of St Andrew's War Memorial Hospital and I'm responding to your application for the position of organising secretary. My apologies for the short notice, but are you available to join me for lunch tomorrow at the United Services Club?'

Keeping my calm, I thanked him and said that it would be a privilege.

I was 24 years old and had just successfully completed my final examinations for the Australian Society of Accountants after years of evening study. At the same time, I had completed my studies for admission to the Australian Marketing Institute, also at night. Back in those days few students qualified for study at the University of Queensland and I missed out. There were no other universities in Queensland and it took decades for that unfortunate obstacle in the quest for excellence to be changed.

I was an active church member at that time and have been ever since. But in applying for the job of establishing St Andrew's Hospital, I thought I had no chance of being appointed. Nevertheless, I could see no reason why I should not give it my best shot.

After a long discussion over lunch about the challenges to be overcome before St Andrew's Hospital could become a reality, Dr Crawford told me that the job was mine if I chose to accept. Which I did in less than a second.

Years later, I discovered that there had been many applicants for the position, some of whom had far more experience than me, but Harold Crawford had said to his committee a few days before our lunch, 'We are taking a considerable risk, but I think we should give this young bloke a go. He could give our project the spark that it needs right now.'

Often, I wonder what direction my life would have taken at that point if Dr Crawford had not taken a punt on me.

Thankfully, it all worked out wonderfully successfully. In four years, we raised enough money to build and open the first two sections of the hospital that would eventually grow to be one of the largest in Brisbane.

Sadly, Harold Crawford died soon after of a heart attack. He was only 68. In writing his obituary for the media, I stated that the hospital would not have happened without his powerful leadership and utter commitment.

Not long after his death, I began the search for new fields to conquer.

The invaluable experience of having a leading role in founding a great hospital would become the cornerstone of my career as an organiser of community projects worldwide.

The major lesson that I learned from my first campaign at St Andrew's was that it is never possible to raise significant money for any project unless you establish around you a team of volunteers who believe in the cause, are willing to become givers themselves and then use their influence to involve others. I have never forgotten it and have worked to organise the involvement of dedicated volunteers in every venture of my long career. It is not possible to raise funds solely by your own efforts, no matter how powerful your personality may be.

As the years passed, I lost contact with St Andrew's Hospital. Most of those whom I worked with had moved on or died, but last year I had some minor surgery there on my old heart and the theatre nurse asked me if I had ever before been a patient at the hospital.

I only partially answered her question.

'Well, I can actually go a bit better than what you are asking. Sixty-four years ago, I signed the contract that enabled this operating theatre to be built.'

She was astonished.

'You couldn't possibly be that old.'

'I was only 26 at the time.'

'Wow, you must have had some powerful inside influence to get an important job like that at such a young age.'

'I must confess that I did have a real good mentor.'

The fact is that I'm getting a bit old but, no matter how many more years I may yet age, I will never forget Harold Crawford. He bravely opened the doors to my life's work and indelibly proved to me that partnerships produce far better results than personal ego.

I will also never forget that it was just before Harold Crawford gave me a chance to shine that I met my life partner, Helen Wyllie. As well as bringing purpose to my life, Helen worked as a volunteer in the fundraising events that I organised at St Andrew's and also as a volunteer in my office when I was struggling to stay on top of all the challenges that arose regularly. It will not surprise you to learn that she became the cornerstone of my life and I hope that I was able to do likewise to sustain her life and her aspirations.

My memories of St Andrew's Hospital prompt me to make two comments.

Back in the era when I was there, volunteers by their thousands worked and gave their money generously to create and maintain hospitals and they felt that the hospitals belonged to their community, not any government.

Now, they are mostly run by governments, or entities heavily subsidised by governments. There is only a moderate sense of community involvement in their work and this is a tragedy.

Back in the 1950s when I began my work at St Andrew's, there was also a strong belief that Christianity was much more than just going to church on Sundays so as to save your own soul and ensure a passage to heaven. We were called to a lifetime of community service powered by the influence of Jesus of Nazareth as our role model.

St Andrew's Hospital would not have happened without thousands of Presbyterians believing that this was their personal calling and devoting countless hours to working with great enthusiasm to make it a reality.

Essentially, they were wonderful days during which Christians worked together to create the type of caring community that they believed was essential to the good life of Australia as a nation and was at the forefront of the ministry of Jesus to all of humanity.

2: Fundraising

I departed from St Andrew's Hospital with goodwill all round and entered the wider world of philanthropy.

I was able to witness how people, rich and poor, used and misused their money.

I soon learned how money represented power and realised that this is not good for most of humanity.

The successful establishment of St Andrew's Hospital caused influential people to enquire as to whether I would be available to organise and finance projects in which they were involved. This flattered my ego and led me to start thinking about the wide range of possibilities that my future could hold.

My lengthy consideration of opportunities led me to accept an offer from Bill Rudder, a highly skilled public relations consultant, to join with him in establishing and financing the Queensland Cancer Fund. Together, we launched the Cancer Campaign in 1960, which became the most successful fundraising venture in the history of Queensland at that point in time. The Fund still operates effectively to this day.

Just as Harold Crawford had done a few years earlier, Bill Rudder became my mentor.

With the good result of our work at the Queensland Cancer Fund as evidence of our skill and potential as fundraisers, Bill backed me in establishing a fundraising consultancy called Compton Associates, which eventually became Everald Compton International. Encouragingly, we were offered contracts to organise fundraising campaigns interstate. Then we won an assignment in New Zealand, which led to us gaining an assignment in England. Eventually, we worked on every continent around the world.

Now, I can happily look back on my 40 years as a fundraiser and feel pleased about successes in so many different places while lamenting my occasional failures when everything went wrong no matter how hard I tried. At the peak of my fundraising career, I had 15 campaign managers working with me out in the field, men and women who organised and managed the campaigns locally while I planned and supervised their work.

Altogether, we would become involved in over 500 campaigns located across 26 nations. Some were large campaigns lasting a year, but most were smaller, with timing usually being from one to three months for each. They covered a wide range of causes such as hospitals, aged care homes, schools, universities, cathedrals, churches, theatres, art galleries, political candidates, industrial development associations, tourism promotion, medical research, mental health, domestic violence education, and so on.

I've referred to some of those campaigns in earlier chapters of this book and it will bore you if I list all of them, so I'll just say here that the best campaigns were the ones that were the toughest to organise. It was often the finest of worthy causes that were the most unpopular with donors simply because they broke new ground and were not socially fashionable.

I didn't ever seek or receive payment of a commission as a percentage of funds raised. I quoted fixed fees for time spent on an assignment and gave a guarantee that if the campaign did not raise the amount of my fees, I had to repay the difference. This occurred only once and I repaid the entire fee on that sad occasion. For other campaigns that did not go well, I provided additional services free of charge for as long as was practical to do so.

The point that I want to make here is that there's no such person as a fundraiser who has a perfect record of success. Anyone who tells you that suffers from self-delusion. I experienced failures that still cause me regret.

What did I learn from it all and did it make my life worthwhile? Did I create footmarks in the sand for others to follow? Only time will tell. However, there are some things worth noting at this point.

The first is that people don't donate money because they have lots of it. If, when growing up, a person does not learn to share everything with their brothers and sisters and friends, they will never become significant givers no matter what their wealth.

Just as important is the undeniable fact that people gain personal spiritual power when they give generously without any expectation of reward. Giving is one of the huge motivators of achievement in life.

Most important of all is that every nation needs a strong and active not-for-profit sector that becomes the conscience of society through which people can serve the community voluntarily and in a wide variety of ways. Any nation that has strong government and business sectors, but a weak not-for-profit sector, has no chance of being a compassionate and cohesive society that is worth living in.

Eventually, I sold Everald Compton International to the 'young Turks' in my team who had suggested to me that I was starting to look a bit old and should sell to them. I did, but retained the right of private practice. Even so, I have since accepted only a few occasional assignments here and there for special reasons from time to time.

I worked with vigour to create a second life career in my senior years that was different to my career in fundraising, a pathway that I recommend to you all. This shift would prove to be a huge learning experience, one that renewed my life and expanded my mind in what otherwise would have been my twilight years.

But I will never forget a fundraising career that took me on challenging journeys to work on fascinating projects around the world, often three to five times every year for many years and enabled me to work with influential people from all walks of life to achieve visionary goals for the good of the human race.

Nor have I forgotten Bill Rudder who, like Harold Crawford, was a significant cornerstone of my career. I have lunch with his sons every year to recall the great days I shared with their father who was an extraordinary person of considerable integrity and achievement.

My most indelible message to you from my experience as a professional is that you must make sure that you have mentors on all of your life journeys and then become a mentor yourself so as to repay your debt to friends by creating more friends.

The exercise of the power of money in society is enormous and its impact is largely underestimated by most of us.

I have too often witnessed people using money to dominate others and control decision-making in politics, charities, churches, sport or indeed their own families, all for their own benefit.

And I have not yet worked out how to stop it or even change it.

But the indisputable fact is that if money is used in the right way at the right time, it can create such incredible benefits for society.

Used solely to achieve dominance and power, it is a plague on society that eventually ends in grief, often for its instigators.

3: National Seniors Australia

My venture into the world of longevity, privately and professionally, has had a huge impact on my life and I hope it enhanced the lives of many others.

I regard the impact of longevity as a crisis as great as climate change but the world is unprepared for it, especially Australia.

We are irresponsibly sleepwalking into a social and economic disaster.

Way back in 1975, a longstanding friend, Bert Martin, nominated me to become a member of the Brisbane Rotary Club. On the day of my induction to the club, we chatted over lunch about how we could be active Rotarians out in the community.

Bert said to me, 'You know, Everald, older Australians have no union that looks after them. Everyone else has a union of some sort or another, but oldies don't.'

We talked about it for a while and I responded by saying that we should do something about it. I then organised a small meeting at my office a few days later.

I invited two friends, Alan Kohler and David Deans, to meet with Bert and myself and work out a strategy.

After a long debate on the positives and negatives, we decided to establish a company that we called Later Years. We launched it in 1976 at a function at the Brisbane Park Royal Hotel where our keynote speaker was Dame Enid Lyons. You will remember that I talked about this great Australian in an earlier chapter.

We then publicly invited anyone over 50 to join Later Years for a small annual financial subscription and we organised financial discounts for them to purchase a wide range of goods and services.

Unfortunately, we struggled to get this concept off the ground. People wanted more than discounts. They sought action for political reform of government services to the ageing. So, we got the message and acted quickly to get reorganised to achieve this. We eventually managed to do this successfully and began to make an impact on governments.

Then we found that being solely a Queensland organisation was insufficient to significantly impress upon politicians in Canberra that we were a force to be dealt with.

So, we had no option but to go national. We commenced this by merging with similar struggling organisations in Perth and Sydney and, in doing so, we changed our name to National Seniors Australia.

Eventually, we hit our peak, reaching a national membership of 280,000 and establishing 200 branches across Australia that our members could attend and convey to us their views about political actions they wanted.

A permanent and powerful political presence in Canberra was also established as well as a research facility that studied the social issues that ageing created.

We notched up many achievements in reforming and improving pensions, superannuation, aged care, affordable housing, telehealth, mature age employment, age discrimination and elder abuse just to name just a few.

I served on the board of directors as founding director for 35 years, 25 of them as chairman. This meant that I became well known as a pleasantly formidable presence around the corridors of power in the Australian Parliament.

When I reached my 80th year, I made an irrevocable decision to resign from the board before someone asked, 'When will this silly old goat retire?'

As soon as I did, Wayne Swan called me with an invitation to chair the Federal Treasury's Advisory Panel on Positive Ageing. I accepted the challenge and served for three years in a great team with Susan Ryan and Brian Howe. We produced a report called 'Turning Grey into Gold' that was well received in professional circles.

When Tony Abbott became prime minister, he sacked me for no reason other than the fact that I had been appointed by Wayne Swan. Strange that, as some years earlier, Abbott had said publicly that I was 'a great Australian'.

So, shall we put the insincerity of politicians aside and get back to the main agenda of the social and economic impact of longevity?

I no longer have an involvement with National Seniors other than one of mutual goodwill. This is deliberate. There is absolutely nothing to be gained by having a former chairman hanging around casting a shadow over his successors.

Nevertheless, National Seniors Australia and similar organisations face difficult times that call for constant innovation of strategy.

The oldies of my era are falling off the perch as I soon will. The baby boomer generation are a different people — they don't join organisations in the way that my generation did. They are much better off financially and prefer to enjoy life in a more modern way that avoids attending meetings. While I must admit that this is a great idea, it means that older Australians are increasingly unrepresented in the halls of power.

So, National Seniors is once again reinventing itself. It invites the trendier oldies to take up individual causes that need political action at a particular time. This strategy is going well even though financial membership has declined as it has been for almost every other community organisation in Australia, especially political parties that are now the realm of a few warped powerbrokers.

So, what of the future. Longevity is a greater threat to the world economy than COVID-19.

The ageing population will by 2040 have a huge impact on society. Over 50,000 Aussies will be 100 years of age or older. Of these, 5000 of them will be aged 110. The largest segment of the Australian population will be aged between 85 and 100. The second largest segment will be 70 to 85. The smallest segment will be 0 to 5.

Will we survive socially and economically? Yes, provided we remove the deadwood from all political parties in the Australian Parliament and start implementing a positive and comprehensive plan to turn grey into gold.

This task remains an important challenge of my life as I concentrate on reforms to retirement incomes, aged care and affordable housing

---

My personal experience is that growing old is a wonderful time of life so long as my mind remains young and I still seek to achieve goals.

I have worked out that my wisdom is only of value if I continue to learn from the experience of others, especially those who are younger than me.

The indisputable fact is that life is a fascinating journey of never-ending education and enterprise.

I reckon that when the day comes that I stop learning and innovating, it will be best for all concerned if I just quietly die since, in cricket terms, I'm just playing out time until stumps and this is a terribly boring way to play cricket. Indeed, lots of cricketers who try it usually get themselves out.

When I wake up every morning, I quickly work out that I must be in front and think about what goals I must kick for the day, just in case it happens to be my last. Indeed, one day it will be.

4:
Inland Railway

Australia has always significantly underinvested in the inland of our continent.

Because most of the nation's population live in capital cities and along the coastline, it is inevitable that this is where our investment dollars go.

There are not enough votes out in the bush for politicians to take rural life, and its enormous potential for productivity, seriously.

This has been as huge a mistake as has ever been made in the history of Australia.

It is time for a similar attitude change as I suggested when discussing longevity.

My involvement in the Inland Railway is a most painful tragedy of my life's work, but now there is a light at the end of a long tunnel.

Let me tell you how it all happened.

My original mentor in this venture was Ross Miller who, back in 1996, was mayor of Toowoomba. He created in my mind the vision of an inland railway from Melbourne to Darwin via NSW and Queensland and strongly encouraged me to take it up. Which I did. He remains a strong supporter to this day.

I went to Parliament in Canberra to visit John Howard, who had just become prime minister, and he said that he would give political backing to an attempt to achieve the Inland Railway by utilising private capital. So, with the aid of my friend Don McDonald, we enlisted a high-level team of eminent business leaders who saw it as an inspirational, nation-building exercise and, together, we got the project started.

Over the next two years, I organised and attended 52 public meetings in rural communities along the intended path of the railway all the way to Darwin to ensure that we had public support. These were the most enthusiastic gatherings I have ever attended, an overflow of attendance everywhere. They wanted a fast, efficient, standard gauge railway that would give them access to trading ports along the way.

They had no doubt that it would develop the Inland Railway economically and socially but, like me, they were unaware that primitive politics could strangle their dreams. It did.

There followed two decades of hard slog in trying to motivate five pedestrian governments (Canberra, Victoria, NSW, Queensland, Northern Territory) to stop quarrelling about who would pay for it, who would run it, what gauge it would be, and how hard it would be to get all their parliamentarians and bureaucrats onside and active. They stubbornly disagreed on just about everything pertaining to the railway and advocated widely differing means of achieving it along a range of possible corridors that would have had different rail gauges that would doom it to inefficient operation. This was incredibly unbelievable.

Eventually, in 2016, the Federal Government decided to financially back the first section of the Inland Railway from Melbourne to Brisbane via Parkes, Goondiwindi and Toowoomba, but they dispensed with me and my team and gave the assignment to their own rail corporation, ARTC, without there being a competitive process. They did not give me even an advisory role based on two decades experience of dealing with stakeholders along the track.

Nor did I ever get a letter of thanks, nor any thought of compensation for the pioneering work since the Liberal National Party wanted voters to think the railway was their vision, not mine. This does not worry me greatly at age 91. I have acquired enough life experience to duck and weave with the punches no matter how hurtful their intent may have been.

Then ARTC wilfully destroyed my original concept of giving rural regions access to ports without which the entire railway is pointless.

Inland Rail, which is now the official name of the first section, does not begin at the Port of Melbourne nor finish at the Port of Brisbane. It is totally useless to rural importers and exporters. It will only allow local consumer freight to be carried from one capital city to another and does not serve the Inland in any meaningful way that will ensure its growth.

The reckless work in building the railway has destroyed the livelihood of hundreds of farmers along the poorly chosen route. They knew that I'd already prepared a plan that used existing corridors of roads, railways, power lines and stock routes. I had conclusively proved the railway was viable and workable. They could have used our plan far more efficiently at less cost and with minimal public inconvenience.

In addition, and because they gave management positions to incompetent political hacks to whom they owed some favours, they have wasted billions of dollars in gross mismanagement so that the construction cost is now double what it should have been, and will possibly treble before the task is completed.

Nevertheless, one day, probably a decade late, it will be built as far as Toowoomba, which will become the freight hub for South-East Queensland, and it will forever stand as a wonderful example to the world of how government in Australia still dwells in the dark ages of primitive politics and appalling bureaucratic management.

Be this as it may, I'm now concentrating my efforts on pioneering a freight railway from where Inland Rail reaches Goondiwindi and build it direct to Miles and Gladstone, which will make Gladstone the 'Rotterdam of Australia'. Gladstone is the only port in eastern Australia that can efficiently handle the world's largest super-freighters and then efficiently distribute freight to and from the southern states faster than any boat could do the job.

As you will have already noted, this has always been planned as step number two of the original vision of a great transcontinental railway from eastern Australia to Darwin and the Kimberley.

It may not be completed in my lifetime, but I plan to make it unstoppable.

At my advanced age, I have no fear of politicians destroying my future or my reputation and I think I may have learned how to put some fear and common sense into their hearts and evoke some positive action.

So, what have I learned from this debacle?

Life for everyone has its ups and downs, but, "Tis better to have loved and lost, than never to have loved at all.'

Nevertheless, the fact remains that Australia is finally moving forward on the construction of its second transcontinental railway.

At last.

Giving it a go has been worthwhile.

Unbelievable as it may sound, it costs Australian farmers far more dollars more to freight their produce from farm to port than it does to ship it from there to the most distant part of the planet.

Yet, no government in the history of our nation has ever seriously attempted to do anything significant about solving this ridiculous situation.

Australia has the potential to become the food bowl of the entire world if we get serious about conquering what historian, Geoffrey Blainey, famously called the 'tyranny of distance'.

But leadership is absent.

Perhaps one day soon we'll finally see some nation-builders emerge.

5.
Advocate

I discovered in my later years that it is important in achieving quality of life to have several careers.

The fact is that each career has given me a new life.

In all, I have enjoyed my five careers as a banker, accountant, fundraiser, corporate director and community advocate, and have a sixth underway as an author.

I am somewhat apologetic in saying it but I must admit that my fifth career in life has been the task of making a lot of purposeful noise, sufficient to make myself heard in the halls of power in Australia and achieve some long overdue changes that will better contribute to the needs of society.

The reality of doing this reveals that I devoted many hours of my life to making speeches, doing media interviews, writing articles and books, posting messages on Twitter and Facebook as well as much negotiating, planning and organising — and I have enjoyed it all immensely.

What is heartening is that even my harshest critics (and there are many) have quietly and graciously told me that I have made a reasonable fist of it all despite losing as many battles as I have won.

This begs a primary question: why did I choose to get so heavily involved in the public arena?

The answer is quite simple.

I worked out early in life that it was an act of criminal negligence not to make maximum use of whatever talents I had the good fortune to be born with. Additionally, my conscience has constantly prodded me into realising it is a vital part of good citizenship to get involved in finding solutions to some of the challenges that face the society in which I live.

So, I focused primarily on using my talents for five important spheres:
- Creating new projects
- Raising money for great causes
- Developing rural Australia
- Making ageing an asset
- Fostering religious faith as a cornerstone of national life

You will have already found references to all of these throughout this book and will have worked out that I needed to develop my skills as a communicator or I would never have achieved anything that was worthwhile.

I made it my business to become basically proficient in handling the hazardous realm of the mainstream media and then, as its influence waned, I have tried to learn how to become effectively and responsibly involved in social media.

This is so complex that I decided to concentrate mainly on Twitter, Facebook and podcasts while ignoring the countless other options that are available in the ever-expanding world of communication.

Twitter is the prime avenue to debate politics, money and ethics while Facebook has its emphasis on all that is social and personal. Podcasts give a chance to use spoken words rather than written ones. Sadly, there are too many nasty, illiterate and juvenile people using all of them. I constantly block the worst of these sad people. They are simply primitive thugs.

I have a growing number of followers on all three and I reckon it has occurred because I've had a clear purpose in using social media. I constantly advocate my five crusades and enter into public debates about them. If I had just indulged in idle chatter and general gossip, it would be a waste of time and effort while accumulating no influence.

Now, I have added the writing of books to my armoury and in creating them I always involve a team of six friends, different ones for each book, as my advisers and critics. They seem to enjoy it as much as I do.

There are four of my books out there in the marketplace at the moment, making this current book number five.

I wrote *The Man on the Twenty Dollar Notes* because John Flynn, founder of the Royal Flying Doctor Service and School of the Air, has had a huge influence on my life as an inspirational role model. I hold the view that he is the greatest nation-builder that Australia has ever produced and I have tried to follow in his footsteps even though I have fallen a long way short of the high mark that he set.

Dinner With the Founding Fathers derived from the fact that few Australians know much about how the Founding Fathers created our nation in 1901 and what words they put in the Australian Constitution. One hundred and twenty years later, this great Constitution requires updating to meet the needs of a rapidly changing world, especially recognising the heritage of our First Peoples. My personal plans are to cause referendums to be held to achieve those reforms. This will occur only if we are aware of the contents of the Constitution and why they were valid at that time, but not now. I wrote this book to achieve that purpose.

A Beautiful Sunset is a novel about how an eminent Anglican priest who is dying of a terminal illness was able to make the last three months of his life the greatest. I regard it as my finest work as an author since I enjoyed creating its major characters, who are Christian, Muslim, Jewish, Buddhist, Confucian, African, atheist and lesbian. They have differing views about life and death as well as holding widely varying fears of both, thereby creating a very relevant guide to life as people come to terms with voluntary assisted dying as well as the lethal impact of COVID-19 and the eventual inevitability of death.

The Power Gift was actually my first novel and it still sells occasionally. It is the tale of the achievements of a philanthropist and the spiritual power that he generated by his generosity and vision.

In addition to those books above, that I hope you are now reading, my plan is to write at least four more during my tenth decade. I enjoyed the task of writing immensely. Each book will be related in some way with the goals of my life and the faith that drives it.

The first of the four will be *Everald's Bible,* based on 100 texts I have chosen from the four gospels of the New Testament that relate to my personal theology as well as 50 powerful sentences from writings and sermons of great Christians down the centuries who have helped grow my faith, plus my own Lord's prayer and creed that replace the original ones which are quite selfish in content. My hope is that this book will help my readers to find a more interesting and powerful life as working partners of Jesus of Nazareth. The traditional Bible smothers the power of his life with trivia.

The second book will be based on a major political event in Australian history and its consequences.

It will be followed by a fictional book about a heresy trial held by a church in a bigoted attempt to silence a First Peoples female pastor who challenges the white version of Christianity and its affinity to Western capitalist culture.

The fourth book will be a novel about a murder in the Australian Parliament. The victim is the prime minister of the day. Its purpose is to highlight the significant risks a person takes in becoming a national leader and the hatred that politicians unnecessarily generate in their quest for power.

In-between my happy and relaxing hours of writing, my job as an advocate of public causes will consume valuable time and it will never end.

Neither will yours.

There are some huge issues on which we can work together and the preservation and enhancement of democracy is one very urgent issue.

But, in the final analysis, advocacy of anything must lead to achievements that are genuine, effective and long lasting or it will all be just an exercise in public posing.

Thankfully, my advocacy over the years has enabled me to have had a significant input in a few important areas in addition to the ones listed in the earlier chapters. These have included having a national leadership role in creating the Uniting Church in Australia 45 years ago and saving Moreton Bay College from closure, as well as establishing the Brisbane Lions Australian Football Club, achieving the largest increase in the age pension in history of Australia, and organising the campaign to get voluntary assisted dying legislation through Queensland Parliament, plus some other worthwhile human needs here and there such as the establishment of three retirement villages.

I should have achieved much more, but I've tried to give it all my best shot.

Advocating a cause in which one can sincerely believe is one of life's greatest adventures. It requires some tenacity and an unshakable belief in what it's all about.

Just identifying with a cause is a waste of time and, in reality, is just an act of showmanship.

You are either in or out. Fence-sitters are useless and hopeless people.

Achieving a dream as part of a team of fervent believers is an absolutely wonderful experience.

Working alone is just a selfish and dreary way to achieve anything.

May you and your team kick many more goals than I have in mind.

Do I Have a Future?

So now I'm left to wonder if I have a future. I do hope so and I intend to make sure that it's a memorable close of life experience so long as it's not achieved at the expense or detriment of others.

Indeed, my aim is to have an active role in creating a caring and cohesive society with minimal divisive elements in it.

I can see no point whatsoever in being alive if I have no more goals that I want to try to kick. I don't believe that I have earned a restful retirement. Indolent relaxing is essentially a boring pastime. Even at the best of times that ensures an earlier death.

Helen and our family are aware of my irrevocable wish that, if my body and brain deteriorate to the point where I am geriatric and useless, then I will quickly find some painless and dignified way to die with dignity. If I do not qualify to use voluntary assisted dying laws, I will find a legal alternative. Most probably with the pleasant assistance of a massive overdose of the finest whisky I can find from a historic distillery deep in the highlands of Scotland. A couple of bottles consumed with some intensity will seize up my old heart.

In my own mind, I feel that I have had a productive and purposeful life. A life that I have enjoyed in company with Helen and I can see no point in filling in time just for the sake of doing so when there is no quality left in my existence.

In that case it will be best to declare my innings closed and dream that I may leave the field to a standing ovation.

Right now, I am a couple of years into a 10-year plan that I have carefully prepared that will take me to my century. I am determined to make it a pleasant and interesting productive decade that benefits other people far more than it does for me.

Join me on the journey.

I will welcome your company.

In fact, I reckon I won't get there without your help.

And it will be lonely without you.

F: WALKING THE LINVILLE TRACK

Catching the Linville train was a wonderful experience.

Sadly, I'm unable to catch it back again since they have pulled up the rail tracks.

But this did not stop Helen and me from coming back to this pleasant rural village in 2021 to give thanks that it gave me a solid start in life and ponder where it would lead me next.

It has been a privilege for me to say thank you to Linville, the village that was, and still is, the ground of my being.

On my 90th birthday in October 2021, I came back to this quite special community in the Brisbane River valley to lead a 14 kilometre charity walk to raise funds for ACTS.

ACTS is a charity that I chair that has been established by the Aspley Uniting Church to make direct financial grants to people hit with significant personal problems, especially people who do not belong to our church or live anywhere near Aspley.

Accompanied by many friends, I walked along the old railway corridor from Linville to Moore, part of the railway on which I travelled on my original rail journey from Linville to Toogoolawah to go to rural school eight decades before. It is now a walking and cycling track with a few creek crossings that were a bit difficult for hikers when they knocked over the bridges several decades ago.

That is a seven kilometre journey. After a cool drink, I walked back to Linville with much help and encouragement from those who kept me company. We did it in just under three hours and Helen helped me make it across the line.

People from all over Australia, some of whom are strangers, sponsored me financially and we managed to raise $36,000 for ACTS.

I was greatly moved by the experience of good fellowship that was in the air that day. My gratitude for this generosity of spirit is enormous.

After enjoying a cold beer in the village garden at the end of the walk, I hosted a lunch in the community hall for 90 people. The Linville Progress Association prepared the food and my guests paid them for their great country lunch, so we all made a small financial contribution to the future of Linville.

It was a happy occasion filled with memories of long ago, made better by sharing it with valued friends.

This extraordinary personal experience made me think again of the role that small towns have performed so ably in the history and development of Australia and what new role they can have in ensuring a prosperous and peaceful future for our nation as a cohesive and caring society that achieves things. It's a subject about which I'm giving thought and action to as the years roll on. It's important since visiting the Aussie bush is a unique way to enjoy life.

Birthday number 90 also made me think of the basics of my heritage, where this has led me in life and what direction it may take me in the years ahead as I walk with positivity through the 10th decade of my existence. This will, hopefully, take me to my century and open doors along the way that enable me to continue to be a constructive contributor to society.

I will never forget what my life was like in Linville back in the days of the Great Depression and subsequently in many other places during those other 29 world events that I have described to you. Nor will I cease to remember what I learned from 20 extraordinary people I worked with or took inspiration from and walked with or the 20 historic places I visited and from which I learned so much about what has created the world of today. Or my work experience and religious journey and political experience as well as all I learned from books or the impact of the many campaigns I organised and enjoyed.

Much has evolved in my thinking on these matters since my first days at the Linville State School and my time at Sunday school at the local Methodist church that is now someone's home. The world of the 1930s no longer exists in the 2020s, but its events still have genuine value whenever we stop to ponder their contribution to history and culture.

So, let me have an objective look at where am I in my life journey and where I am heading in the last lap.

Right now, I live by three sets of values that are important to me and may be of some worth to you as you ponder your journey.

Those values are a moving feast of learning and growing. I review and renew them regularly on the basis of constant reading, listening, study and application plus lots of human contact. I try to avoid ever having a repetitive day or a fundamentalist mindset or a fear of change or a moment of depression.

The first of those values relates to my ever-growing and reforming faith and my personal ethics as I ponder their meaning and purpose every day.

It is based on creative thinking that is somewhat similar to that of Thomas Jefferson, the third president of the United States of America and author of the American Declaration of Independence.

Thomas Jefferson was a nominal Christian who rejected dogmas and creeds and miracles and who created his own Bible that the world now calls the Jefferson Bible. It comprises extracts from the four gospels: Matthew, Mark, Luke and John, and contains parables attributed to Jesus that relate to morals and ethics.

Jefferson based his personal faith on his choices of passages from those gospels. it's notable that it includes no mention of miracles or the virgin birth or the resurrection.

Notably, his principal comment is that the words of Jesus are of an intellectual level over and above those of Socrates and Cicero and Plato who spoke mainly to intellectuals, not the ordinary people whom Jesus lived with. I readily agree with his thoughts and, as mentioned above in the chapter I called *Advocate*. This has challenged me to create my own Bible in texts rather than the passages he used. Texts have more power than passages of scripture. Significant for me is my addition of comments by great Christians spread over 2000 years of spiritual experience since the Bible was written. This emphasises the fact that God is not dead and Jesus of Nazareth becomes a role model, not a fiction created by churches.

While I work on that, my life goes on and so I want to tell you where I am with my personal faith right now.

For good or ill, here is my set of spiritual values at this moment in time on my constant and never-ending journey of life experience:

Jesus of Nazareth is the role model of my life.

Powered by THE GREAT SPIRIT, I am a committed working partner of his as we walk together to create a world of sharing, caring and justice.'

While it is not a particularly trendy title, I'm now able to proudly describe myself a POJON — a Partner of Jesus of Nazareth.

I have taken this further and developed a personal prayer to replace the traditional Lord's Prayer, which I reject as a selfish plea that asks God to provide me with the basics of life while protecting me from all harm.

Here it is:

'*Great Spirit, empower me to walk with Jesus of Nazareth as I do my best to help carry out his mission to create a world of justice, compassion and peace.'*

The second relates to my civic responsibilities:

'I am a citizen of the world. Australia is the nation of my choice.

I work with family and friends to achieve the goal of a world in which all people have a home shared with those whom they love and secured by a job, food, school and hospital made possible by all having a fair go on a level playing field where there is no discrimination.'

Then, there is this pledge to myself:

'My twilight years are devoted to achieving humanitarian goals. I will not use my advancing age or declining health as an excuse for failing to continue to serve the society that has given me every opportunity to enjoy a good life.'

In forming those spiritual values, I came to acquire respect for religions other than Christian, doing much reading about other faiths, especially Muslim, Jewish, Hindu, Buddhist, Confucian, Sikh, Mormon and Bahai, as well as the philosophy of atheists, humanists and rationalists. It has been a mind-opening experience that I plan to continue.

Finally, I especially thank the village of Linville for not just giving me a start to my journey all those years ago, but also for reviving in my soul many fresh thoughts about all the possibilities that abound in an ever-challenging future.

I firmly believe that the world needs more communities like Linville where it is possible to know everyone who lives or works there and join happily with them in creating a close caring society that is not possible in a crowded city.

Above all, I revere my vivid memory of the first day I caught the Linville train. Its incredible excitement opened for me a door to an amazing and endlessly incredible world that I have been able to share with Helen.

I grasped life with both hands and have never let go.

So, using the language of the bush where I grew up in Linville, may God bless Linville 'real good'.

There it is.

Nearly one hundred thousand words of a life.

The ramblings of an old soul.

The writing of all of these many words has taught me much about life.

I have tried to gather together my personal experiences of a life journey and quietly reflect on them.

It has fired me up to do much better in my final years.

I plan to make them the most productive and constructive and meaningful of my long life.

May you and I meet along the way and kick a few goals together, and may I thank my friends Greg Cary, Barry Renaud, Noela Lowien, Dean Gould, Jonathan Holland, Alison Courtice and Marcus Fielding for their help in guiding the Linville train on its final journey..

Until then,

SHALOM

www.ingramcontent.com/pod-product-compliance
Lightning Source LLC
Chambersburg PA
CBHW050100170426
43198CB00014B/2401